ENGLAND IN THE AGE OF HOGARTH

ENGLAND IN THE AGE OF HOGARTH

Derek Jarrett

YALE UNIVERSITY PRESS
NEW HAVEN AND LONDON

This book is dedicated to the memory of my sister Doreen, who first awakened my interest in historical writing but did not live to see me try my hand at it.

First published in Great Britain by
Hart-Davis, MacGibbon Ltd, 1974.

Reprinted 1992, 1996

Printed in Great Britain at The Bath Press, Bath.

ISBN 0-300-03608-6 (cloth)
ISBN 0-300-03609-4 (paper)
LC 85-52071

Contents

Acknowledgements

The illustrations in this book are reproduced by kind permission of the following: Department of Prints and Drawings, the British Museum; the Trustees of the National Gallery; the Trustees of the Tate Gallery; the National Portrait Gallery; the Trustees of the Sir John Soane Museum; Hogarth's House, London Borough of Hounslow; Crown Copyright: HMSO; Crown Copyright: National Monument Record; National Trust, Upton House; the Leger Galleries; the Guildhall Museum and S. F. Sabin Esq. Illustration Research Service supplied the pictures.

List of Illustrations

Preface to This Edition

When this book was first published many kind things were said about it and reviewers greeted it as a contribution to social history. I very much fear, however, that I lack those advanced demographic skills which are now essential if one is to write the history of societies. All I have been able to do is to write about people, real people who flourished or failed to flourish in eighteenth-century England, and my aim has been to give the reader some idea of what it must have been like to live at that time.

For this Yale edition, the text and notes remain unaltered. I have added a small number of supplementary references, and the section on further reading has been expanded and brought up to date.

DEREK JARRETT
September 1985

Preface

When first it was suggested that I should write this book I was busy with what is usually called 'political' history. Influenced by the work of Sir Lewis Namier and his school, I had been encouraged to seek the truth about eighteenth-century England in the intrigues of politicians and in the details of the parties and the groupings which they formed.

But the questions which Namier prompted us to ask about politicians were calculated to lead us far beyond the confines of politics. They were questions about unconscious as well as conscious motives, about the myths and prejudices which ordinary people cherished and which politicians exploited. My own particular interest, which concerned England's involvement with France, very soon showed me the importance of xenophobia and aggressive nationalism and self-deluded insularity. Other obsessions, inward rather than outward turned, were equally potent. Although Namier's field has come to be thought of as merely the 'structure of politics', his approach to history revealed the importance of the foundations of prejudice and preconception upon which that structure was reared.

I have therefore set out to describe those foundations in this book, not simply as an introduction to eighteenth-century political history but as a way of showing what it must have been like to live at that time. It was a dour and unromantic age, quick to recognize the pathos and the absurdity of human life. Its view of itself was harsh and it was always ready to remind men and women how little they could expect on this earth and how much they must bear. Nobody saw these things more clearly than Hogarth and it was for this reason that Englishmen continued to gaze, for many years after his death, into the mirror which he had held up to them. His work provides a starting point for the examination not only of the generation he portrayed but also of the generation which followed him and which was so deeply influenced by his picture of English society.

I am deeply indebted to Andrew Best, who suggested the title of this book and has done much to smooth its passage. My debt to other historians working in the field is very great indeed and I trust that I have made it clear in my notes and bibliography. I have been especially helped by the work of Professor Ronald Paulson, who has shed much new light on Hogarth's life and work, and by that of Mrs Dorothy George and Dr Dorothy Marshall, both of whom have bridged with authoritative ease the gap between political and social history in this period.

DEREK JARRETT

1 The Freeborn Englishman

ENGLAND in the 1750s was a patchwork of distinct and separate local communities, within which the great majority of Englishmen and Englishwomen lived and died close to the places where they had been born, knowing very little of other counties or other towns. The propertied minority, noblemen and freeholders in the counties and aldermen and freemen in the towns and cities, were able to move about more freely and to acquire a wider and less fragmented view of the England which between them they owned and governed. Although roads were often atrocious, uncomfortable even in dry weather and almost impassable when it rained, the carriages of the rich were nevertheless constantly to be seen trundling their owners off to places of business or places of pleasure, administrative centres or fashionable resorts. A nobleman with lands in some northern county might well travel the length of the country two or three times a year, taking in watering places and race meetings, cathedral cities and garrison towns, as well as his necessary visits to London.

Ordinary country gentlemen seldom made such elaborate progresses, but they usually came to London fairly regularly on business and often took their families to Bath or some other spa town as well. Quite a few of them sat in the House of Commons at some time during their lives and most of them were justices of the peace, which meant that they met together four times a year in their county towns to enforce laws which other propertied men in Parliament had already made in order to keep the poor in their proper places. The magnates of the boroughs and cities, from lord mayors to ordinary tradesmen and manufacturers, ranged less widely: for the most part they were concerned only with the discipline of their own workpeople and the maintenance of their own business contacts. But the principle was the same: whatever you owned you also governed, whether it was an estate with thousands of tenants or a workshop with a few journeymen and apprentices. And to govern you had to know something of the great world, to see the country and its problems from above and not merely from below. As for those who owned nothing and governed nobody, it was their business to stay dutifully where God and their superiors had placed them, even though their numbers made up the bulk of the population and their labours produced the bulk of its wealth.

We know well enough what the men of property thought about this state of affairs. It might not be the best of all possible worlds but it was at least, in their opinion, the best of all practicable ones. Kingly tyranny must be resisted at all costs; and such resistance could only be effective if men of real substance asserted their rights individually in their own localities and collectively in Parliament in London. By forcing the central government to respect their own very extensive freedoms and privileges, they automatically guaranteed to those beneath them as much freedom as it was proper for such people to have. What we do not know is what the vastly greater ranks of the unpropertied thought about things. Hardly anybody considered it worthwhile to record their lives, let alone their views. It was not for nothing that the poet Gray wrote of the 'noiseless tenor' and 'destiny obscure' of the great majority of his fellow countrymen.

But even the obscure were not always entirely noiseless. When they were really discontented or really excited about something they were capable of a good deal of noise and even a good deal of violence. Their riots and commotions were noted, even if their views and complaints were not. And from the evidence of those riots it is possible to discover quite a lot – to discover, for instance, that there was a remarkable degree not only of acceptance, but even of unity among these people who had such good cause for discontent and dissension. Northerners and southerners, Cornishmen and East Anglians, villagers and townsmen, were isolated from one another in a way which their more closely integrated descendants find hard to imagine. They were also subject in many cases to local tyrannies and injustices about which the law of the land could do very little. And yet all were conscious of being Englishmen and of possessing, because they were Englishmen, liberties which had real value and for which they had good reason to be thankful. Their violence, when it came, was seldom directed against the inequalities of the existing system or the powers of their rightful masters. Almost always it was provoked by innovators and interlopers, by those who seemed to threaten that splendid English constitution which in fact guaranteed social subordination but which seemed to many to guarantee personal liberty. Most English labouring men were traditionalists, zealous in their defence of freedoms which seemed as relevant to them as to their superiors.

As for the lawyers and politicians who were the appointed guardians of these freedoms, they seemed able to think and act with remarkable facility on two completely different levels. On the one hand they made impassioned speeches about English freedom in general and about the rights and liberties of the people as a whole, while on the other they advanced their careers and their fortunes by exploiting the particular and exclusive freedoms of those rich enough to fight cases in the law courts or be represented in Parliament. 'The prerogatives of princes', Parliament had told King James I many years before, 'may easily and do daily grow; the privileges of the subject are for the most part at an everlasting stand.'[1] But now it was the privileges of some subjects, rich and influential subjects, which were easily and daily growing, while the liberties of the poor were for the most part at an everlasting stand. This was especially true of those liberties which might stand in the way of the enrichment of their betters. In the 1720s Defoe had noted that the poor were still able to assert their rights over common land, if necessary by force; but now local magnates and their men of business in London had changed all that. Parliament was busy passing, at their behest, Enclosure Acts which turned the English countryside into a pattern of privately owned fields with precious little land of any value left as common.[2]

What then remained? What was it that made so many Englishmen cling to the belief that they, and not merely their social superiors, were truly freeborn and could rely on a remote Parliament of property owners to guard for them their birthright? Part of the answer lies in words and phrases, legal terms which defined in obscure English or even more obscure Latin the liberties which in practice clever lawyers and determined magistrates could often circumscribe. 'Habeas corpus', the most famous and most cherished of these phrases, meant that no Englishman could be imprisoned without trial – unless, of course, he was too poor to put up bail or had committed the heinous crime of being in debt. But the legal tags and Latin phrases did not really come to the heart of the matter. The real secret of English freedom in the eighteenth century was not to be found in the lawyers' commentaries or the constitutional histories, but in the streets. It was contained in something which was ordinary enough to Englishmen but very extraordinary and even awe-inspiring to foreigners: the English crowd.

When Voltaire first came to England in 1728 and saw the crowds in Greenwich Park on a Sunday he assumed that this must be a pleasure garden in which the rich and the powerful were taking their ease.[3] It was with some surprise that he realized he was in fact watching ordinary men and women, even apprentices and streetwalkers, dressed up to imitate their betters and strolling about as though they were fashionable idlers. And whatever may have happened to the rights of the poor in the country, the rights of the crowds in the towns had if anything increased rather than diminished during the 1730s and 1740s. By 1752 Henry Fielding, by no means a sympathizer with the rich and the powerful, was suggesting in some alarm that the rabble now regarded the pavements as their own preserve and were ready to push decent people into the gutter.[4] His fears were exaggerated: in fact the crowds who claimed their rights on the pavements of London were usually imitating, rather than defying, other and more substantial citizens. In 1750 a fashionable lady found her coach invaded by a jeering procession of all sorts and conditions of men, some of them extremely dirty and smelly, because she had obstructed the footpath by parking outside a trinket shop at Charing Cross. But the leader of this human chain, the man without whom the incident probably would not have taken place, was a polite and respectably dressed gentleman who had asked her civilly to move and had been haughtily refused. In such cases the sympathies of most Englishmen, propertied as well as unpropertied, were with the rough humour of the crowd rather than with the arrogance of the individual.

The same was true of another liberty which the English crowd regarded as peculiarly its own: the right to laugh at pretentiousness and ostentation. This was exercised increasingly in the streets of London and other towns as fashions became more and more extreme. Even in the middle of the century leaders of fashion were beginning to envelop themselves in large black bags, partly to preserve their secrets and partly to avoid being mocked and hooted after by the crowd. By the late 1760s there was a concerted campaign, not only in the streets but also in the print shops, against the extremes of fashion introduced from Italy by the so-called 'Macaronis'. The late 1770s and early 1780s saw a return to more sober fashions, but those who chose to appear in anything out of the ordinary still ran the risk of public humiliation. Sophie von la Roche, a rather prim German lady who visited England in 1786, noted with some satisfaction that the entire audience at the Haymarket theatre made fun of four ladies who entered one of the boxes dressed in fantastic head-dresses, with their faces almost hidden behind vast neckerchiefs and their nosegays sprouting from their bosoms like young trees. After a quarter of an hour of merriment in the auditorium the campaign of ridicule spread to the stage: the action of the play was halted while four actresses appeared dressed in a similarly exaggerated fashion and greeted the ladies with mock salutations. The whole theatre was by now rocking with mirth and finally the would-be leaders of fashion had to leave amidst 'universal ridicule'.[5]

This episode seemed to Sophie to be a salutary example of the freeborn Englishman's readiness to give utterance to his innate good sense and his contempt for pomp. She was equally enthusiastic about the presence of working people in the public parks, something which was as surprising to her in the 1780s as it had been to Voltaire half a century earlier. And she pointed out that it reflected not only the economic and social facts of English life, the comparative absence of class distinction and a fairer distribution of wealth, but also the political and constitutional arrangements of the country. The freeborn English were able to chastise the folly of the rich because their forefathers had chastised the arrogance of the powerful and had forced their kings to accept constitutional limitations. English labouring men were better off than their counterparts in France or Germany because their country's constitution was based upon 'a republican spirit welded with a monarchy'.[6]

Most eighteenth-century Englishmen would have bridled at being called republicans; and most of those who have studied the English revolutions of the seventeenth century would doubt that the constitution which finally emerged from those upheavals, the constitution of the year 1688, did much to guarantee the liberties of ordinary men or to ensure a fairer distribution of wealth. Nevertheless, there was something in what Sophie said. In 1688 the men who actually owned England, from great noblemen down to ordinary freeholders and freemen, had decided that King James II was threatening their ancient and undoubted rights and liberties. They had therefore recognized his daughter Mary and her Dutch husband William III as joint sovereigns in his stead. They had argued at the time, and were still arguing now, about the precise significance of this change. Some said that it meant the people could elect their own kings, others that men of property in Parliament could limit the powers of kings but could not alter the essentially divine, rather than elective, nature of their right to the throne. But no amount of argument could conceal the fact that the succession to the English throne had been determined by violence or the threat of violence. And this threat sprang not merely from the indignation of property owners, but from the actions of the people they controlled or failed to control. The English revolutions of the seventeenth century may not have been popular revolutions, but they had nevertheless had the effect of giving the populace a political importance such as it had in no other European country. The unabashed turbulence of the English crowd was indeed one of the outward and visible signs of the English system of limited monarchy.

The crowd was not always as good-humoured or as fair-minded as Sophie seemed to think. Weakness and infirmity often got as rough a handling as arrogance and ostentation. A Frenchman who visited London in 1763, a venerable and distinguished scientist who had had the misfortune to become rather deaf in his old age, was followed about the streets by a large crowd jeering at his ear trumpet.[7] In France itself such things did not happen. Hans Stanley, while he was travelling from Paris to Orleans a few years later, had to drive for many miles behind a carriage piled high with an extraordinary assortment of luggage which was capped by an enormous parrot cage. In England such a sight would have produced jeers and catcalls all along the roads; but here, wrote Stanley in some surprise, it passed 'without the least animadversion from the populace, so much quieter are they than in England'.[8] The French, particularly the aristocratic French, could not understand why the English failed to keep the poor in their proper place. In France, as Mrs Thrale remarked when she crossed the Channel on the eve of the French revolution, 'everyone seems to belong to some other man and no man to himself'.[9] The 'masterless man', the man for whom nobody could be held responsible, seemed as dangerous to propertied men as a stray dog who had no owner to muzzle him. European governments took steps to see that such men were as rare as possible and they expected the English to follow their example.

In fact the English did – in theory. They were terrified of the 'mob', a word which they were fond of using and which derived from a Latin phrase denoting the shifting populace, people who had no fixed place in society and nobody to control them. For more than two hundred years Parliament had been busily passing laws which ensured that there should be no masterless men and therefore no mobs. In theory almost every labouring man in England was tied to his place of work, unable to leave without his employer's written permission and liable to be turned back by the Overseer of the Poor in any neighbouring parish into which he tried to cross. But practice was very different from theory and many of those who had the job of enforcing the laws found it more convenient or more profitable to let them slide a little. Thousands of labourers moved with steadily increasing freedom across the country, attracted by new jobs offered by landowners or industrialists or merchants who were sufficiently influential to see that the law was not too literally interpreted. The social theories of the propertied classes required fixity and stability, a state of affairs in which every man had his place and kept to it. But their business interests often required movement, the sort of movement which could provide readily available reserves of labour. And the end product of all this movement was the London crowd, at once the supreme symbol and the ultimate guarantee of English freedom.

It is for this reason that the England of the 1750s was in a very special sense the England of Hogarth, an immensely popular artist who was then at the height of his powers. Hogarth did a lot of things very well, but the thing he did best was the portrayal of the London crowd. Others have painted more dramatic crowds, crowds whose statuesque silence adds to the horror of the martyrdom they are watching or crowds whose swirling movement denotes the fervour of the revolution they are enacting; but nobody in the whole history of painting has ever excelled Hogarth in the art of building up a crowd out of real people, people who jog one another's elbows or pick one another's pockets or turn aside at the smell of one another's breath. His street scenes suggest the excitement and the potential violence of the crowd, but they also suggest the loneliness and the pathetic absurdity of the individuals who make it up. These are people who assert the liberties of freeborn Englishmen readily enough in the streets but who will probably regain their sense of hierarchy, their crippling consciousness of their own importance or lack of it, once they get back indoors again. Hogarth put into pictorial form the underlying paradox of eighteenth-century English society, the society that claimed to keep each individual Englishman in his proper place and yet could at times be overawed by the spectacle of Englishmen as a whole claiming their ancient birthright of freedom.

Hogarth died in 1764, the last few years of his life clouded by a bitter and very damaging quarrel with John Wilkes over their rival interpretations of this same paradox. But his prints and engravings continued to sell and his influence and reputation grew steadily – at any rate as long as English life and politics continued to be dominated by the boisterous and uninhibited attitudes which he had reflected. It was not until the 1790s that things really began to change: then, for a variety of reasons which will be discussed later, life in England became more earnest, more straitlaced and above all more complex. Then and then only did Hogarth begin to evoke shocked revulsion or sniggering nostalgia rather than the more straightforward pleasures of recognition and self-congratulation. And even then the world of the streets, especially the London streets, was still his. Those who illustrated it did so under his influence and those who inhabited it kept alive the world which he had created and which had created him. Most of them still came regularly into contact with his work, either in their own homes or in the places in which they worked or took their leisure. In the countryside at large his influence, though more diffused, was still very considerable. Comparatively few people in late eighteenth-century England, wherever they lived, can have failed to see at least one picture by Hogarth. No single human being – not even John Wesley, for all his indefatigable journeying and preaching – touched so many lives or touched them in ways that were more likely to have a lasting effect. The English were a self-conscious nation, openly proud of their virtues and secretly fascinated by their vices. And it was all reflected in Hogarth, virtues and vices alike: the sterling qualities of independence and hard work and good sense, coupled with the strange melancholia and the preoccupation with pain – two unpleasant national traits upon which foreigners never tired of commenting. The pictures of Hogarth, and the hundreds of pictures which imitated him, spoke to Englishmen with a directness which the written word could never achieve and which sermons and other harangues could seldom match. They spoke directly because they spoke in private as well as in public, reflecting the secret preoccupations of the individual as well as the protestations of the crowd. This was indeed Hogarth's England; and he ruled it in a way that was curiously intimate, even domestic. To imagine the second half of the eighteenth century without Hogarth is like imagining a close-knit family without its collection of snapshots.

Not all the images in this album were obviously or immediately reassuring. One of the most popular of them was not even a picture of England at all, but of France, a view of the town gate at Calais (Plate 1). Most of the figures in it were French: strutting and leering soldiers to represent military tyranny, cringing and emaciated workmen to represent the misery of the people. A religious procession in the distance indicated the superstition and priestcraft of the Roman Catholic church, while an obese and slavering monk in the foreground indicated its greed and sensuality. Crouched in a corner was a Scotsman, a tartan-clad refugee who had had to flee to France after the failure of the 1745 rebellion* and who was now joining in the lugubrious orgy of wretchedness which was Hogarth's view of French life. The only two things English in the picture were Hogarth himself, busily sketching in the middle distance but with the heavy hand of French tyranny already upon his shoulder, and an enormous joint of beef. It was this last that gave the picture the rather cumbersome title under which it was first published in March 1749: *A Print*

* In July 1745 Prince Charles Edward Stuart landed in Scotland to claim the British crown on behalf of his father, James Stuart, son of the James II who had been dethroned in 1688. He conquered Scotland and invaded England, but had to turn back at Derby and was finally defeated at Culloden in April 1746. See p. 35.

1 (*Above*) Hogarth: *The Gate of Calais*, 1749. Originally entitled 'O the Roast Beef of Old England'.

2 (*Overleaf*) A statuette of George III by Hardenberg, showing the king as a plain country gentleman, a role which suited him and endeared him to most of his subjects.

Presented
by H.R.H Princess Elizabeth
Langravine of Hesse Homburg

designed and engraved by Mr Hogarth, representing a Prodigy which lately appeared before the Gate of Calais. O the Roast-Beef of Old England, &c.[10] Not all Hogarth's customers shared his passionate devotion to the rituals of beef-eating and the songs associated with it, so that the engraving soon came to be known simply as *The Gate of Calais.* It was reissued many times and attained immense popularity.

The reason for this popularity was obvious enough. For years the English had underlined their own freedoms by dwelling on the horrors of Continental enslavement. If Englishmen ever became restive under the rule of their freeborn squires, they could always be reassured by the cry of 'Popery and Wooden Shoes', by the reminder of the miseries of the priest-ridden and clog-wearing peasants on the other side of the Channel. As an artist Hogarth knew that the best way to indicate bright light was to paint dark shadows; as a propagandist he knew that the best way to indicate English liberty was to paint French slavery. And now he had produced the definitive example of this particular kind of propaganda by antithesis. In fact he could have found better and more dramatic material if he had gone farther afield, to countries such as Prussia or Russia where tyranny had a far sharper edge than in France. But Berlin and St Petersburg, unlike Calais, could not be seen from England on even the clearest day. France was the neighbour, the enemy, the rival; and so she became also the archetype of that Continental tyranny which freeborn Englishmen regarded with mingled contempt and fascination.

For Hogarth himself the picture was genuinely autobiographical. He had indeed felt the heavy hand of the French authorities, for he had been arrested while sketching in Calais and carried before the governor as a suspected spy. Until that time his behaviour when abroad had always been noisy and offensive: he had made two short trips to Paris (the episode in Calais took place on the way back from the second of them) and on both of them he had displayed gratuitous rudeness about all things French. One of his companions later told how he would constantly make embarrassingly loud remarks, drawing attention to the poverty and sluttishness of the women or the tastelessness of the architecture: French houses, he insisted, were 'all gilt and beshit'.[11] But now he was made to realize that even a freeborn Englishman could be subjected to the laws of the country he was visiting, however harsh they might seem. If he was free it was because of the society in which he lived and not because of any innate valour of his own. The governor told him that he might well have been hanged then and there if the peace treaty between the two countries had not been concluded a few months earlier. He was finally released, but under humiliating conditions; and once he got safely back to England he stayed there, never again venturing across the Channel to parade his sturdy John Bullishness in the face of the enslaved French. He continued, however, his relentless campaign against foreign influences of all kinds, particularly in the arts. One of the things that endeared him most to his fellow countrymen was his staunch opposition to foreign fripperies and to all the Frenchified tastes which richer and more impressionable and better-mannered young men brought back from their Grand Tours* on the Continent.

Thus Hogarth was more than just the painter of crowds, the artist who illustrated and reflected the supreme symbol of English liberty. He was also himself an archetype of the freeborn Englishman, coming very close in many ways to that most basic and influential of all archetypes, John Bull. In his original form John Bull had been a cloth merchant, a fictitious figure created by John Arbuthnot in his pamphlet *Law is a bottomless pit* in 1712. Arbuthnot's purpose was to show how England had gone to war with France some years earlier in order to safeguard her cloth trade and how in the event she had been cheated by clever politicians and unscrupulous foreign allies. He therefore made John Bull into anything but a heroic character: this imaginary Mr Bull was a hot-tempered but short-sighted blunderer, henpecked by his wife and gulled by most of those around him. He did not represent the freeborn Englishman at all, but merely the commercialism and greed of a certain sort of Englishman. But by the time Hogarth shook the dust of France from his feet and started to paint a massive joint of beef as a symbol of English freedom amid the misery of French enslavement, John Bull had changed his character and immensely enhanced his stature. He had become less like a cloth merchant and more like the animal from which he took his name: strong, virile, a country dweller rather than a commercially minded townsman. And, of course, he was superbly stubborn and intractable, always ready to toss and gore those who tried to tame him. When he first started to appear in prints and caricatures, which was not until the 1760s, it was either as a bull or as a man with bull's horns or a bull's head, rather like the minotaur of ancient Crete.[12]

Hogarth's only contribution to this particular line of development was his almost mystical insistence on the eating of beef as a means of acquiring the virility and the virtues of the sturdy, freeborn Englishman. Earlier in the century loyalists in London had been scandalized by the goings-on at

* See pp. 167–8.

the Calves Head Club, where eager young Whigs* held banquets at which the severed head of a calf was used in order to mock the memory of King Charles I, executed by the triumphant parliamentary army in 1649. 'The meat shall represent the tyrant's head,' ran the club's boast, 'the wine, his blood our predecessors shed.'[13] High Church Tories were angered by such things not only because they regarded Charles I as a royal martyr rather than a tyrant brought to book, but also because of the deliberate parody of the Communion service which was involved in the club's ritual. In 1735 the Calves Head Club was closed down after an infuriated crowd had attacked it on 30 January, the anniversary of Charles I's execution.[14] A couple of weeks earlier Hogarth and some of his friends had founded the Sublime Society of Beefsteaks, a club which continued to assert, though in a less offensive manner, the connection between the eating of the horned beast and the acquisition of the virtues it was supposed to represent – strength, independence and the love of freedom. 'Beef and Liberty' was the club's motto; and since its members' pranks were calculated to mock authority as a whole rather than the church and the monarchy in particular it lasted a good deal longer than the Calves Head Club had done.[15] Indeed, the Beefsteak Club still exists today, an eminently respectable though occasionally high-spirited body of men.

The precise significance of all this bovine symbolism is not easy to determine. Hogarth himself used the bull's horns in another context as a symbol of servitude rather than freedom, a device to indicate that the man in question was a poor craven thing, terrorized and cuckolded by his domineering wife.[16] Originally the horns which symbolized cuckoldry were probably the spurs of a cockerel, but the use of the horns of a bull was also very ancient and was sanctified by Shakespeare himself in *Much Ado About Nothing*.[17] Many of the cartoons which showed John Bull as a bull represented him as yoked rather than free, a heavy and rather pathetic creature who could be led by the nose even when he bellowed most loudly.

The really significant question was: who could lead him? The point about the bull was that he represented the Englishman as subject, whereas the lion represented the Englishman as ruler. When the caricaturists wanted to indicate the nation in arms, the nation triumphing over the French or exerting itself against rebellious American colonists, they showed

* During the 1670s those who wanted the monarchy to be subordinated to Parliament and to the Common Law came to be called 'Whigs', a term of abuse meaning ungodly Scottish rebels. They in their turn called the loyalists 'Tories', meaning superstitious Catholic Irish outlaws. The labels stuck and served to define the two opposing political attitudes of the time.

it as the royal lion of England; but when they wanted to comment on the nation's domestic troubles, the taxes it had to pay or the corrupt politicians it had to endure, they showed it as a bull. And bulls need to be led by a particular sort of man: someone with firmness yet humour, someone not afraid to get his clothes dirty, someone used to the honest toil of country life. The moral of it all was that the ordinary freeborn Englishman would take almost anything from those who respected him and understood him but would paw the ground ominously in the presence of canting moralizers or villainous courtiers. The image of the bull as the national symbol of England was a comment on the art of the government, on the particular sort of government which you had to practise when you were dealing not with cringing French slaves, but with true freeborn Englishmen.

It was certainly true that some of the most successful and some of the most popular men in eighteenth-century English government were those who looked as though they could manage animals as well as men. The English crowd might be an urban phenomenon but the art of managing it was not entirely an urban skill. Sir Robert Walpole, one of the most effective politicians of the first half of the century, was always careful to avoid any appearance of over-sophistication: the image he sought to cultivate was that of the bluff country squire who brought to the business of central government the same straightforward earthiness which served him in good stead in local affairs. And King George III, effectively vilified and misrepresented by hostile propagandists during the first half of his reign, finally won through to a position of unprecedented popularity because of his apparent resemblance to a simple countryman. (See Plate 2.) In fact there was something almost schizophrenic about the freeborn Englishman and the political tradition for which he stood. On the one hand he was a townsman, his liberties rooted in urban resistance to feudal overlords and his independence symbolized by the free movement of the urban crowd as opposed to the stratified servitude of the countryside. And yet on the other hand he was also the sturdy countryman, slow to anger but implacable when roused and a doughty champion of traditional liberties against the trickery and corruption of politicians in London.

It was this 'country' aspect of his personality that predominated when the freeborn Englishman was invoked in political terms. There were 558 members of the House of Commons at this time and most of them were career politicians, men who had come in as the clients of some great patron and who intended to advance their careers by following him into office when the time came – if, indeed, it had not come already. Many of the 421 members for the boroughs and cities of England, as well as most of the forty-five members who represented Scotland, fell into this category. They tended to vote either in the interests of the government that was in office or in the interests of an opposition group whose real object was to occupy the corridors of power rather than reform them. But the ninety-two members for the counties (two each for the forty counties of England and one each for the twelve Welsh counties) were in a rather different position. For the most part county electorates were too large to be dominated by any patron, however powerful, and so the representation of the counties was usually settled by agreement among the freeholders. The ninety-two knights of the shire, together with thirty or forty other independent country gentlemen who sat for those borough seats which had so far escaped the influence of the great patrons, formed a chosen band which in its own eyes was the only true guardian of the country's interests. Indeed, they often called themselves the Country Party, dismissing the other four-fifths of the House as courtiers or office-seekers, men who were the minions of government rather than the champions of the governed. Only country gentlemen who were truly independent, content with their broad acres and unambitious for power and office, could speak out boldly for the freeborn Englishman against those who sought to lead him by the nose.[18]

Hogarth's comment on this particular aspect of John Bull was made in four magnificent paintings, all of them probably completed in 1754, showing various aspects of a county election. (See Plate 3.) One of them contained a milestone indicating that the county town in question was only nineteen miles from London; but in fact the paintings were clearly based on the tumultuous and scandalous Oxfordshire election of a few months before. It was more than forty years since the county had gone to the polls; but now a local Whig magnate decided to challenge the hold which the 'Tory' or 'Country Party' gentlemen had had over Oxfordshire for so long. The resulting contest was marked by riots that turned in some cases into pitched battles, with men killed and prisoners taken on both sides. The independent gentlemen of Oxfordshire were so furious at this invasion of their traditional preserves that they trotted out every possible slogan in order to smear the Whigs and their government. The cry against calendar reform was revived – in 1752 the government had switched from the ancient Julian calendar to the Gregorian calendar and there had been violent protests at the apparent loss of eleven days when 2 September was followed by 14 September – and so were the complaints about Lord Hardwicke's Marriage Act of 1753. This comparatively innocuous measure merely sought to prevent clandestine marriages and stop the exploitation of heiresses, but it was represented by the opposition as an intolerable invasion of the liberties of the freeborn Englishman.

There were other and nastier cries. In 1753 the Government had had to repeal an Act recently passed allowing for the naturalization of Jews, because of a rabid campaign of anti-Semitism waged mainly by those same country gentlemen who were always so ready to defend the freeborn Englishman against real or imagined foreign influences in high places.[19] Other stock targets for the Country Party also came in for their share of defamation during the fight against the Jew Bill. The King's younger son, the Duke of Cumberland, commander-in-chief of the army and victor over the Jacobite rebels at Culloden, was hated by the honest squires of England not only because he was the symbol of Hanoverian militarism, but also because he was suspected of wanting to usurp the throne now that his elder brother was dead and the heir was the future George III, a boy of fifteen. Cumberland therefore made his appearance in scurrilous prints, queueing up to be circumcised and declaring that it would make little difference to him – a reference to his supposed impotence.[20] Now, in Oxfordshire, all this was dragged up again as the indignant country gentlemen encouraged their freeborn labourers to riot against the threat of Whig domination. Hanoverian wicked uncles, universal circumcision and a dismal future of stolen days and regulated marriages. The result was a close-fought battle in which the Tory candidate was returned, only to be unseated by a Whig-dominated House of Commons on charges of intimidation and corruption which were, in this case at least, only too well founded.

With his usual sardonic humour Hogarth filled his four election pictures with characters busily making nonsense of the slogans which they used so brazenly: the country gentlemen's candidate is supported by banners against the Jew Bill, yet he himself quietly buys trinkets from a Jewish pedlar in order to tempt the ladies. Every picture is crammed with references to the absurdity of political slogans and the degradation of political morals. It is not easy to discover the artist's own political allegiance. Like most intelligent men of his time, Hogarth professed to look down on all party politicians, including those independent men who pretended to represent the Country Party but whose convictions and prejudices were in fact Tory, as the Oxfordshire election had shown. Men as intelligent as Hogarth but with more optimism and less cynicism still believed that it might somehow be possible to preserve the liberties of England without such squalid political bickering: the constitution could best be defended, they thought, if all men united around it instead of dividing within it.

There is no reason to think that Hogarth entertained idealistic notions of this sort, but he certainly deplored the violence and stupidity of contemporary politics and he seems to have been marginally more depressed by the mindless prejudices of the country gentlemen than by the suave trickery of their Whig opponents. These honest squires who claimed to champion John Bull were readier to make capital for themselves out of his intransigence than to secure for him any real freedom.

During the twenty years that followed Hogarth's election pictures the squires steadily became more important in politics. The Seven Years War, fought between 1756 and 1763, secured for Great Britain vast new territories and an improved trading position, but it also brought with it a crippling load of debt which enabled the country gentlemen to argue that the country had been brought to the verge of bankruptcy in order to accumulate private profits for the Whig politicians and for the greedy merchants and Jewish financiers by whom they were surrounded. The commercial interests fought back against propaganda of this sort, stirring up the London crowds with as much skill as the infuriated squires had shown in Oxfordshire. By the autumn of 1763 the young George III, who had succeeded to the throne in October 1760, was remarking gloomily: 'We hear of insurrections and tumults in every part of the country; there is no government, no law.'[21] Whig politicians blamed the squires: in the spring of 1765 one Whig leader went so far as to prophesy that a measure to give the country gentlemen more power over the poor in their localities would 'set all the counties of England in a flame'.[22] But in the event it was the squires who saddled the politicians with the responsibility for the discontents and disturbances of the time. By the early 1770s Parliament and the party leaders who controlled it were lower in public esteem than they had been for a lifetime. As the career politicians blamed one another, the Government insisting all would be well if the opposition were less irresponsible and the opposition insisting that all would be well if only they were in power, independent men throughout the country blamed the very fact that politics was a career.

It was the American revolution that brought things to a head, giving the country gentlemen of England their greatest moment of glory and at the same time pointing inexorably to their decline and to the decline of the particular concept of English liberty which they represented. They had themselves done much to make the revolt of the American colonies inevitable, because they steadily refused to contribute any further to commercial expansion or to the military and administrative expenditure which it brought with it. It soon became clear in the 1760s that no ministry could survive for long unless it could solve the American problem without raising any new taxes in England and without creating any new administrative machinery which the independent men in Parliament could represent as an unwarranted extension of government patronage. In other words, the squires made a peaceful solution of the American problem impossible, while posing – for the most part successfully – as the champions of all freeborn Englishmen against governmental attempts to enmesh them in an extended and expensive administrative network run for the benefit of commercial men and overweening colonists.

The absurdity of this pose was pointed out by Sir William Meredith, member for Liverpool and himself an independent for many years. While the country gentlemen were congratulating themselves on the Stamp Act, arguing that it was fair to lay a tax on the American colonists in order that freeborn Englishmen should no longer have to pay taxes for a commercial empire they resented, he reminded them solemnly: 'The safety of this country consists in this . . . that we cannot lay a tax upon others without taxing ourselves. This is not the case in America. We shall tax them in order to ease ourselves.'[23] And this was indeed the great weakness of the squires: their determination to ease themselves. Just as the freeholders of the apple-growing counties had been prepared to jeopardize the government's finances a year or so earlier rather than see excise extended to cider, so now the whole body of English landed men would put the overseas empire at risk rather than pay a penny more than they must towards the cost of running it. The truth was that they were not really interested in freedom in general, or indeed in abstractions of any sort – hence their contempt for the abstractions to which the Americans had recourse in their Declaration of Independence in July 1776. They were interested in their own particular freedoms and franchises and privileges and they believed, probably quite sincerely in many cases, that these would broaden down from precedent to precedent to ensure in the end the liberties of all. In the meantime they would fight their own corner.

The glory of the country gentlemen was short-lived, not simply because they were selfish and prejudiced and irresponsible but because they were swiftly becoming obsolete, a rumbustious and amateurish anachronism in a world which was moving inexorably towards bureaucracy and professional standards of government. The war with the American colonists, fought between 1775 and 1783, turned out to be not an end but a beginning. Far from halting the country's progress towards an ever-increasing dependence on foreign trade, it accelerated it. By the time it was over the country gentlemen's ideal of England as a self-sufficient and self-governing land had vanished for ever. Capitalist investment, in industry and agriculture as well as in foreign trade, was producing a level of economic growth which made a rapid increase in population both possible and necessary. In many parts of the country the self-contained parish system was breaking down, and with it the old undisputed rule of the local landed gentleman. When he met with his fellow justices of the peace at the quarterly sessions in his county town, he found that there was more to do than simply judge a few neglectful parish authorities or send a handful of wrongdoers before the judges of assize. The government of the county was becoming more complex and it needed professional administrators rather than amateur country gentlemen. Still less were the gentlemanly amateurs able to comprehend the governmental problems of the county as a whole: their rather naïve belief in local independence and weak central governments as the secret of national success looked rather silly in the new age of capitalism and statistics. Nor were the squires themselves always able to opt out of this new and bewildering spiral of economic growth and governmental control. However self-contained their little landed empires might seem, they usually needed capital to maintain them and wider markets to extend them. Independent men whose fathers had stood together because they had been indifferent to government office found that they themselves could not afford to be indifferent to government policy, even on complicated matters of finance or foreign trade which they would rather have ignored.

By the end of the War of American Independence the decline in the political importance of the independent men was an accepted fact at Westminster. 'The independents', wrote the younger Pitt scornfully in February 1784, 'are ... as ineffectual as ever.'[24] Politicians who could understand and manipulate the complicated patterns of the new capitalism no longer needed to worry very much about the frustrated fulminations of a hundred or so country gentlemen whose independence had been undermined and whose claim to represent the country was falling apart in their hands. And while politicians in office quietly wrote off the independent men as a nuisance that need no longer be endured, politicians in opposition lamented the passing of a resource of which they had often been able to make good use. In 1789, when King George III recovered from a serious illness and thus prevented the opposition Whigs from coming into power as the ministers of his son, some opposition leaders refused to believe that his recovery was genuine and spoke of him being 'carried about in a state of idiocy' in an attempt to fool the people and prevent his son being made Regent. It was in this connection that Edmund Burke, one of the most embittered of the would-be ministers, produced his famous remark that 'John Bull has been long dead and is succeeded by something not very much meriting that firm, blunt, thick-headed but well-meaning title'.[25] The mere fact that opposition politicians could not get independent men to share their doubts about the king's recovery was enough, in Burke's eyes, to indicate that the great age of the freeborn Englishman was over.

The really sad thing was that Burke was right. The eighteenth-century concept of English liberty *was* dependent on the truculence and irresponsibility of the local magnates and upon their readiness to champion the prejudices of the crowd against the so-called wisdom of the government in London. In the past there had always been a fair chance that the prejudices might be right and the wisdom wrong; but now, in an age of statistics and bureaucracy, this chance was becoming more and more remote. Nor was this only an age of statistics: it was also an age of uncertainty. Rebellion in America, unrest in Ireland and finally revolution in France all made the squires far less ready to rouse and encourage the turbulent crowds they had manipulated so confidently in the past. Whether he was landowner or factory owner, countryman or townsman, the man of property found that he could only defend his own privileges and freedoms by sacrificing those of his social inferiors. If the order of society was to be preserved, it must be preserved by the efforts and by the methods of the central government. Parliamentary committees began to be appointed to look into things which previously had been the jealously guarded preserve of the local justice of the peace: poor law, public health, apprenticeship regulations, hours and conditions of work. The freeborn Englishman with his genial and amateurish and haphazard authority was gradually elbowed aside and his place was taken by the professional administrator. Clerks in government offices in London, armed with invincible batteries of statistics and calculations, came to wield greater authority than the eighteenth-century gentleman had ever known. His reign was over. He was dying with the century that had created him.

The system that set up gentlemanly amateurs as the cornerstones of English law and administration had always had its critics. 'I own I have been sometimes inclined to think,' wrote Fielding ironically in 1751, 'that this office of a Justice of the Peace requires some knowledge of the law . . . and yet certain it is, Mr Thrasher never read one syllable of the matter.'[26] As a justice of the peace himself – he had taken his oath as one of the justices for Westminster in October 1748 – Fielding knew only too well how difficult it was to introduce professional standards, or even proper impartiality and efficiency, into the day-to-day administration of justice in

Hogarth: *Canvassing for Votes*, 1754. While others drum up votes for him the Tory candidate makes nonsense of his promises by buying trinkets from the Jews he has vowed to drive out of the country.

PW
Defence of Publick Stews
Injection

England. His predecessor at the court in Bow Street, Sir Thomas de Veil, had been attacked and threatened not only by the mob but also by his fellow justices because he had tried to turn the haphazard system of informers into a proper organization for the detection and apprehension of criminals. In 1749 there had been a violent public outcry against Fielding himself because of the part he had played in putting down some serious riots at a brothel in the Strand.[27] (See Plate 4.) He would have liked to see a proper police force, at least in London if not in the country as a whole; but to most Englishmen in the 1750s such an idea was tantamount to suggesting an importation of French tyranny. Even in 1780, after propertied men had been scared and sobered by the ferocious Gordon riots in June of that year,* Lord Shelburne was still regarded as an apologist for French despotism because he suggested in the House of Lords that the time had now come for London to have a police force.[28] By 1788 there were open attacks in the *Gentleman's Magazine* on the kind of justice of the peace who knew nothing of the law and therefore 'gives up his neighbours to pettifoggers and half gentlemen, who torture the laws to base purposes of petty quarrels, low prejudices and mercenary cabal';[29] yet in the same year justices of the peace for Hertfordshire could still react violently when the central Government dared to interfere in the business of putting down riots in their county.[30]

When the people of Paris stormed the ancient prison of the Bastille on 14 July 1789 many Englishmen believed, perhaps rather naïvely, that this signified the end of the French system of strong centralized tyranny. Many of them also thought, with rather more justification, that their own traditional system of local self-government was crumbling in the face of steadily advancing governmental powers. The caricaturist James Gillray, one of Hogarth's most talented successors, went so far as to produce a cartoon entitled *France Freedom, Britain Slavery*, which showed Englishmen cringing in chains before Pitt, now firmly established as first minister, while exultant Frenchmen celebrated their new-won liberty. The chains were part of the cartoonist's stock-in-trade, as were the axe which Pitt waved aloft and the gibbet which appeared in the background. They symbolized invasions of the liberty of the subject, invasions which had been long feared and which were in fact about to take place as a result of the war against the French revolution which began in 1793. By 1797, when John Bowdler came to write his impassioned *Reform or Ruin*, there was something almost pathetic about the jaunty defiance with which he declared, 'I am a freeborn Briton and an independent man . . . I have the

* See pp. 55–6.

right to think and speak for myself and will do so.' Having made the claim, he took care not to press it. 'Having no more desire to see the inside of Newgate than to try the air of Botany Bay,' he wrote, 'I shall be cautious in what I have to say about Parliament.'[31] He had good reason for caution, for by this time men were indeed being sentenced to imprisonment and transportation for advocating parliamentary reform. Severe inroads had been made upon the liberty of the subject and of the press – inroads which propertied men disliked but which they felt constrained to accept as necessary prophylactic measures to ward off the contagion of revolution.

Dramatic though these developments were, they were not to prove in the long run the really essential factor in the decline of the rumbustious and irresponsible traditions of eighteenth-century liberty. The repressive measures of the 1790s were eventually repealed or allowed to fall into disuse; but the advance of bureaucracy could not be halted. English life, particularly English economic life, had come of age: it was too mature, too sophisticated, too complicated, to be managed any longer by the hit-and-miss methods of the local magnates. It was this truth, and not the lurid activities of sadistic despots, that lay behind the contrasts between Hogarth's *The Gate of Calais* and Gillray's *France Freedom, Britain Slavery*. Caricaturists and pamphleteers might argue as to whether the obsession with chains was a French or an English predilection, but in fact English liberty was not languishing in a torture chamber or hanging from a gibbet: it was smothered under a mass of statistics and regulations, some of them regrettable but most of them necessary. Back in the 1750s, while Hogarth was still indulging in his public shudders about the lack of liberty on the other side of the Channel, a French writer had prophesied that eventually English avarice would destroy English liberty.[32] That prophecy was now being fulfilled. By making themselves the richest nation on earth the English had created in their own country problems which could no longer be solved by the old easy-going methods of local management. Government, informed and professional and efficient government, had come to stay. If the freeborn Englishman was to survive, his liberties would have to be guaranteed by the government itself and not merely by the government allowing his landlord or employer to assume responsibility for him. It was to this end that there was carried out in 1801 the exercise that marked the advent of modern government and the passing of the old world of amateurism: the taking of the first proper census of the population of the kingdom.

A proposal for a census had been put before Parliament as early as 1753, in the middle of those turbulent years that saw independent English gentlemen fulminating against Jewish naturalization and calendar reform and the proper regulation of marriages. Its chief opponent in the House of Commons had been William Thornton of Cattal in Yorkshire, a country landowner but also a man with some political ambitions who was politically rather more sophisticated than the ordinary crusty country gentleman. 'I was never more astonished and alarmed,' he cried, 'I did not believe that there had been any set of men, or indeed any individual of the human species, so presumptuous and so abandoned as to make the proposal which we have just heard.' He attacked the Bill because it would give dangerous information both to enemies abroad and to enemies at home. The latter, he explained, were 'place-men and tax-masters'; and he thought that he would ill deserve the confidence of his constituents if he agreed to anything that would increase their power. As far as he was concerned the central government was the open and declared enemy of every local community. If freeborn Englishmen did anything to help it they would deserve 'the canvas frock and wooden shoes, which will inevitably be put on'. 'As to myself,' he said, 'I hold this project to be totally subversive of the last remains of English liberty . . . If any officer, by whatever authority, should demand of me an account of the number and circumstances of my family, I would refuse it; and if he persisted in the affront, I would order my servants to give him the discipline of the horse-pond.'[33] Thornton's fiery words served their purpose: nobody dared to make out a proper case for the proposal and it was dropped.

But in 1800 the measure authorizing the census of the following year passed through both Houses amidst almost universal acclaim. On all sides the proposer was complimented on his initiative and good sense, while opposition speakers confined themselves to points of detail.[34] Even more than the contrast between Hogarth's picture of French tyranny and Gillray's image of English enslavement, the contrast between the census debates of 1753 and 1800 illustrates both the strength and the weakness of the eighteenth-century English idea of liberty. Both in their original unaccountability and in their final resignation to being counted, the English bore witness to a progress from turbulence to regimentation which influenced every circumstance of their lives during this half-century.

2 Valour and Violence

'EVERY man thinks meanly of him self,' Dr Johnson once remarked, 'for not having been a soldier, or not having been at sea.'[1] Even at the best of times it is not easy for literary men to confess to secret guilt feelings of this sort; and in Johnson's case there was an added difficulty, for he was a Tory, a man who carried the independence of the eighteenth-century gentleman to a point verging on disloyalty and treason – at any rate in theory. 'If the English were fairly polled,' he growled, 'George III would be packed out of the kingdom by nightfall and his adherents hanged by morning.'[2] In fact his contempt for the Hanoverians and nostalgia for the good old hereditary monarchs of the Stuart dynasty seems to have been more rhetorical than real: when he actually met George III face to face the aura of kingship, even of Hanoverian kingship, had such an effect on him that he behaved with a deference bordering on servility. But however inconsistent he might be about kings, he could not afford to be inconsistent about soldiers. As far as Tories were concerned soldiers were the lowest of human creatures, poor enslaved beings who were good for nothing but making slaves of their fellow men. England was an island – like Shakespeare's John of Gaunt, the gentlemen of the eighteenth century tended to forget that it was actually joined to Scotland – and therefore could have no other possible use for armies but as instruments of tyranny. The Tories never forgot that the outcome of the Civil War, the nemesis of impious rebellion and regicide, had been the military dictatorship of Oliver Cromwell. Nor did they forget that the overthrow of James II in 1688 and the elevation of Dutch William to the throne had dragged the country into expensive Continental wars which had revived once again the sinister power and influence of military men.

The English contempt for soldiers and military glory was not confined to Tories. Most Englishmen considered that there were only two possible reasons for a man becoming a soldier: either because he was forced to, or because he was so poor and destitute that he had no other choice. Native English soldiers were therefore inadmissible, since their very existence implied either the tyranny of conscription or the scandal of widespread poverty – both of them things which the English claimed to have banished from their land for ever. Foreign soldiers, German troops imported by the Hanoverians or Dutchmen serving William III, were even worse since they symbolized a foreign military yoke. Whigs were often as anxious as Tories to avoid any suggestion of enthusiasm for military matters, however glorious and victorious they might be. Horace Walpole, a man nurtured and sustained by the Whig political establishment that the independents and the Tories hated so cordially, did his best to remain unimpressed by martial pomp and circumstance. In September 1759, when even the unenthusiastic English were beginning to stir to the news of some of the greatest victories their country had ever known, Walpole managed to remain cool and detached, ironically comparing English successes with the arrogance and militarism of ancient Rome. 'We want but a little more insolence and a worse cause to make us a very classic nation,' he concluded. But even Walpole was elated by the events of the next few weeks as news of yet more victories poured in from all over the world. 'Thus we wind up this wonderful year!' he wrote excitedly at the end of November. 'Who that died three years ago and could revive would believe it?'[3] However much they might differ in other things, particularly in their religion and in their politics, Johnson and Walpole were alike in their typically English ambivalence towards the grandeurs and the servitude of the military life.

Hogarth reflected this attitude in his *The March to Finchley* (Plate 5), painted in 1749 and published as an engraving in the spring of 1750. Military matters were very much in the air just then, as Parliament was debating the Duke of Cumberland's unpopular and eventually unsuccessful plan to impose a Prussian style of discipline upon the British army. Hogarth had painted a couple of pictures of Cumberland as a boy many years earlier and now his comment took the apparently complimentary form of a reminder of the Duke's finest hour, his defence of England against the Jacobite invasion from Scotland in 1745. While Cumberland had concentrated his army in the Midlands to intercept Prince Charles, George II had ordered the establishment of a camp at Finchley, a few miles north of London, to act as a second line of defence in case the capital should be attacked. The London militia and other volunteers had marched out there, stiffened by such regular troops as could be spared; and it was the farewell of the Londoners to these brave defenders that Hogarth now chose to portray. The scene was the Tottenham Court Road, only a short walk from Hogarth's own house in what is now Leicester

Square. In the distance a column of troops could be seen winding its way towards Finchley in a reasonably orderly fashion; but in the foreground the soldiery was behaving very differently. Crowded between two taverns, the Adam and Eve on the left and the King's Head on the right, the men were clearly ready to partake of all that these establishments had to offer – which was more than just drink, at any rate in the case of the King's Head. It had been taken over for the occasion by one of the more enterprising of the Covent Garden brothelkeepers, who had installed her girls at the upstairs windows so that they could show themselves off properly. As the troops broke ranks and mingled with the crowds they were beset by all manner of street vendors and camp followers – some of them Jacobite spies and conspirators. As a picture of Englishmen defending their freedom *The March to Finchley* was sadly lacking in dignity and patriotic fervour; but as a picture of Englishmen enjoying their freedom it had few equals.

When war broke out with France again in 1756 Hogarth produced two plates called *The Invasion* (Plate 6), in which he brought together the two themes he had already explored in *The Gate of Calais* and *The March to Finchley*: the deadly seriousness of French militarism and the carefree fortitude of England's response to it. In the first plate French soldiers gathered on the coast of France, waiting to embark for the invasion of England, while a tonsured monk gloated over the instruments of torture which he hoped soon to use on the stiff-necked English heretics. In the second those same heretics prepared their resistance in their usual light-hearted way, drawing rude pictures of the King of France and frolicking with their womenfolk. The tavern outside which this merriment was taking place was called the Duke of Cumberland; and underneath the duke's picture on the inn-sign Hogarth hung the legend 'Roast and boiled every day'. This could perhaps have been taken as a compliment, identifying the duke – who was certainly meaty enough in all conscience – with the symbolic beef of English liberty, which all good innkeepers served and all good Englishmen devoured. But it was much more likely to have been meant as a sly reference to the popular nickname of 'Butcher Cumberland' and to the bitter attacks made on the duke by the caricaturists and the pamphleteers, who did indeed 'roast and boil' him nearly every day. As in *The March to Finchley*, the implication was clear enough: the valour which would defend England's liberties would spring not from the regimentation and discipline so dear to Hanoverian hearts, but from the English tradition of jostling insubordination which German kings and their soldierly sons would never understand.

5 Hogarth: *The March to Finchley*, 1749. Detail showing the scene four years earlier when the troops, marching off to save London from the rebels, were distracted by the temptations of the flesh in the Tottenham Court Road.

Soup Meagre
a la
Sabot Royal

Plan pour un
Monastere dans
Black Friars à
Londre

St. Antoni

Duke of Cumberland
Roast & Boil'd every Day

7 (*Above*) Hogarth: *Strolling Actresses in a Barn*, 1738. As well as commenting on the Licensing Act of the previous year (see p. 161) this picture provides some interesting sidelights on methods of infant feeding.

6 (*Opposite*) Hogarth: *The Invasion*, 1756. The first plate shows the French preparations to invade and the second the English reaction. Nothing in eighteenth-century art illustrates better the Englishman's conviction that his light-hearted defiance could cope with any threat, however sinister.

8 Hogarth: *Gin Lane*, 1751. A print intended to 'reform some reigning Vices peculiar to the lower Class of People'. Shortly after its publication the first effective Act against gin drinking was passed.

Once again it was Dr Johnson who underlined the point. 'They who complain in peace of the insolence of the populace', he wrote, 'must remember that their insolence is bravery in war.'[4] As long as Englishmen themselves were prepared to defend the liberties of England, coming forward like the grinning lad in Hogarth's picture to swell in moments of peril the skeleton force maintained in normal times, all would be well. Freeborn Englishmen would be able to have it both ways, applauding bravery and endurance because these virtues were born of the freedom they cherished and not of the militarism they despised. But unfortunately it was not quite as easy as that. The invasion scare of 1756 in fact drove home lessons far sharper and harsher than Hogarth's carefree picture of carousing suggested. The old strategy, whereby England maintained a small army of some 17,000 men and relied on mustering volunteers in an emergency, had really depended on the readiness of England's continental allies to tie down France's land forces. Now she had lost those allies, with the result that even the most desultory invasion preparations on the other side of the Channel could render England impotent in all foreign theatres of war while she struggled to raise enough men to defend her own shores. Nor was the struggle particularly successful: in spite of the supposed enthusiasm and patriotism of the freeborn Englishman, extra Hanoverian regular troops had to be drafted in to ensure the defence of the country. Propertied men discovered that even the 'insolence of the populace' was not sufficient to protect them against the twin dangers of French militarism and Hanoverian militarism. By 1760 the wealthy citizens of London had subscribed over £7,000 at Guildhall in order to bribe men, at four guineas a head, to join the army.[5]

It was William Thornton, the same man who had threatened to have census officials thrown into his horse-pond, who put forward the answer to this dilemma. In 1752 he had published *The Counterpoise: being thoughts on a militia and a standing army*; and he followed this up by bringing a Bill into Parliament for the establishment of a militia.[6] His Bill never got beyond the report stage, but the invasion scare of 1756 led many influential politicians, including the elder Pitt, to think that the establishment of a militia might be a useful move, pleasing the country gentlemen and helping the defence of the country at one and the same time. A Militia Act was passed in 1757 which was designed to reassure the squires and to show that the proposed militia would indeed be a counterpoise, and not an adjunct, to the standing army of which Englishmen were so deeply suspicious. Only those with a certain amount of property were to be officers, while those enlisting in the ranks were to be as free as possible to carry on their normal trades and jobs. Although drilling was to be on weekdays – a proposal to drill on Sundays was defeated on the grounds that it would offend the Almighty and thus make French victory in the war certain – it was to be limited to the summer months and it only amounted to a few days a year. So far from arming the people and making them dangerous, as opponents of the measure had feared, the Militia Act seemed to confirm the local power of the landed gentleman as the ruler of English society. Moreover, he would not even have to pay for the new and prestigious privilege of playing at soldiers with his tenants and servants: the costs of the militia were to be met from general taxation and not from the localities themselves, as had been the case with the traditional militia arrangements of earlier times.

Nevertheless, the country gentlemen of England showed little enthusiasm for the plan and their labourers showed even less. It proved almost impossible to get officers, while in many counties there were serious riots when local parish authorities tried to draw up the lists of those liable to serve in the ranks. In Yorkshire the high sheriff was besieged by an armed mob which threatened to pull down his house and those of his neighbours if he tried to implement the Act. In Bedfordshire the local justices abandoned the attempt to ballot for militiamen after they had been told that they would be murdered by the mob if they went ahead. It took another Act and another invasion scare, the more serious one of 1759, to get the militia properly organized. And even then there were many counties in which the forces raised were never actually embodied for service. It was not until 1778, when the French intervened on the side of the colonists in the War of American Independence, that the militia first turned out as a really national force. It was still far from popular and ministers feared that their proposals to increase its numbers would lead to 'tumults and insurrections'; but at least it was now fashionable. Young aristocrats, as well as ordinary country gentlemen, found that time passed pleasantly at various militia camps that were set up throughout the country. One such camp, at Coxheath near Maidstone in Kent, was represented in meticulous detail in the backcloth for Richard Tickell's play *The Camp*, which ran successfully for two seasons at Drury Lane Theatre.[7]

The militia provided Englishmen with a useful escape route from their quandary about the demands of freedom and the demands of military security. Military training in the eighteenth century did not have to be very lengthy: even in the highly disciplined armies of Prussia it took only a month or two to teach recruits to handle their weapons and learn the basic formations which were necessary in battle or on the march. In the

British army standards were much lower and more amateurish. Many army officers had neither the inclination nor the knowledge to drill their men properly, so that it was not difficult for the militia to equal and even in some cases to surpass the regular troops in efficiency and keenness. From 1762 onwards twenty-eight days drill a year became standard practice; and this gave English gentlemen an opportunity to indulge their military enthusiasms while still retaining their amateur status and their right to rail at the enslaving propensities of standing armies. They fought mock battles and they practised Indian methods of bush fighting; they wheeled and charged and organized ambitious field days and other exercises. And at the end of it all they felt they could look any regular army officer in the face without flinching. Whatever Dr Johnson might think, they no longer thought meanly of themselves for not having been soldiers or not having been to sea.[8]

It was the sea that provided the other escape route from the dilemma about freedom and security. For while soldiers were simply soldiers and nothing else, men who had no peacetime trade but the repression of free-born Englishmen, sailors were also seamen. They could be usefully employed extending in peace the fisheries and the commercial riches which they defended in war. Besides, the island history of Britain had fostered a belief that seapower, unlike military power, was an attribute of liberty rather than a danger to it. The seamen were the real defenders of the island fortress, standing on the battlements (or perhaps in the moat itself, for the sake of a consistent metaphor) and facing outwards towards the foe. Soldiers, on the other hand, were the cowardly bullies who ran around inside the fortress harrying its civilian occupants under the pretence of organizing a defence in which they themselves were careful to take very few risks. Like the militiamen, the mariners who guarded England's shores had a regular peacetime occupation: braving the elements in order to bring back the harvest of the sea or the produce of foreign lands. Like the militiamen, they were a living proof of the English contention that fighting emboldened the free men who undertook it occasionally but enslaved and corrupted the military men who made it into a full-time occupation.

Sentiments of this sort inspired a masque called *Alfred*, written by James Thomson and David Mallet and first performed in 1740. Like most of the successful London entertainments of the time, it had political overtones. It was produced under the patronage of Frederick Prince of Wales, the elder brother and political rival of the Duke of Cumberland. Cumberland himself was only nineteen at the time and had not yet become the country gentlemen's favourite scapegoat for the sins of Hanover and Hanoverian militarism: that position was still occupied by King George II himself. But the Prince of Wales was already well launched on his own career as his father's chief opponent and the champion of the country gentlemen and their prejudices. Thus *Alfred* – for which incidentally, Hogarth was commissioned to engrave the tickets of invitation – celebrated the traditional concept of English liberty as something to be defended by honest English seamen and not by alien Hanoverian soldiers. Its most striking feature was the song 'Rule Britannia', soon to become one of the most popular of Britain's many patriotic and jingoistic songs. Its famous refrain urged Britannia to rule the waves, in order to ensure that Britons should never be slaves; but it left it conveniently to the discretion of the politicians and the naval commanders to decide just which waves would have to be ruled. It contained both the sturdy defiance of the freedom-loving island race and also the arrogant imperialism of the most rapidly developing commercial and industrial nation in the world.

As it turned out it was the mariners and not the militiamen who ensured the defence of England in the second half of the eighteenth century. The invasion threat of 1756 never really materialized; but when the French did bring together an invasion force, in 1759, it was the British navy which scattered and destroyed the ships that were to have escorted it. There was a nasty moment in 1779, when the combined French and Spanish fleets rode unchallenged in the English Channel, and another in 1797, when the navies of France, Spain and the Dutch Republic were all turned against England at a time when her own fleets were weakened by serious mutinies. But these crises were surmounted – in 1797 the mutineers even offered to suspend their mutiny in order to fight the enemy if he should put to sea – and the period ended with Nelson's great victory at Trafalgar in 1805, which finally put paid to Napoleon Bonaparte's invasion plans. In strategic and tactical terms, at any rate, the English had vindicated their claim to be able to defend themselves without recourse to a full-scale professional army.

The social implications of the claim were less easily vindicated. In theory English society provided the ideal foundation upon which a superstructure of seapower could be reared, even though the enslaving power of armies had no place in it; but in practice things were rather different. English gentlemen had gloried for many years in what they called their 'blue water' policies, by means of which their wars could be fought purely at sea, in the interests of English trade and English security rather than for the sake of the military ambitions of the Hanoverians. But in fact those same gentlemen and their representatives in Parliament had fought doggedly against any attempt to increase the naval estimates to a realistic level, with the result that the country rubbed along in peacetime with a navy of some 16,000 men and was then faced with the task of increasing this establishment fivefold whenever war broke out. Every war revealed the terrible dangers of naval unpreparedness in the early stages, yet every peace treaty brought a clamour for retrenchment which forced the government into shortsighted and perilous economies. Meanwhile the various interests and pressure groups in Parliament argued bitterly about the usefulness or otherwise of the commercial and territorial gains that sea-power had produced. This was particularly true in the 1760s, when landed men insisted that the victories of 1759, glorious though they might have been, had bankrupted the nation and produced 'public poverty and private opulence, the fatal disease which has put a period to all the greatest and most flourishing empires of the world'.[9]

For the ordinary sailor these disagreements about the value of his services meant that his life was one of hardship and injustice. He was paid roughly one pound a month, a rate which had been originally settled in the 1650s and was now totally unrealistic. Even this miserable sum was not given to him in cash: he merely got a ticket which entitled him to payment in full if he presented it at the pay office on Tower Hill in London, but which was subject to swingeing deductions if he tried to cash it anywhere else – which of course he had to do, since he was often landed at some port distant from London. The ticket touts who swarmed around the quays at Chatham and Portsmouth and Plymouth, offering sailors cut rates for the pay tickets which were the country's only reward for the war they had won, were the outward and visible signs of the iniquitous system of private profit upon which naval administration was based. What little money the grudging taxpayer granted was sucked into a morass of corruption and inefficiency. 'You may rest assured,' said Admiral Lord St Vincent, 'that the civil branch of the navy is rotten to the core.'[10] Victuals, like pay, were subject to the private profit-taking of unscrupulous contractors. Just before he won his magnificent victory off Quiberon Bay, the naval battle which did more than any other to end the invasion threat of 1759, Admiral Hawke reported that the 'bread' (i.e., hard ship's biscuit) he had taken on board at Plymouth 'though not altogether unfit for use' was nevertheless 'so full of weevils and maggots that it would have infected all the bread come on board this day'.[11]

Just as weevils and maggots did not render biscuit unfit for use – you could always bang it against something hard to jolt some of them out, or alternatively you could eat it in the dark so that you didn't see them[12] – so illness did not render men unfit for duty. Men fed on a diet of ship's biscuit and dried meat or fish, with small quantities of oatmeal, butter and cheese to supplement it, suffered almost continuously from scurvy and other deficiency diseases; while the extremely cramped quarters allotted to the ordinary seamen meant that there was little hope of stopping the spread of infectious diseases. It was reckoned that in the Seven Years War, from 1756 to 1763, nearly a hundred times as many sailors died from disease or other unidentifiable cause as were killed in battle.[13] James Lind's experiments with lime-juice and lemon-juice as remedies for scurvy were made soon after the Seven Years War was over, yet it was not until the end of the century that the Admiralty made proper use of his discoveries. In the meantime captains whose ships were already undermanned could not afford to be too squeamish about such things. The novelist Tobias Smollett had sailed as a surgeon's mate himself, so that he knew only too well the horrors that could result from the disciplinary instincts of the captain and the ignorance or servility of the surgeon. His account of a ship's sick parade in *The Adventures of Roderick Random* probably contains therefore an unpleasant germ of reality within its melodramatic exaggerations:

> The third complained of a pleuritic stitch, and spitting of blood, for which doctor Mackshane prescribed exercise at the pump to promote expectoration; but whether this was improper for one in his situation, or that it was used to excess, I know not, but in less than half an hour he was suffocated with a deluge of blood that issued from his lungs. – A fourth, with much difficulty, climbed to the quarter-deck, being loaded with a monstrous ascites, or dropsy, that invaded his chest so much, he could scarce fetch his breath; but this disease being interpreted into fat, occasioned by idleness and excess of eating, he was ordered, with a view to promote perspiration and enlarge his chest, to go aloft immediately: it was in vain for this unwieldy wretch to allege his utter incapacity, the boatswain's driver was commanded to whip him up with the cat and nine tails: the smart of this application made him exert himself so much, that he actually arrived at the foot-hook-shrouds; but when the enormous weight of his body had nothing else to support it than his weakened arms, either out of spite or necessity he quitted his hold, and plumped into the sea ...[14]

Smollett's imagination undoubtedly outran the truth: Britannia could hardly have ruled the waves if she dropped her men into them with such abandon. But she certainly did not, on the other hand, rule them by promoting the kind of merry hornpipe of Jolly Jack Tars which the patriotic songs suggested. Many of these songs were in fact written much later, in the nineteenth century, when the great days of Nelson could be recalled in a safe glow of romantic nostalgia. Then it was that poets began to talk of hearts of oak and of flags that braved the battle and the breeze. During the eighteenth century itself most people knew well enough that ruling the waves was a grim and difficult business; and they also knew that they did not propose to make it any less so by granting more money to the king's navy or by improving the conditions under which his sailors had to live.

No one knew these harsh truths better than the ordinary merchant seaman, the man upon whom the navy relied to make up the complement of its ships in time of war. Having been turned loose at the end of one war because the country felt no further need for him and therefore no further responsibility either, the seaman found himself courted at the beginning of the next. Captains desperate for crews would mount recruiting campaigns in the seaports of the country, sending their officers out with stirring music and honeyed words to persuade patriotic sailormen to join the king's navy. The sailormen remained almost totally unconvinced: very few ships in the eighteenth-century navy had more than fifteen per cent of volunteers in their crews. The rest had been gathered in by one of various means of compulsion, among which the press gang was the most notorious and the most effective. Officers would lead parties of their men into the streets of the port, there to seize and press into service any seaman they could find. Alternatively, they would put out in small boats to intercept and board homecoming merchant ships in order to seize members of their crews. One gentleman in Northumberland in 1801 sent his young son on a trial voyage to London, simply in order to see if the seafaring life agreed with him; but 'in the Nore he was impressed and dragged away by oppression's savage grasp and sent to Egypt or elsewhere to be butchered . . .'[15]

Other methods of recruitment relied on a theoretically free choice exercised in circumstances which made it in effect compulsory. Men imprisoned for debt were allowed to opt for the navy as an alternative, a practice which led Dr Johnson to remark, in one of his more realistic moments, that 'No man will be a sailor, who has contrivance enough to get himself into a jail; for being in a ship is being in a jail with the chance of being drowned.'[16] Most debtors agreed with him: they chose to be imprisoned on land rather than on the high seas. Other men, too poor even to get the chance of running into debt, had less choice. Any vagabond or beggar or person without fixed abode and regular employment could be brought before a justice and drafted into the navy. A similar fate befell some 30,000 poor and destitute boys in London during the second half of the century, though in their case it was classed as charity. Jonas Hanway, a kindly gentleman who popularized umbrellas and reformed prostitutes, busied himself also with this benevolent work. He founded the Marine Society, which snatched these lads from the squalid and dangerous but possibly remunerative criminal lives which they would otherwise have led. Instead it sent them to a life in the navy which was just as squalid and dangerous but safely unremunerative and therefore socially acceptable. Many of these boys, cowed early in life and incapable of aspiring to any other sort of existence, grew up to be reliable and obedient sailors. Together with the volunteers they formed a small core of relatively compliant men, perhaps a quarter of the ship's company all told, to make up for the sullen reluctance of the conscripted majority. The navies of England reflected the realities of her social system rather than the cherished myths woven around it. Men rich enough to exercise freedom forced those poorer than themselves into fleets which the propertied classes were too mean to pay properly and too corrupt to administer efficiently. Even the despised foreigner was not forgotten in this scramble to get maritime protection on the cheap. Liberty might be English, but its happy possessors did not scruple to include the benighted subjects of foreign tyrants among the men whom they forced into fighting for it. Most ships had ten to twenty per cent of foreigners in their crew, many of them pressed men.[17]

However hard his life and however humble his origins the sailor was nevertheless able to take a pride in himself, something which the soldier as a hated instrument of military tyranny found rather more difficult. When Hogarth and four of his drinking companions went on an impromptu jaunt into Kent in 1732 they came across some sailors who had been abandoned by their officer, a callow midshipman, after the boat in which they had been rowing him had become stuck in the mud. He had left them with no food and no money, so the travellers gave them a shilling and made merry with them.[18] Incidents of this sort with soldiers rather than sailors are seldom recorded and it is hard to imagine them taking place. The weatherbeaten figure of the sailorman might inspire distaste and sometimes even fear, but basically he was seen as a friend and not an enemy to the liberty which Englishmen cherished. The same could not be said of the soldier, who was scarcely thought of as a person at all. Once he had been conned by the recruiting sergeant or forcibly drafted by the justices of the peace – for the power of these gentlemen extended to the army as well as the navy – he became merely a unit in the menacing juggernaut of military power. While the sailor appeared in cartoons and popular prints as Jolly Jack Tar, a cheery and confident figure who filled the picture with his bluster and his bravery, the soldier was usually an anonymous member of some serried line on a parade ground or – less frequently – on a battlefield.

The traditional English hatred of standing armies was the main reason for this difference in status, but it was not the only one. After all, the sailor in the navy had usually been a seaman before he had been pressed, so that he had a trade to go back to. He might be a slave for the duration of the war, but at least he could hold up his head and brag about the great things he would do once he got back to his proper calling. And in the meantime he had the ship itself to provide him with a home and a sense of belonging. The soldier had none of these things. His only trade was soldiering itself, something which most of his countrymen regarded with contempt, and his only home was an inn or other billet in which he was very far from welcome. There were barracks in Ireland and in Scotland, because those countries had no Parliament independent enough to defy the soldiery sent to overawe them;* but in England there were scarcely any. In London and in one or two other garrison towns there was lodging of a sort officially designed for soldiers, but for the most part they were dumped in small groups upon reluctant innkeepers who were forced to feed and lodge them for fourpence a day. Parliament maintained this system not simply to disperse the army but also to keep a check on its numbers. Opposition speakers argued that if the soldiers were hidden away in barracks their numbers might be surreptitiously increased, whereas under the billeting system the people would be 'sensible of the fetters which are preparing for them' and so could act before it was too late.[19]

The soldier was thus forced to live cheek by jowl with civilians who despised him and who were always ready to denounce him to his superior officers. Drunkenness and violence on the part of ordinary people were often tolerated, sometimes even admired as signs of that sturdy independence of which Englishmen were so proud; but if a soldier dared to get drunk or show signs of disorderliness he was immediately seen as an example of that unbridled militarism against which the country was always on guard. Only the most barbarous punishments could preserve discipline in such circumstances or placate the civilian wrath once it was aroused. In the navy floggings seem to have been comparatively moderate in the early part of the century, steadily rising to levels of sickening cruelty by the

* There was an Irish Parliament in Dublin until 1800, but it was effectively under the control of the English authorities for most of the period. Scotland had lost her Parliament in 1707 and sent representatives to Westminster instead – sixteen to the Lords and forty-five to the Commons.

1790s: an offence which would have resulted in fifty lashes at the time of Queen Anne was punished by two or three hundred by the reign of George III.[20] But in the army the levels were always much higher. One soldier boasted in 1727 that he had received 26,000 lashes during the past fourteen years. His officers were not sure that he was telling the truth, but at least they made sure that he improved his average: during the next year they sentenced him to a further 4,000 lashes.[21]

Atrocities of this sort did not cease once the soldier was posted abroad. Joseph Wall, appointed governor and commander-in-chief of Goree in West Africa in 1779, had one of his soldiers flogged to death on the voyage out. Another, Sergeant Armstrong, died in hospital in Goree after a flogging he had received because he had dared to lead a deputation to inquire about arrears of pay. In this particular case Governor Wall was eventually tried and executed for murder, but this was largely because he had neglected to hold a proper court-martial in Armstrong's case and because he had subsequently pointed to his own guilt by fleeing from the law.[22] Officers who stood their ground and were careful to go through the proper forms could not normally be held to account if the punishments they ordered turned out to be fatal. Nor could anyone hold to account those responsible for the mismanagement and corruption which resulted in thousands of soldiers dying of malnutrition and disease and neglect. During the British attack on Cartagena in 1741 the force employed was reduced from 8,000 to 3,500, mainly as a result of deaths from fever, before the offensive was even properly launched.

There had been times in the past when a soldier could take a pride in his exploits; and there were to be such times again. Marlborough had inspired his men at the beginning of the century, during the War of the Spanish Succession, and Wellington was to do so again in the 1800s. One of the most memorable of the fictitious soldiers of the period was a proud and loyal man, Laurence Sterne's Corporal Trim in *Tristram Shandy*. Another and more poignant figure was the disabled soldier whom Oliver Goldsmith described in one of his *Citizen of the World* essays. He had originally got into trouble for killing a hare because he was destitute and starving: for this he had been sentenced to seven years' slave labour in the American colonies. On his return he had been picked up again by the authorities, because he had no fixed abode, and had been forced into the army. He had finished up with a wound in the chest, a severed leg and four fingers missing from his left hand. Now he had to beg for his living, because he was not technically entitled to apply either to the military hospital at Chelsea or the naval one at Greenwich. 'However,' concluded this resilient character, 'Blessed be God, I enjoy good health, and will for ever love liberty and Old England. Liberty, property and Old England for ever, huzza!'[23] And real soldiers could be as loyal as imaginary ones to the system that exploited them. It is recorded that when General Burgoyne's army surrendered to the American rebels at Saratoga in 1777 the men wept when their officers were marched away and cried 'God bless your honours' until they were out of earshot.[24] It was loyalty of this sort that Marlborough had inspired and that Wellington was to make the basis for a virtual regeneration of the British army during the Peninsular War of 1808–14.

But Marlborough and Wellington and even Burgoyne had advantages that most eighteenth-century military commanders lacked. They were fighting sustained and reasonably continuous campaigns in countries where Britain had a comparatively firm foothold and where climatic conditions were not extreme. For the great majority of soldiers in the late eighteenth century things were very different. Long spells of duty at home, in the midst of a hostile and contemptuous civilian population, were relieved only by postings to some remote colonial station where conditions were almost unbearable even when there was no fighting. When they were not being despised as lackeys of militarism they were being packed off to win a commercial empire for which the sailors got most of the credit. The maritime wars of the period showed clearly enough that if Britannia wanted to rule the waves she would have to conquer the ports and fortresses and trading stations of other would-be rulers. And these conquests had to be made by soldiers, soldiers who were crowded into ships for weeks on end in conditions even worse than those of the sailors and who were then subjected on disembarkation to hardships like those of the Cartagena campaign. The army and navy were both fighting for their king and country, but the country for its part tended to separate the two concepts, seeing the soldiers as instruments of a despotic king and the sailors as champions of a free country.

One of the reasons why the riots in the Strand in 1749* caused such an outcry was that they produced an apparent confrontation between these two sets of men. The trouble began when some sailors accused a brothel-keeper of cheating them and it ended, after a weekend of ugly disturbances, when a detachment of forty soldiers marched in with drums beating. In the absence of a police force the hard-pressed justices usually turned in the end to the army when the turbulence of the English crowd, the prized 'insolence of the populace' of Dr Johnson's phrase, threatened

* See p. 31.

to turn to violence. The results could well be unpleasant for the justices, since they would be attacked for breaking the constitution if subsequent events suggested that the violence had not justified military intervention; but it could be a great deal more unpleasant for the soldiers. English juries were notoriously reluctant to find against anyone accused of attacking the military, just as they were notoriously anxious to find against any soldier accused of using undue force upon the civil population. Soldiers ordered to fire upon a crowd might well be indicted for murder if they obeyed or shot for disobedience if they refused. The position of the officers who gave the orders was equally hazardous. In 1736 a certain Captain Porteous commanded his men to fire upon an Edinburgh crowd which threatened to get out of hand after the hanging of a particularly popular smuggler. Porteous was condemned to death by the Edinburgh courts and when the government in London tried to intervene, postponing his execution while it looked into the case, the mob broke into his prison and lynched him.

The significant factor in the Porteous case was the thing which was most difficult to determine: the composition of the crowd upon which the soldiers fired in the first place. Johnson's phrase – and, indeed, many of Hogarth's pictures as well – suggested that it was the populace as a whole whose insolence was but a manifestation of freeborn courage. A brave and sturdy people was always ready to take to the streets and defend its liberties, baring its breast to the cowardly attacks of armed oppression. The valour, it seemed, was on the side of the governed and the violence on the side of the government. But in fact criminals in eighteenth-century England could be pretty cowardly and pretty violent themselves. The crowds that gathered to see a smuggler hanged might consist of ordinary men and women, but those who led and manipulated the crowds were anything but ordinary. They were in many cases thugs, out to revenge themselves on the authorities who had managed to catch and convict a smuggler – which was in itself a very considerable feat in an age when smugglers and other criminals were both feared and admired by many people. It was always easier to join a mob protesting against a hanging than it was to put yourself on the side of law and order – as Daniel Chater found when he decided to give evidence against a gang of smugglers in 1748. He was riding with the exciseman to whom he had given the information, one William Galley, when both men were set upon by the gang:

> They began with poor Galley, cut off his nose and privities, broke every joint of him and after several hours' torture dispatched him. Chater they carried to a dry well, hung him by the middle to a cross beam in it, leaving him to perish with hunger and pain; but when they came, several days after, and heard him groan,

they cut the rope, let him drop to the bottom, and threw in logs and stones to cover him. The person who gave this information, however known to the magistrates, was in disguise lest he should meet the like fate.[25]

The murder of Galley and Chater produced a temporary revulsion against the smugglers, as a result of which the authorities got some measure of co-operation from the public and were able to smash several of the most dangerous gangs, including the notorious one based at Hawkhurst in Kent. But it was not long before the traditional romanticized view of smuggling reasserted itself: the gangs were seen as merry bands, genial rascals with whom even such godly and respectable men as Parson Woodforde had regular dealings,[26] while the authorities were seen as tyrants to whom nobody but a mercenary informer would ever give any help. Gentlemen continued to drink their smuggled brandy and smoke their smuggled tobacco, inveighing the while against all revenue officers as instruments of despotism. In 1765 the Crown bought the Isle of Man from the Duke of Athole, thus removing from the smugglers an important base from which they had previously operated with impunity. Meanwhile troops were posted along the coast to deal with smugglers, an unheard-of innovation which brought protests from the soldiers themselves as well as from the public, even though less than seven hundred men were involved. These measures had little effect and during the War of American Independence smuggling increased alarmingly – by something like three times, according to one official estimate. Proper steps were at last taken during the 1780s: extension of the excise system, rationalization of tariff levels, increased powers for the navy. Underlying the new attitude to smuggling was a new attitude to trade itself, an attitude which sprang from more enlightened economic theories and a greater understanding of the statistical evidence involved. As in so many other aspects of English life, it was the extension of bureaucracy that finally tamed the savagery lying behind the romantic myth of the merry smuggler.[27]

Other romantic myths died less easily. In 1786, nearly half a century after the execution of the notorious Dick Turpin, Sophie von la Roche heard yet another version of the 'gentlemanly highwayman' story – this time a respectable young man who had been forced to take to the road because of his gambling debts and who was brought to repentance and reform by the kindness of his lady victims, who subscribed 150 guineas for him.[28] Two years later William Brodie was hanged in Edinburgh for a series of robberies which seemed to have been motivated, in the beginning at any rate, by a simple love of excitement and danger for its own sake.[29] Brodie was said to be a great lover of *The Beggar's Opera*, a source from which secure and respectable men had for more than sixty years drawn their colourful fantasies about a criminal underworld which they could afford to idealize because they did not have to live in it. Few of these fantasies were translated into reality as dramatically as those of William Brodie, but they all played their part in glamorizing the criminal and the code of honour by which he was supposed to live. Real-life informers like Daniel Chater were soon forgotten, as were the appalling risks they ran; but fictitious informers like Jemmy Twitcher of *The Beggar's Opera* lived on, despised by gallant criminals and freeborn Englishmen alike, to perpetuate the myth of 'honour among thieves'.

In fact *The Beggar's Opera* was never intended to idealize the criminal life. It was originally produced at the Lincoln's Inn Fields theatre in 1728, some three years after the execution of the notorious Jonathan Wild; and there can be little doubt that its author John Gay based his character of Mr Peachum upon that famous gangster and thieftaker. Like Peachum, Wild had claimed to be a devoted servant of the public, maintaining his dangerous contacts with the underworld simply in order to help in recovering stolen property and bringing thieves to justice. In reality he had been a leader of thieves himself, taking a profit on the goods which they stole and which he so virtuously 'traced' and returned to their owners for a fee. He had kept control of his gang by the simple expedient of betraying to the authorities any member of it who gave him any trouble – and indeed several who did not, since there were substantial rewards for information leading to the conviction of criminals.

Whether the informer was rich or poor, villainous or public-spirited, he was still the central figure in the process of controlling crime in an unpoliced society. The really appalling thing about the infamous Wild and his fictitious counterparts was that their claim to be useful and necessary members of society was to a large extent justified. If men of property would not appoint a police force to catch thieves for them, then they must rely on the thieves themselves. And they must take their share of the blame for the reign of terror which this system produced, not only among smugglers and pickpockets but among large sections of the poorer classes as a whole. Some twenty years after the murder of Daniel Chater another Daniel, Daniel Clark, found himself a witness for the prosecution at the trial of some weavers accused of cutting silk in looms. The weavers were hanged; and as a result their friends hunted Clark down and finally, after he had lived in terror for more than a year, they set upon him in the street and dragged him to a pond. They threw him in, with his hands tied behind his back, and pelted him with stones and brickbats for some time.

Then they took him out, pulled a cord tied around his neck and threw him back. The stoning was then continued until his brains were beaten out.[30]

Public confidence in the system of informers and thieftakers was shaken in 1754 and 1755 by the extremely unpleasant case of Macdaniel and Berry, two gangsters who blackmailed three other men into staging a fake robbery simply in order to betray their accomplices and collect the reward. One man, Blee, picked up the unsuspecting victims in the Fleet Market and persuaded them to join him in robbing Salmon, a breeches maker in Deptford. Salmon, who was part of the conspiracy, allowed himself to be robbed without any resistance and Blee then introduced a man called Egan, who would buy the stolen property. Egan took it to Macdaniel, who had organized the marking of the goods so that Salmon could swear they were his and prove the case. Needless to say, it was Macdaniel who then dragged the victims, Kelly and Ellis, before the justices of the peace at Greenwich. All the other members of the conspiracy turned king's evidence and Macdaniel prepared to collect his reward as soon as the two men he had framed were duly hanged. But unfortunately for him a certain Mr Cox, the extremely astute constable for the lower hundred of Blackheath, wormed the truth of the matter out of Blee. The whole gang was sent for trial at the Old Bailey and the episode ended, suitably enough, in public violence coming to the aid of the retributive majesty of the law. Egan and Salmon were sentenced to stand in the pillory, where they were stoned to death by the mob. Having sown the seeds of violence by its reliance on the system of informers, the law then presided over the harvest by its reliance on the punishment of the pillory.[31]

However unpleasant the deaths of Egan and Salmon may have been, there were others who suffered even more exquisite agony in the pillory. In 1780 a coachman named Read and his friend Smith, a plasterer, were sentenced to the pillory for homosexual practices. Read was a very short man, so that when his head and hands were forced through the holes in the pillory his feet could not reach the ground and he 'hung rather than walked' as the instrument of torture was turned round and round. Those in the crowd were amused to see his face go black and the blood force itself out of his nostrils and his eyes and his ears; but the sight moved them to increased anger rather than to pity. Both men were pelted mercilessly and Read was dead by the time he was released. Smith was so horribly maimed that he was given up for dead.[32] They were unfortunate, of course – not only because they had made love in a way which aroused the most bestial of the Englishman's prejudices, but also because they had been born into the wrong social class. When gentlemen indulged in 'sodomitical practices' they could be reasonably sure that even if they were brought to court their punishment would be light and their identity would be discreetly concealed by the newspapers.[33] But however exceptional the case of Read and Smith may have been, it was nevertheless a sobering demonstration of the price that had to be paid for liberty. Englishmen liked to think that their freedom meant less barbarity rather than more, a society in which wrongdoers were merely pelted with a few rotten eggs or were at the worst sent to a quick death on the gallows rather than to the lingering torments of Continental torture chambers. But all too often it meant a society in which public vengeance of the most abominable kind took the place of justice.

These things could always be dismissed as unhappy accidents, spontaneous outbursts of public indignation which must be expected occasionally in a free country. Certainly they were occasional and unpremeditated when compared with the systematic judicial barbarities of some Continental countries. Even George Selwyn, who took an erotic pleasure in watching pain and torture, seldom knew in advance whether his excitement would be heightened by the mob throwing bricks and jagged metal or dulled by their use of dung and dead cats. In France, on the other hand, he knew exactly what he was about: when he went to Paris in 1757 to see Damiens tortured to death for wounding Louis XV the programme of events was carefully planned and he was not disappointed. In most European countries the use of torture to extract confessions was still legal, but in England it had been abolished. There was still the terrible penalty of *peine forte et dure*, by which a man could be pressed to death if he refused to plead to an indictment: in 1741 a special press had to be constructed in order to inflict this torture upon Henry Cook, a shoemaker of east London who had refused to answer a charge of highway robbery.[34] *Peine forte et dure* was abolished in 1772, but other forms of lingering death remained legal. Women could be burned to death until 1790, though the executioner usually took steps to shorten their sufferings. When the *Gentleman's Magazine* described the burning of a woman at Newgate in 1789 it took care to reassure its readers that she had in fact been strangled before the flames reached her.[35] Most executioners were reasonably competent and humane men who did their best for their victims. The law prescribed that traitors should be cut down from the gallows in order to have their bowels burnt before their eyes while they were still alive; but when this sentence was carried out on some Jacobite rebels in 1746 the hangman made sure that they were dead before he cut out their bowels.[36] Even the worst of traitors were not subjected to the agonies that Read the coachman suffered. Englishmen were proud of their freedom to inflict on one another the barbarities which were, in less enlightened countries, the prerogative of a despotic government.

Not everyone agreed that the steadily mounting violence of the times was a price worth paying for freedom. Many thought by the 1750s that law and order were breaking down altogether and that criminals were, in Smollett's words, 'more desperate and savage than they had ever appeared since mankind was civilized'.[37] A whole series of books and pamphlets was published on the subject, some of them frankly sensationalist and others piously optimistic – one writer chronicled all the cases he could find in which the hand of God seemed to have been at work, striking malefactors down and bringing their evil deeds to light. Others saw divine intervention operating in a different way: it was suggested in 1750 that a recent outbreak of gaol fever at the Old Bailey was God's way of showing his disapproval of a penal system which made too much use of the death penalty. In England there were more than two hundred offences for which a man could be hanged, more than in most European countries and certainly far more than were mentioned in the Bible, as one shocked correspondent of the *Gentleman's Magazine* pointed out.[38] Another reader suggested that hanging should be replaced by castration. 'Intemperate lust', he argued, 'is the most frequent cause of such crime, and what more adequate punishment? 'Tis an operation not without a suitable degree of pain, sometimes danger; and perhaps Newgate would tremble more at the approach of such an execution than at the parade at Tyburn.' He also proposed that the newly-made eunuchs should be branded with a capital C on each cheek and that for female offenders a more liberal use should be made of the punishment of transportation to slave labour in the colonies.[39]

In the midst of this frenzied and rather prurient debate a few voices argued for a little less freedom and a little more control, for more effective detection of crime rather than for more ingenious punishments. Henry Fielding and his half-brother, blind Sir John Fielding, who succeeded him as justice of the peace at Bow Street, campaigned for some kind of police force to patrol the streets in London and apprehend criminals. No government dared to entertain publicly such un-English proposals, but the Fieldings did manage to extract from the Treasury some Secret Service funds with which they paid a small force of volunteer thieftakers known as the Bow Street Runners. Within two years this body of men had made such an impact that one writer said that 'the reigning evil of street robberies hath been almost totally suppressed'.[40]

But by this time there were other manifestations of violence as well as the activities of footpads and gangsters. The Seven Years War brought high taxes, high prices and the interruption of normal trading conditions – all of which contributed to mounting unemployment and therefore to mounting unrest and rioting. The worst disturbances were in London, but George III was not being entirely fanciful when he complained in 1763 that there were 'insurrections and tumults in every part of the country'.* In the summer of 1765 there were serious riots in Suffolk in which several people were killed after the military had been called in to deal with the situation. In this case the danger was so great that even the justices of the peace, usually so jealous of any invasion of their local self-sufficiency, begged the government to send a special commission to try the rioters and 'strike terror into the people'. An even uglier situation developed a month or so later in Yorkshire and Durham, where miners attacked the collieries in force and had to be fought back by three troops of dragoons. Poor harvests added to the government's problems, forcing up food prices and producing extremely serious food riots in 1766 throughout the land. It was several years before bread prices fell to their normal levels again, so that the poor became more and more determined to defend their standards of living, by violence if necessary. In May 1768 the Home Secretary† told the Secretary of War to send a detachment of troops from Romney to deal with the situation in Tenterden, where a notice had been pinned to the inn-sign of the White Lion tavern inciting the poor to force down the price of corn by destroying the mills of those millers who paid more than a certain amount for it. By 1769 the prevailing mood of turbulence and unrest had even spread to the Channel Islands. 'As the mob ruled in England,' said rioters in Jersey in September 1769, 'they would also govern in the island.'[41]

Being freeborn Englishmen, the rioters for the most part convinced themselves that their liberties as well as their livelihoods were at stake. In London unemployed weavers and sailors and coalheavers cried not for work but for Wilkes, the opposition journalist who had become a martyr because the government's proceedings against him for seditious libel had been declared illegal by the law courts. Governments whose real fault was that they governed too little, allowing the problems of the Seven Years War to grow almost unchecked into the problems of the American Revo-

* See p. 27.

† Until 1782 the work of the two secretaries of state was divided between Northern and Southern, rather than Home and Foreign, Departments; but in this ministry Shelburne, Secretary for Southern Department, took charge of home affairs.

lution, were constantly under attack for governing too much and for wishing to snuff out the liberties of Englishmen. And all the while the shadow of violence lengthened across the unpoliced land of England. In 1748 Daniel Chater had been tortured to death for informing against unemployed weavers. To some extent the gentlemen of England were beginning to react to the change: they were beginning to see that unemployment was as much their concern as smuggling. They were even beginning to suspect that both these evils might be more effectively cured by the centralized professionalism they distrusted than by the localized amateurism they cherished. But they were still a long way from accepting the need for a police force as a means whereby violence might be prevented rather than cured. One thing at least they had in common with the rioters they feared: they believed that English liberty in its existing form was the friend and not the enemy of public order and the public good.

The crisis came in 1780. In May of that year opposition politicians were still running true to form, attacking justices who wanted to police public demonstrations with troops and even suggesting that such action on the part of the authorities would make it necessary for those attending the meetings to arm themselves against attack. A government spokesman who defended the justices was told that they were 'infamous characters' and that he should not even be seen in the same room with them, let alone allow himself to defend their actions.[42] A month later there was an opportunity for these doctrines to be put into practice, for an anti-Catholic mob urged on by Lord George Gordon got out of hand and started burning down houses instead of merely protesting against legislation, the purpose for which it had originally assembled. With frightening speed the protest demonstration turned into a riot and the riot into a reign of terror. Prisons were broken open and the prisoners released to swell the ranks of the rioters; distilleries were attacked and looted to provide a means of exciting the crowds to yet more violence. Ordinary citizens, who had had nothing to do with the Catholic toleration laws which had originally inspired the Protestant fury of Lord George Gordon, found their houses destroyed and pillaged. Other ordinary citizens, poorer and humbler men who had been turned into rioters by the slogans of the bigots and the headiness of the stolen gin, were burned alive as they lay helplessly drunk in the ruins of the buildings they had looted. Within a week over four hundred people had been killed or wounded and large areas of London had been turned into a shambles.[43]

There could be no doubt that the principal reason for the horror of the Gordon riots was the implementation of the theories which had been aired in Parliament a month earlier. Some members of the government did indeed behave as though they thought that justices calling out troops were offenders against the constitution, and that freeborn rioters treated in this way had a right to arm themselves. Certainly some of the king's ministers told him flatly, and quite erroneously, that the military could not act until they had got a justice to read the Riot Act to the crowds first. Since the justices who had suggested such a thing had already had their houses burned down, other justices were understandably reluctant to follow their example. The forces of law and order in London during the first couple of days of the riots consisted of frustrated soldiers looking in vain for frightened magistrates, most of whom had gone to ground and were determined not to be found. It was George III himself who took control, issuing a royal proclamation ordering the troops to open fire and bring the riots under control. This was accordingly done and after a week of terror men of property in London could once more return to their houses without fearing for their lives. Among them were some of those same opposition politicians who had spoken so eloquently in May of the vices of soldiers and justices and of the virtues of demonstrators and protesters. Needless to say, they were humbled and converted by their unpleasant experience – so much so that they immediately approached the Government to suggest that law and order could best be re-established by the widening of the administration and their own admission to office.[44]

The conversion did not last long. Immediately after the Gordon riots the newspapers were full of discussions on the need for a police force, but when the government introduced a Bill in 1785 to set up such a body for London and Westminster it was decisively defeated, even though the proposed force was to consist of only 225 men and was to cost a modest £20,000 a year. A considerable step forward was taken in 1792, when it became possible to pay the justices of the peace in London and Westminster a proper salary. This did not entirely eliminate the activities of men like Justice Blackborough, who took protection money from prostitutes and threatened to punish any constable who bothered them, but at least it meant that there was now a fair chance that the capital city, at any rate, would get justices who thought they had a job to do rather than an opportunity to exploit. In country areas, it was thought, there were fewer opportunities for corruption and gentlemen were in any case less corruptible: the position of justice of the peace continued to be a matter of local prestige. It was significant, however, that in 1794 Thomas Gisborne should think fit to remark, in his influential book on *The Duties of Men in the Higher and Middle Classes of Society*, that nobody ought to seek this position simply because of 'solicitude for personal pre-eminence and political weight in the circle of his connections'.[45] Meanwhile the forces the justices had at their disposal continued to be totally insufficient: in London a few enthusiastic but hard-pressed Bow Street Runners and in other areas the reluctant figure of the parish constable, appointed usually against his will to his unenviable office and anxious only to save his skin and avoid offending his neighbours. London did not get its police force until 1829 and it took another thirty years for the rest of the country to follow suit.

Attitudes of mind changed more rapidly than administrative methods. Although England went into the nineteenth century with her actual means of controlling disorder unaltered, her thinkers and legislators had developed, during the twenty years that followed the Gordon riots, a new approach to the problems which disorder posed. The wars against the French revolution and against Napoleon, lasting on and off from 1793 to 1815, brought with them a new and unprecedented pride in military achievement which helped to modify the old eighteenth-century belief that the violence was always on the side of the soldier and the valour on the side of those whom he sought to control. The very fact that England was fighting a revolutionary régime, linked in most Englishmen's minds with mob violence in the streets of Paris, meant that such turbulence was seen increasingly as an offence against English propriety and stability rather than as a guarantee of English liberty. Burke's funeral oration on John Bull proved to be premature:* that redoubtable character rose from the grave refreshed and refurbished, well on his way to becoming the nineteenth-century John Bull who was to stride so purposefully across the pages of *Punch*, defying other nations but seldom defying his own government. Like the Englishmen he represented, John Bull turned his aggressions dutifully outwards, changing for the purpose into a sober costume of black and white relieved only by the beflagged waistcoat with which he daunted impertinent foreigners. His ferocity was now directed to the maintenance of imperial glory rather than to the maintenance of civil liberty. The soldier was his friend and not his enemy. Valour and violence had at last been reconciled.

* See p. 30.

3 Childhood's Pattern

FOR the great majority of people in eighteenth-century England the most urgent problem in life was how to prevent it. Men of property were often glad to have large families, either because they enjoyed the process of begetting them or because they wanted to make quite certain of the continuation of their line; but the poorer classes had to be more careful. There were, indeed, some fortunate parts of the country where children could be turned fairly speedily from a liability into an asset: Defoe had noted in 1724 that in Taunton and the villages around it there was not a single child over five years of age that could not earn its own bread, as long as its parents had taught it the basic skills which the cloth trade of that area demanded.[1] But prosperity of this sort was exceptional. In most of the towns and counties of England there was only just enough work to keep the adult labouring population in employment. The best that young children could hope for was a succession of poorly paid odd jobs, many of them temporary and seasonal: stone-picking, bird-scaring or the collection of mushrooms or blackberries from the fields and hedges. The mechanization of the textile industries during the second half of the century was to change all this and open the way to an industrial society in which even the youngest children could help to swell the family's earnings. But in the meantime there was no escaping the harsh truth that family limitation, in some form or other, had to be practised by most married couples.

Recent developments in the techniques used by historians studying population have made it clear that such limitation was habitual not only in England, but in many Continental countries as well. The methods employed were neither sophisticated nor pleasant. The only effective way of preventing conception – other than sexual abstinence, which some moralists seemed to regard as one of the duties of the poor – was to cut short the act of love itself: *coitus interruptus* was certainly practised very widely. Contraceptive sheaths were crude and coarse things, uncomfortable as well as unreliable, and used by men about town anxious to avoid disease rather than by married couples anxious to avoid parenthood. Unwelcome pregnancies were all too common among the married as well as among the unmarried, so that most communities included a clandestine abortionist who claimed to be able to terminate them. Her methods might well be bizarre and even brutal, but they were perhaps less brutal than those which would have to be adopted if she failed. However desperate they might be, however worried at the prospect of an extra mouth which they were too poor to feed, labouring men and women were not normally murderers of their own children. But there is, as one historian has pointed out, only a thin and uncertain line between deliberate infanticide and the kind of harassed neglect that makes no great effort either to kill or to keep alive. Neglect of this sort was very often the last resort of the eighteenth-century family planner.[2]

Conclusions of this kind, now emerging from a careful study of marriage and fertility among the labouring classes of the eighteenth century, are very different from those reached by some contemporaries. William Cadogan, who was appointed physician to the London Foundling Hospital in 1754, had published some years earlier *An Essay upon nursing and the management of children from their birth to three years of age*; and in it he made a comparison between the healthy fecundity of the poor and the over-anxious sickliness of the rich. It was a comparison which was to be repeated over and over again during the next fifty years, until it became part and parcel of that idealization of the so-called 'simple life' which we associate with the Romantic Movement of the late eighteenth and early nineteenth centuries:

> In the lower class of mankind, expecially in the country, disease and mortality are not so frequent, either among the adults, or their children. Health and posterity are the portion of the poor, I mean the laborious: the want of superfluity confines them more within the limits of Nature: hence they enjoy blessings they feel not, and are ignorant of their cause. The mother who has only a few rags to cover her child loosely, and little more than her own breast to feed it, sees it healthy and strong . . .[3]

Certainly it is pleasant to think that in warm weather the babies of the poor were 'covered loosely with a few rags', instead of being bound into little parcels as more fashionable children were. These tightly drawn swaddling clothes were intended, as one writer put it, 'to receive and retain all the evacuations of nature',[4] so that they produced appalling discomfort as well as serious skin conditions. In cold weather, however, the few loose rags may have been less beneficial; and if the penurious mother had no rags to spare for cleaning the child up (and, of course, no running water in her cottage) the discomfort and the skin disease were probably as common among the poor as among the rich. And the rich could at least guard their children against cold and damp, which were always present in the earth-floored cottages of the poor.

Cadogan himself revealed, indirectly and perhaps unconsciously, one of the ways in which harsh economic reality modified his rosy picture of the fortunate labouring classes and their broods of sturdy children. He stressed continually the vital importance of breast-feeding and he advised that children should not be weaned until they were a year old; and then he went on to say that if the mother did not want to feed her child herself she should employ a wet-nurse from among the poorer classes to suckle it for her. This substitute should be, he said, a woman of between twenty and thirty years of age who had given birth not more than three months before.[5] But he made no mention of the fate of the woman's own child. Was it to be weaned at three months instead of twelve and put on to those 'paps, panadas and gruels' which he himself condemned so strongly? Or was it presumed to have died already, a victim of those hazards which bulked so much larger in the lives of the poor than Cadogan and other idealists imagined?

Some thirty years later William Alexander, another medical man, made a more specific and more closely calculated comment on the custom of wet-nursing. He assumed that the nurse's own child did not die but was weaned at nine months, allowing its mother to go on for another nine months providing milk for her employer's baby. This meant, he said, that a woman among the poorer classes was only able to have a child every twenty-seven months, since she was unlikely to conceive while she was feeding. While the interval between the pregnancies of the poor was thus artificially lengthened, that between those of the rich was shortened: a woman who farmed out her children could easily have a baby every year. As the birth-rate declined among the poor and rose among the rich, the disparity would feed upon itself: the increasing number of rich mothers wanting wet-nurses would have to make greater and greater demands upon the poor. In the end the English would become, he forecast gloomily, as decadent as the Spaniards – a nation of gentlemen, too proud to work and too poor to be idle.[6]

In fact it became increasingly fashionable, towards the end of the century, for gentlewomen to suckle their own children. 'Believe it not,' said one handbook, 'that your bosoms are less charming for having a dear little cherub at your breast.'[7] The children of the rich did not suck dry the breasts of the poor, as Alexander had feared, and they did not have to exist on the sugary slops and spiced gruels which Cadogan had accused indulgent parents and harassed nursemaids of using to excess. There were still many strange superstitions connected with the diet of infants and of pregnant mothers. As late as 1784 an English traveller in France was surprised to find that the abundance of strawberries and lobsters in that country did not produce a crop of strawberry marks and deformed claw-like hands among the children of mothers who indulged themselves in such treats while they were pregnant; and the custom of feeding a day-old baby on roast pork, 'to cure it of all the mother's longings', seems to have taken a long time to die out.[8] But on the whole the feeding of infants among the propertied classes was probably more sensible than the censorious tone of the nursing handbooks would suggest.

Conversely, the treatment of babies by those mothers who were too poor to buy the handbooks was less enlightened and also less 'natural' than the romantic idealists thought. Towards the end of the century the mechanization of the textile industry was to make young children healthier as well as more profitable: cheap washable cottons improved the personal hygiene of the mother as well as the child, so that infant mortality was sharply reduced. But in the meantime most labouring women wore padded petticoats and leather stays which harboured all kinds of infections, while the baby linen itself was usually too precious to be risked too often in the wash-tub. Nor did the overworked mothers of the poorer classes always have the time or the inclination to feed their own children in the natural way which Cadogan admired so much. Hogarth's horrific image in the corner of his print *Strolling Actresses in a Barn* (Plate 7), dating from 1738, provides a useful corrective to the romanticized pictures of buxom country-dwellers with contented infants at their breasts. Hogarth's strolling actress cannot think of suckling her child: it must take its dose of pap now and like it, even though it is terrified by her eagle's costume and is vomiting out the pap as fast as she spoons it in. The porringer from which the mother is feeding the child stands on a stage crown on the floor of the barn, while in the opposite corner of the picture a monkey is urinating into a stage helmet. Perhaps next time the monkey will use the crown and the mother the helmet, after both pieces of head-gear have picked up another layer of grease and germs from the wigs of the players who wear them.

It may well be that the child is taking in something else with its feed as well as dirt and infection. Just above its head another actress is taking an opiate of some sort to deaden her toothache; and this serves as a reminder of the habitual use which the eighteenth century made of strong drugs, for children as well as adults. Some mothers were compassionate, drugging their children to ease the pain which they seemed to be suffering, while others – including possibly Hogarth's eagle-headed actress – were more practical. Their work or their situations required that their children should be quiet at certain times and so they took steps accordingly. Susannah Wesley, mother of the founder of Methodism, was made of sterner stuff: she made sure that all her children were taught to 'fear the rod' by the time they were a year old, so that the 'most odious noise of the crying of children' was never heard in her house.[9] But among the poor there was usually less beating and more pacifying. Gin, perhaps the most widely used of all drugs during this period, was often taken in, quite literally, with the mother's milk. In 1751 Hogarth produced *Gin Lane*, one of a pair of prints designed, as he himself said, 'to reform some reigning vices peculiar to the lower class of people'. (See Plate 8.) The central figure in his composition was a woman who lay in a drunken stupor while the child she had been suckling fell from her arms to its death. Other children, perhaps more fortunate, survived to take their gin in a more direct form and to have it supplemented by other sedatives, principally laudanum. In 1769 William Buchan's immensely popular tract *Domestic Medicine* asserted that half of the children who died in London each year were killed by laudanum, spirits or proprietary sedatives.[10]

There were of course other and less drastic means of stopping babies from crying: rocking in the cradle, dandling on the knee, cuddling in the arms. Cuddling was frowned upon by some among the upper and middle classes, who thought that it was bad for children to show them too much affection. 'The common people', declared one London journal in 1732, 'generally express more fondness for their children than persons of rank and distinction: the good sense of the latter prevents their affection from being troublesome.'[11] Dandling was less reprehensible, but it had its dangers: French visitors, in particular, were convinced that the English habit of jolting infants up and down on the knee, and even of tossing them into the air from time to time, was a cause of water on the brain.[12] Rocking was by far the most general method of pacifying babies and some rich households even possessed clockwork cradles which would give up to forty-three minutes, continuous rocking once they were fully wound. The other part of the ritual, the singing of a lullaby, could not be carried out by clockwork and so the traditional cradle songs were handed down from generation to generation. Only very gradually did it dawn on mothers that their babies need not necessarily cry all the time and require constant soothing. By the early nineteenth century advanced theorists were claiming that continual crying was the result of swaddling and of general mismanagement: careful attention to toilet training and feeding routines would prevent it, making for happier and more serene children without resort to rocking and lullabies. Needless to say, such ideas were not supposed to apply to the poor, who should in any case concern themselves only with the physical development of their children, 'the formation of their minds being quite out of their sphere'.[13]

In fact all children, rich or poor, had their minds formed by the soothing routines of the nursery and by the songs and rhymes that went with them. 'Hush-a-bye, baby, on the tree top', equally useful for rocking children in the cradle or dandling them on the knee, was already well established and went to a tune which closely resembled that of 'Lilliburlero', the ballad which was indissolubly linked with the revolution of 1688 and the freedoms which it was supposed to have secured. Other nursery rhymes helped to inculcate the standard English attitudes of mind: contempt for the French, satisfaction with existing liberties, belief in the social hierarchy. Even the five little piggies who were counted out on innumerable sets of fingers and toes bore witness to their nationality: as the century progressed the third little piggy tended to be given the roast beef of old England rather than the unspecified viands of earlier versions. Moralists and antiquarians, as well as booksellers with an eye for the profits to be made, began to interest themselves in this popular and very influential culture of the nursery. Many collections of nursery rhymes appeared during the second half of the century, beginning with *Tommy Thumb's Pretty Song Book* in 1744 and going on to include various versions of *Mother Goose*, an impressive array of popular ballads and a daunting number of cautionary and moralistic versions. The editor of *Mother Goose's Melody*, published in 1765, was even prepared to tack a moral on to 'Hush-a-bye baby': 'This may serve as a warning,' he declared, 'to the proud and ambitious, who climb so high that they generally fall at last.'[14]

From nursery rhymes the child progressed to children's stories, which were just beginning to emerge as a distinct literary form. Undoubtedly there were still many thousands of families in which parents and children continued to enjoy together traditional ballads and stories of marvels; but among the propertied classes it was fashionable to look down on tales of the fantastic and the miraculous as relics of that popish superstition which rational Englishmen had left behind. If such tales were still told they were told either as vehicles for satire, as was the case with Swift's *Gulliver's Travels* in 1726, or they were told specifically for children. Some perennial favourites like Defoe's *Robinson Crusoe* were enjoyed by adults and children alike, though by the end of the century even *Robinson Crusoe* was being condemned as an unsettling and escapist book which would make children discontented with their everyday lives. Similar criticisms were made of the stories of Cinderella (which was thought to be unfair to stepmothers), of Bluebeard and of the Sleeping Beauty – all of which were contained, along with many others, in Perrault's *Contes de Ma Mère l'Oye*, first translated in 1729. Booksellers like John Newbery of St Paul's Churchyard, for whom Goldsmith is said to have written *Little Goody Two Shoes* in 1766, made handsome profits by striking a balance between moral content and genuine interest; but during the last thirty years of the century the moralists triumphed. Thomas Day's three-volume novel *The History of Sandford and Merton*, a dreary succession of pompous precepts and humourless writing which was published between 1783 and 1787, was typical of the moral tracts with which children were supposed to improve their minds now that so many of their elders had decided that fairy stories were bad for them.

Whatever might happen to stories and nursery rhymes, children's toys and games were reasonably safe from the moralists. From rattles and teething rings, some of which were very elaborate creations in silver and coral, the child would progress to dolls or perhaps simple mechanical toys: Hogarth's painting of Daniel Graham's children (Plate 9), done in 1742, shows a baby carriage which incorporates a moving toy bird. Whipping tops were among the most popular of all toys for boys. At one end of the social scale we see the harlot's little boy playing with his top in Hogarth's *A Harlot's Progress*, seated under his mother's open coffin; at the other we hear of sixpence being spent on whips and tops for the children of the Duke of Bedford in 1753.[15] Nursery games were usually simple and traditional, but in the upper ranks of society they sometimes became more ambitious. In 1732 Hogarth was commissioned to paint a picture of children's amateur theatricals at St James's Palace, before the younger members of the royal family.

If the child actors in this picture appear rather stiff and self-conscious it is probably because they actually looked that way rather than because of any failing on the part of Hogarth.[16] Although his own marriage was childless he had a great love of children and a considerable understanding of them. Together with another childless lover of children, Captain Thomas Coram, he played a considerable part in the campaign to set up a charitable institution to take in the innumerable children who were abandoned by their parents in the streets of London and in the countryside around. In theory the parish authorities were responsible for the children

9 Hogarth: *The Graham children*, 1742.

of the poor, whether born in wedlock or out of it. An unmarried mother was supposed to appear before a justice and name the father of her child, whereupon the justice and the parish officials would force the man either to marry her or to pay for the upkeep of the child. A man named in this way usually found it difficult to deny that the child was his: it was better, said one writer, 'to make the best bargain he can with the church wardens to take it off his hands, which is commonly done for a treat and ten or twelve pounds'.[17] But there were many cases in which neither the woman nor her child had a claim on any parish, just as there were many more in which the parents, whether married or not, preferred to leave the baby to its fate rather than face an official inquisition. Since the majority of children taken over by the parish died within a few years in any case, such parents were perhaps less callous than they seemed.

In Catholic countries there were charities run by the religious orders which dealt with the problem of abandoned children: English visitors to France, for instance, were forced to admit that their own country was put to shame by the French hospitals for *Enfants trouvés*.[18] Coram and his helpers determined to follow the example of the French and establish a Foundling Hospital in London. When they finally opened their doors in March 1741, after many months of fund-raising, the response was overwhelming. The doors were besieged by crowds of women with babies in their arms and it took only four hours to fill up the hospital. The governors – Hogarth among them – were then forced to plead with those mothers who had been disappointed and beg them 'that they would not drop any of their children in the street, where they most probably must perish, but to take care of them till they could have an opportunity of putting them into the Hospital which was hoped would be very soon and that everybody would immediately leave the Hospital without making any disturbance'. The women accordingly left, 'with great decency', and the governors were able to examine their new charges more carefully. They found that the great majority of the children were clean and neatly dressed, 'from whence and other circumstances they appeared not to have been under the care of the parish officers', and they also found that many of them 'appeared as if stupefied with some opiate'.[19] These observations provided an insight into the desperation of the parents and the reputation of the parish authorities. Within a few years the Foundling Hospital had done such excellent work that the government determined to extend its sphere, giving it a grant on the condition that it took in children from the country as well as London. This proved to be a disastrous experiment, which had to be discontinued after four years. During those years the hospital's resources were hopelessly overstrained as a result of the ever-growing number of children who were dumped, often more dead than alive, into the basket at its doors.

While the children at the Foundling Hospital were a matter of public concern, the great majority of children lived lives that were private and enclosed. Their happiness or unhappiness depended entirely on their parents or, in the case of those who had been sent away from home, on their schoolmasters or the families to which they had been apprenticed. In theory the Church of England was supposed to supervise the spiritual lives of the children in the community, but in practice it did very little once it had baptized them. Even baptisms occasionally had a suggestion of unconcern and incompetence about them: in 1730 a country parson christened a little girl Robert, only finding out subsequently that the midwife had been too 'crazed with liquor' to get the baby's sex right.[20] Many bishops failed to hold regular confirmation services and music did not yet play a large enough part in church services to warrant the children of the parish being associated with the church as choristers. They took part in popular festivities on saints' days and at other important points in the church calendar, but these were often more pagan than Christian and they were not always pleasant for the children who were involved in them. In many parishes the annual ceremony of beating the bounds meant beating the village boys as well, afterwards 'stopping their crying with halfpence'. It was also customary to whip children, even if they had committed no fault, after taking them to public executions; but one foreign visitor noted with relief in 1765 that this unpleasant habit was falling into disuse.[21]

Because the public life of eighteenth-century children was so circumscribed and their private life so hidden from view it is hard to decide just how harsh their treatment was. Memoirs and autobiographies of the period are full of recollected horrors: Mrs Sherwood remembered having to translate fifty lines of Virgil a day while imprisoned in the stocks, Charlotte Charke said that she was tied to a table leg, Fanny Kemble gave an account of a week's imprisonment in the tool shed.[22] Memories of boyhood were even more lurid, involving frequent and severe thrashings – though the humanitarian Samuel Romilly recalled, significantly enough, that he had 'burned with shame' because he had *not* been flogged as a boy.[23] In general it seemed almost obligatory, particularly for men, to show that they had endured physical ill-treatment when young; and this is in itself a reason to distrust some of their accounts of the beatings that were supposed to have 'made men of them'. The women's recollections, though more bizarre, were probably more veracious: many little girls did have to sit in stocks, just as others were swung by the neck with weights attached to their feet or were made to wear iron collars and backboards. But this battery of tortures was the product not of deliberate cruelty but of misguided attempts to cure defects of posture. As for Charlotte Charke, her autobiography was just a pot-boiler, written at a time when she was desperately short of money and stuffed full of tall stories to make it sell. But if she did indeed do the things she said she did as a girl, including shooting at a neighbour's chimneypots with a musket, it is hardly surprising that extreme measures had to be taken to restrain her.[24]

However much doubt there may be about cruelty to children in their own homes, there is none about the sickening brutality which went on in schools, particularly in the grammar schools. Most grammar schools took in pupils as boarders if required, because the appalling state of the roads meant that children living in the country could not possibly travel to and from the nearest town every day and still have time for any schooling. English parents, as foreign visitors noted with some disapproval, were stoical to the point of callousness when it came to sending their children away from home. In Somerset in the 1780s Elizabeth Ham's parents sent her to a cousin's house as an infant, apparently simply because their own house was rather small, and did not take her back until she was nine years old.[25] Once the habit of boarding was established there was no reason for parents to restrict their choice of school: it was as easy to send a boy to a grammar school four counties away, if that school happened to be more fashionable, as it was to send him to the grammar school in the local market town. Eton, Winchester, Westminster and Harrow were already established as places where boys might mix with the sons of rich and powerful people, thus ensuring for them the all-important advantage of proper 'connections' in future life. Grammar schools all over the country struggled to get similar reputations, thus making nonsense of their original function as centres for the education of poor and deserving boys. Those schools that had succeeded in becoming fashionable were refreshingly frank about their achievement: the pharisaical cant that marked the nineteenth-century public school ethos had not yet made its appearance. The governors of Harrow School pointed out in 1800, without any beating about the bush, that whatever the intentions of their founder might have been, 'the school is not now adapted generally for persons of low condition, but better suited to those of a higher class'.[26]

A school did not necessarily have to be brutal in order to be fashionable, but the amount of power given to the older boys – and consequently the chances of their abusing it – does seem to have been directly proportionate to the pretensions of the school. No doubt there was plenty of bullying even in the most lowly country grammar school, but there was not the licensed savagery that left Lord Holland's fingers deformed for life because it had amused his fagmaster at Eton to make him toast bread in his bare hands. In earlier times the fagging system had been regarded as an abuse: even as late as 1668 it was a matter for complaint that prefects at Winchester forced younger boys to make their beds for them and supply them with ink and paper, threatening to report them for imaginary offences if they did not.[27] But by the eighteenth century it had become an accepted principle at England's leading schools that the smaller boys acted as menial servants for their seniors, thus reflecting the hierarchical society which such schools existed to perpetuate. 'I am confident that I derived some of the greatest vices and misfortunes of my life from a fashionable school,' wrote Vicesimus Knox. 'I was placed there when I was but an infant, and lived as a fag under a state of oppression from my schoolfellows unknown to any slave in the plantations.'[28]

In 1778, at the age of twenty-six, Knox became headmaster of Tonbridge School. Three years later he published *Liberal Education*, a plea for a more enlightened curriculum – grammar schools and public schools, whether fashionable or not, concentrated almost entirely on Latin and Greek grammar and versification – and more attention to good manners and civilized behaviour. Similar arguments were put forward in William Cowper's *Tirocinium, or a review of schools* in 1784. Cowper had been at Westminster in the 1740s, at the time when it was described by Chesterfield as 'a seat of illiberal manners and brutal behaviour'.[29] Left to themselves, boys tended to produce a kind of obscene parody of English society, a world in which petty tyrants used their freedom from constraint in order to constrain others. What the reformers wanted was a new generation of schoolmasters, men who would not leave boys to themselves but would control their lives as effectively as the new moralists and the new bureaucrats were coming to control the lives of adults.

Such men were already at work, and had been for many years. The Dissenting Academies, schools set up in the seventeenth century by those sects that had been excluded from the Church of England, taught a wide variety of subjects, technical as well as classical, and opened their doors to Anglicans as well as Dissenters. One of the most successful of them, Warrington Academy in Lancashire, educated the sons of noblemen and gentlemen as well as those of rich merchants and industrialists: the lists of its pupils in the 1760s included Lord Willoughby, Sir James Ibbetson, Sir

John Scott and many other rich and influential landowners.[30] The new nonconformists, the Wesleyans, who were breaking away from the Church of England in the eighteenth century as the Puritans had broken away from it in the sixteenth and seventeenth, were more rigorous. Wesley himself insisted that there must be constant surveillance of the children at the schools he founded and that they should never be allowed any holidays. Nor must they ever be permitted any games or amusements during their long days of labour and prayer – they got up at four o'clock in the morning, summer and winter – because 'he who plays as a boy will play as a man'.[31]

It would be pleasant to think that the more traditionalist schoolmasters, the grammar school and public school teachers who stood out against the ideas of Knox and Cowper, refusing to import the methods of middle-class Dissenters into their upper-class Anglican schools, were motivated by a genuine love of boyhood freedom and a distaste for the totalitarian implications of this new concern about the leisure time of schoolboys. Unfortunately this does not seem to have been the case. Schoolmastering was a despised profession in the eighteenth century and even Joseph Priestley, one of the tutors at Warrington Academy, was originally determined to avoid teaching at all costs: he would have done anything, he wrote later, rather than earn his living in such a contemptible manner.[32] Mr Flack, the schoolmaster whose brutalities made Samuel Romilly ashamed because he was not among their victims, seems to have been a splenetic and frustrated man, consumed with a hatred of his own station in life. Sophie von la Roche, putting up at a hotel in Dover in 1786 while waiting for a boat back to France, shuddered at the sight of the master who ruled over the schoolroom into which her bedroom window looked: 'a large, powerful man, strong enough to strangle four youths at a time, and who, in addition, has his square head bound up in a large cloth which, plus his dark brown overcoat, gives him a disagreeable look which must frighten the children'.[33] There seems to have been very little idealism and enthusiasm among the traditionalists. It was the new ideas, however totalitarian and bureaucratic might be their implications, that attracted those who took a pride in their profession.

At the fashionable schools there were important consolations. Neither the peppery Mr Flack nor the powerful man in the headcloth and brown overcoat would have been quite such ominous figures if they had been sweetened by the prospect of useful connections and patronage, rich benefices or fellowships or private tutorships. At Eton and the other great schools of the land there were careers to be made, careers that might lead on to deaneries and even to bishoprics; but they were not usually dependent on what went on in the classroom. If schoolmasters made their way in the world they did not do so because they were inspired teachers. How, then, did they get any satisfaction from the long hours they spent beating Latin and Greek into boys whom they knew secretly despised them as social inferiors? Samuel Butler had suggested one possible answer many years before in his 'Hudibras':

> The pedant in the school-boy's breeches
> Does claw and curry his own itches.

In 1735 there appeared in the *Gentleman's Magazine* a facetious but extremely enthusiastic 'Dissertation upon Flogging', in which the author rejoiced that there were so many 'professors of this noble art' among the schoolmasters of England. 'I have seen a professor foam with ecstasy,' he wrote, 'at the sight of a jolly pair of buttocks.'[34] The following year the magazine returned to the same theme, this time in a more solemn and critical tone. Quoting the lines from 'Hudibras', it observed that 'if punishment come from self-pleasing, then it will not be just'. Masters who selected 'pretty and ingenious' boys for particularly severe beatings, assuring them that they did so out of the love they bore them, were simply putting a sanctimonious gloss on an erotic and unsavoury reality. 'What shall we think of such liking?' the writer asked indignantly.[35] The eighteenth century had a better understanding of sexual deviations than some of the more condescending post-Freudian writers have imagined.

Within a few years a pamphlet had appeared entitled *The Shameful Discipline of the Schools Exposed*, in which the teaching profession was arraigned in more general terms and was told that its members 'countenanced a very criminal *gout* and cloaked their vice with pretence of necessary correction'. This provoked a furious reply under the title *The Benefit of School Discipline*, by one who signed himself 'A lover of decency and order'. He defended the practice of flogging, saying that it was preferable to caning over the hands because many boys had had their hands permanently crippled after they had been 'so hardly laid on by such a piece of timber'. As to the charges of sadism, he rebutted these with a great show of moral indignation and suggested that, on the contrary, anyone who wished to restrict the whipping of schoolboys must himself be effeminate and unmanly.[36] Thus defended and justified, the schoolmasters continued on their way undeterred. The great schools of England remained places of unbridled brutality and the masters who presided over these blood sports came to be regarded with a strange mixture of fear and affection. Samuel

Parr was such a devotee of flogging that when he could find no excuse for it he would suggest to his boys that he should whip them in advance, promising that the next fault should go unpunished; but he was also a popular and much loved schoolmaster. There was a major riot at Harrow when the governors refused to do as the boys wished and make him headmaster.

The Harrow riots of 1771 were short and sharp. The governors who had refused to appoint Parr were threatened with bludgeons and one of them had his chaise broken to pieces. 'We were drawn back by Mr Parr at last,' wrote one of the ringleaders, 'who came with his hat off, with fear lest our madness should be laid to him. Poor man, his distress hurt me much. If it had not been for him, we should have broke Mr Hern's windows then – another governor; but that did not happen till last night and this morning.' Parr made a touching farewell speech to his supporters: 'He thanked us for the great love we bore to him, which, he said, was made too plain, he was afraid by our mischief on his account . . . A great many of the boys were in tears, and I never restrained them with so great hardship before.' This particular rioter then retired to his tea, only to find that while he was gone his followers burnt the remnants of the chaise and broke the remaining windows in the school.[37] Three years later there was an affray at Winchester because the headmaster disapproved of the boys making public mock of a hunchbacked servant; and for the next twenty years (which were, coincidentally enough, the years of the American and French revolutions) there was a string of uprisings in the great schools of England. They culminated in the Great Rebellion at Winchester in 1793, during which the rebels seized the keys of the school and barricaded themselves in, and an even greater one at Rugby four years later. At Rugby the boys mined the headmaster's study with gunpowder, made a bonfire of their desks and were finally defeated by an impromptu force of militiamen after being besieged on an island in the school grounds.[38]

The advisability of sending girls away to school was a matter for debate. Most people thought that mothers who had sufficient leisure and sufficient learning should educate their daughters at home: even Elizabeth Montagu, a great advocate of education for women, was distrustful of girls' schools and slightly apologetic about making use of them. She put her two young charges, Miss Carter and Miss Botham, into a boarding school in the summer of 1753, when she had to go to Tunbridge Wells for her health; but she told her sister that there were special reasons and that in any case it was only for two months. 'Mr Montagu thought Miss Carter's dancing would be better improved if she went to school,' she wrote, 'and he is as desirous she should be a fine dancer as if she was to be a Maid of Honour . . . in regard to Miss Botham going, she is a fine girl, but so lively and so idle, she requires infinite care.' And she concluded by stressing that she would not relax her own general supervision of the girls' education: 'I believe no *gouvernante* ever took half the pains I have done with these children, explaining to them everything they read and talking to them on all points of behaviour.'[39] Some months later Miss Botham's father received a bill from the school in Kensington where two of his younger daughters were being educated. It was not exorbitant – just over thirty pounds for the two of them for five months – but the items of which it was made up did not suggest a very academic syllabus. Apart from the board and lodging, which came to something over nineteen pounds, the largest item was four pounds ten shillings for the dancing master. The rest was a matter of copy books, spelling books, pins and needles and pomatum powder. Most significant of all was the letter which accompanied the bill. 'I hope, Sir, that you're satisfied of us,' wrote the school's proprietor, 'if so I shall alwise thry, as well as my wife, to do all wee can to improve your daughters in everything, especially in their morals and manners.' He made no mention of intellectual accomplishments, a field in which he was perhaps less confident.[40]

Lady Mary Wortley Montagu, a distant relative of Elizabeth and like her a writer of some distinction, thought that the value of book learning for a girl was in any case rather dubious. Any young woman who acquired such learning should conceal it, she advised, 'with as much solicitude as she would hide crookedness or lameness. The parade of it can only serve to draw on her the envy, and consequently the most inveterate hatred, of all he and she fools'.[41] Even the boisterous Charlotte Charke doubted the value of some of the subjects she had been taught at Mrs Draper's famous school in Park Street, Westminster, early in the century. Of geography she wrote: 'Though I know it to be a most useful and pleasing science, I cannot think it was altogether necessary for a Female.'[42] As girls' boarding schools became more and more numerous there was increasing disquiet not only about the academic aspects of their syllabus but also about the ladylike accomplishments upon which most of them concentrated their efforts. A writer in the *London Chronicle* in 1759 pointed out that it was precisely those parents who least needed such accomplishments in their daughters who were most tempted to make use of the schools which were springing up all over the country. The wives of 'low tradesmen and mechanics', too ignorant and too busy to educate their daughters themselves, put them out to boarding schools and had them returned to them as would-be young ladies, too proud to help their parents about the house and too pretentious to accept their proper station in life. He suggested something more down-to-earth and appropriate:

> I would propose that schools for the education of such girls should be kept by discreet women; those who have been housekeepers in large families would be the properest persons for this purpose; that the young people should be taught submission and humility to their superiors, decency and modesty in their own dress and behaviour. That they should be very well instructed in all kinds of plain work, reading, writing, accounts, pastry, pickling, preserving and other branches of cookery; be taught to weave and wash lace and other linen. Thus instructed, they may be of great comfort and assistance to their parents and husbands; they may have a right to expect the kindest treatment from their mistresses; they are sure to be respected as useful members of society; whereas young ladies are the most useless of God's creatures.[43]

Not everyone was prepared to be as forthright as this crusty gentleman, but his prejudices were shared by many people in all ranks of society. When Arthur Young came upon a piano in a farmer's parlour he wanted to burn it, because to him it was a sign that the poor man had been deluded into overeducating his daughters and encouraging them in 'ladylike' accomplishments.[44] The ambitious middle-class parent, making himself and his daughters ridiculous by trying to turn them into ladies, was a stock figure of fun in caricatures and on the stage and in literature. By the end of the century, however, this concern about the effects of women's education upon the social order was working in rather a different direction. A writer in the *Gentleman's Magazine* in 1789 was very indignant about the punishments used in one London girls' school and about the social attitudes that lay behind them. He was glad to hear that the school had discontinued the use of the birch – 'the impropriety of it is still more apparent', he wrote, 'in places of education sacred to the fair sex' – but he was shocked to learn that instead the girls were made to wear the uniform of a charity girl if they were in disgrace. It was scandalous, he thought, that young ladies from the upper classes should be encouraged to think that poverty was a disgrace. Neither they nor their schoolmistresses had any right to look down on charity girls or to ignore 'the great duties of humility and consideration of the poor'.[45]

By this time some of the 'ladylike accomplishments' were coming under attack as being unsuitable even for real ladies, let alone for aspirants from the middle classes. Writing, arithmetic, music and French were fairly uncontroversial subjects, though some people feared that French might prove the key to undesirable reading. Mrs Cartwright, writing on women's education in 1777, considered that some books written in that language were 'more calculated to amuse the fair' than English ones, but others had their doubts as to the nature of the amusement offered. Italian was 'not at all essential to the education of a private gentlewoman'.[46] Dancing, which had seemed so harmless earlier in the century and which even Mrs Cartwright thought beneficial to the health, became more suspect by the 1780s and 1790s. John Moir, who wrote his *Female Tuition or an Address to Mothers* in 1787, thought that it could only be recommended to those parents who wished to see their daughters 'elegant rather than virtuous'. 'It often happens to the fine female dancer,' he warned his readers solemnly, 'that she is under such temptations to scenes equally fatal to her health and morals as she cannot always withstand.'[47] Ten years later Thomas Gisborne repeated this warning and applied it not merely to dancing but also to anything which might encourage girls to take an interest in 'theatrical representations':

> The lowest orders of the people, mutable, uninformed and passionately addicted to spectacles of amusement, may probably be acted upon through the medium of theatrical representation with greater facility and success than other classes of the community. But to speak of individuals among the upper and middle ranks of life, young women are the persons likely to imbibe the strongest tinge from the sentiments and transactions set before them in the drama.[48]

If dancing and play-acting were valued for the healthy exercise which they provided, then some more improving form of physical exertion must be found to put in their place. He suggested gardening:

> It seems desirable that girls should be allowed, when educated at home, and if possible when placed in schools, to possess little gardens of their own and to amuse themselves in them with the lighter offices of cultivation. The healthiness of the employment would amply compensate for a few dragged frocks and dirtied gloves.[49]

It was left to country schools to heed such advice. The fashionable girls' schools in and around London made sure that their pupils kept their clothes clean and took their exercise in a ladylike manner. In 1786 Sophie von la Roche was charmed by a bevy of girls from a school in Kensington, with their 'simple white uniforms' and their 'light, cheerful gait'. Later she went to see the famous school run by the four Misses Stephenson in their house in Queen's Square, where the fees were more than a hundred guineas a year. She found the girls dancing, a form of exercise which the Misses Stephenson encouraged in defiance of the moralists. They also encouraged their girls to take a proper interest in 'dress and ornament', though they were not entirely without anxiety about the results. They were increasingly worried about the growing custom of allowing girls to go home for a holiday each year: they told Sophie that they would abolish it if they could, 'as one or other of the girls always returned with morally harmful or misguided notions'.[50]

Many traditionally minded people thought that the really harmful and misguided notions were not so much those that prevailed at academies for young ladies of the upper classes as those that led to the establishment of schools for the lower classes. The Bishop of London told the clergy of his diocese in 1724 that they must be careful to see that village schools did not encourage 'fine writing for the boys, fine working for the girls, or fine singing for either'.[51] Farther north, in Northumberland, Thomas Bewick noted towards the end of the century that ordinary labouring men were often more intelligent and better read than the farmers for whom they worked. Farther north still, in Scotland, there was a system of parish schools which made the Scots one of the most literate nations in the world. In England village schools were less numerous and less ambitious: they did not aim to create a literate labouring class and they were for the most part careful to avoid the excesses against which the Bishop of London had warned. The middle and upper classes, upon whose charity such schools often depended, were anxious that education should not be pushed to the point where their own children would have to compete for jobs with the jumped-up sons and daughters of labouring men. As a result charity school children sometimes did little more than learn by rote their catechism and their tables while their hands were kept busy with spinning or knitting or whatever other form of drudgery was to constitute their appointed life's work. Sometimes this principle was extended from the pupils to the teacher: one country curate in the middle of the century taught the village children for nothing and spun at the same time to keep himself alive.[52] Many villages could boast a kindly local pedagogue similar to those idealized by the poets – someone like Goldsmith's schoolmaster, who amazed the rustics by the amount of knowledge he managed to carry in one small head, or like Shenstone's schoolmistress who was skilled at taming 'unruly brats'. Their efforts were supplemented by those of the charity schools, several thousands of which were founded in the course of the century, and by well-meaning attempts to fill the scant leisure of working children, either on Sundays or after work, with scripture lessons and moral uplift.

The *Gentleman's Magazine* told in 1734 of a country lad who weighed over seven stone at the age of five and stood four feet seven inches tall.

The important thing about this prodigy was his usefulness; he could already carry out man's work and was very profitable for his parents.[53] Less fortunate parents usually had to wait longer. There were trades in which young children could make themselves very useful: chimney sweeps used small boys to great advantage, though they had to take care not to stifle them or burn them or get them stuck halfway up a chimney.[54] They also had to keep them half-starved so that they would be thin enough: a well-fed sweeping boy was an absurdity. But chimney sweeping was not just an odd job. It was a trade to which a boy had to be properly apprenticed, so that he might one day practise it himself if he did not succumb to cancer of the scrotum, the occupational disease of climbing boys. Few parents desperate enough to consign their sons to such a fate could afford the premiums, so that sweeps usually went to the parish authorities for their boys. In 1767 and 1778 Jonas Hanway got laws passed laying it down that in such cases premiums should be paid in two instalments, which meant that the sweeps had to keep the boys alive for a period of years if they wanted the second instalment.

Faced with this choice between odd jobs that were unprofitable and regular trades which, however unpleasant, required premiums, poor parents might well agree to their children taking advantage of such schooling as was available. But fundamentally the business of poor children – that is, the children of the greater part of the population of the country – was to work and not to learn. For them, education was merely a symptom of unemployment. When the cotton mills and the coal mines started to swallow up children in their thousands at the end of the century, creating more and more employment until even children of four and five years old were working twelve or more hours a day, some people allowed themselves to believe that in the old days such things did not happen. Romantic poets and other gentlemen of an idealistic turn of mind fled from the horrors of the factories and the mines to the unspoilt English countryside. There they came across innocent children, busy at their simple tasks or merry in their simple games, who moved them to tears and to poetic utterance. For the most part the children they met seem to have been sensible little things, well aware that a judicious mixture of cheerfulness and pathos, combined with much curtseying and scraping of forelocks, would pay dividends. And they were as influential as they were sensible, for they were the unwitting creators of the myth of the Golden Age of pre-industrial childhood. Their beguiling little faces crowded out the memory of the other children, the children who were desperately hunting for work to supplement the family income or who had been threatened with dire punishments if they did not bring home the required quantity of blackberries or mushrooms.

In fact it was the children of the rich, rather than those of the poor, who inherited the joys of the English countryside. Young Thomas Frankland, breaking bounds at Eton in 1761 in order to pick cowslips for his bottle of cowslip wine,[55] probably had more time to appreciate England's pastoral delights than the children of his own age who were working long hours for local farmers as apprentices. In spite of all its brutalities and all its inhibitions, an upper- or middle-class childhood in eighteenth-century England could give a sense of security and well-being that has seldom been equalled since capitalism and bureaucracy changed the face of society. But for the great majority of those who grew up in the age of Hogarth childhood was a luxury in which they could not afford to indulge for long. These were at best only part-time children.

4 Earning a Living

PETER KALM, a young Swedish scientist who spent some months in England in 1748, was surprised to find a rich and successful farmer in Hertfordshire who kept hardly any permanent farm workers: apart from his own son and daughter he had only one boy and one girl to do all the work of the farm, both indoors and out. This was not necessarily because he overworked these children, for in fact he had the reputation of being a very good employer. It was because 'in this place it is the custom that a farmer does not keep many servants, but always employs day-labourers, for which reason in every village there live a great many poor, who hire themselves out to work for pence'. This particular farmer paid eight to ten pence a day; and for that he expected twelve hours' work, from six in the morning until six in the evening. In Essex Kalm found rates that were a little more generous: one farmer paid nine shillings a week to the men whom he hired to help with the threshing. But in both cases the labourers had to provide their own food: all they got from their employer was beer. Nor did they have any certainty of getting work, even in the busy seasons of haymaking and harvesting. Kalm also noticed large numbers of migrant labourers, mainly from Ireland, who descended on the countryside around London in the summer season in order to offer their services and often to undercut the local workers. In Kent there was a great influx of workers from Wales, mainly women and girls, to help with the hop-picking.[1]

Migrant labour was no new thing, even in Sweden. What really surprised Kalm and other foreign visitors was the fact that there seemed to be no permanent relationship, no ties of mutual obligation and responsibility, between the landowner and those he employed. Poor people lived in the villages that clustered around the farms, but they were not the concern of the farmer. He made use of their labour when he needed it and that was the end of the matter. But in the more traditional society to which Kalm was accustomed, and which was the norm in most European countries, the relationship between master and man was something much more than a daily exchange of a few coppers in return for a few hours' work. European hierarchies might be rigid and oppressive, but at least they gave a certain degree of permanence and stability. Noblemen and other landowners exacted service from their 'churls' – a word which Kalm applied, with an uncomprehending lack of discrimination, to every labouring man he met – but in return they were supposed to provide them with a bare living or with the means of getting it. The English labourer might boast of his independence, but there was something to be said for dependence if it meant that the master shouldered responsibilities to which the Englishman's employer seemed indifferent.

But the counties around London were not typical of the country as a whole. If Peter Kalm had travelled farther afield, into the depths of the West Country and the fastnesses of the North, he would have found villages where the local landowner cared for and maintained those who worked on his own land, while at the same time respecting the landed rights of even the poorest villager, who had a share of the common field and a say in the running of the village. But such villages were becoming rare, while the benign paternalism by which they were supposed to be governed was becoming rarer still. In 1770 Oliver Goldsmith published his poem *The Deserted Village*, in which he lamented the passing of the old pattern of agrarian life. He suggested that in times gone by the peasantry and the yeomanry of old England had been the country's pride: each man had had his plot of land and each lord had had his sense of responsibility, always ready both to punish and to protect those who were dependent upon him. This rural paradise, in which men were able to 'crown a youth of labour with an age of ease', was now being eroded by the capitalistic greed of the new landowners, who were breaking up the old village lands in order to build up for themselves great enclosed estates upon which they could employ hired labourers. In fact, however, even the poets had noticed for some time that the English countryside had been rather less than heavenly. Thomas Gray began his *Elegy Written in a Country Churchyard* in 1742, several years before Kalm's visit and nearly thirty years before the appearance of Goldsmith's poem; but even so he remembered that ploughmen were weary, that 'chill penury' was the farm labourer's lot and that there were already 'little tyrants' abroad in the green fields of England. It was a very long time indeed since the country had had the 'bold peasantry' of Goldsmith's imagination. Hogarth's England was an England of landless labourers, many of them totally dependent on daily wages to keep them and their families out of the workhouse.

In harsh arithmetical terms this meant that something over two million people, nearly half the population of the country, had no resources whatever other than their labour – labour which was usually unskilled and very poorly paid. This situation produced a curiously two-edged and contradictory response from the propertied classes. On the one hand they were seriously alarmed by the sheer size of this floating labour force and by the prospect of what might happen if work could not be found for it: those who provided employment for the poor, either by buying more of their products or by setting up new industries, were universally commended. Late in the seventeenth century Gregory King, a self-appointed population expert, had declared that 'labouring people, out-servants, cottagers and paupers' could never be expected to contribute to the wealth of the country in any positive way, since the value of their lowly labour was so little that it could not maintain them and their families and would have to be supplemented sooner or later, either during or after their working lives, by poor relief paid for by their betters. This view continued to be dominant throughout the eighteenth century and it gave support to the kind of sentimental nostalgia which inspired Goldsmith's *Deserted Village*: a dependent peasantry of the old sort was seen as a guarantee of stability, whereas an independent and masterless body of landless labourers seemed to menace the prosperity as well as the security of the realm.

On the other hand men of property saw clearly enough that labourers who had no land and no lords were much more useful to an expanding economy than an old-fashioned peasantry would have been. Arthur Young, whose writings on labour relations and wage levels were extremely influential from the 1770s onwards, was very enthusiastic about the virtues of a propertied peasantry – as long as it was kept safely on the far side of the English Channel. When he was in France he sang the praises of small-holdings and noted with satisfaction every little plot of land which was intensively cultivated, as he thought, because the man who tilled it also owned it. But in England he was the advocate of capitalistic farming, large estates and a labour force without rights or resources. 'Everyone but an idiot,' he remarked testily when there was talk of distress among labourers, 'knows that the lower class must be kept poor or they will never be industrious.' When the price of meat and tea and white bread began to rise in the 1760s and early 1770s he insisted that this was a reason not for higher wages but for greater economy on the part of the poor.[2] They should eschew such enervating luxuries and live on coarse bread and the occasional piece of bacon. And there were many areas in which his callous verdict seemed to be justified by the course of events.

Labouring men and women who had no rights and no place in society, no prospect of advancement and no recognition for work well done, were not prepared to work unless they had to. When times were good, with low food prices and abundant employment, they did enough work to feed themselves and no more; when times were bad they clamoured for poor relief.

The Poor Law was one of the special features of English society, the subject of much self-congratulation among the propertied classes and a certain amount of admiring comment from foreigners. One visitor thought that it was a kind of mutual insurance system, a fund towards which all citizens paid their share willingly in the knowledge that if they fell upon hard times they would be entitled to benefits;[3] but few Englishmen saw it in quite this light. For them, contribution to poor relief was an unpleasant duty and dependence on it an unthinkable disgrace. Each parish had its Overseer of the Poor, who collected poor rates from propertied people and used the money to maintain those in the parish who could not earn their own living for one reason or another: the unemployed and the unemployable, the very young and the very old. Sometimes he gave 'outdoor relief', maintaining people in their own homes, and in other cases it was 'indoor relief', which meant that the paupers had to come into a workhouse or house of correction. This, as Goldsmith well knew, was the reality that lay behind his phrase about crowning a youth of labour with an age of ease. In 1760 his imaginary Chinese philosopher, Lien Chi Altangi, commented that a certain tinker who had brought up seven sons, all of them soldiers in the service of their country, would have been honoured in China, whereas in England 'the sons, when the war is over, may probably be whipped from parish to parish as vagabonds and the old man, when past labour, may die a prisoner in some house of correction'.[4] If gentlemen were to be sure of getting casual labour when they needed it, there must be a certain amount of movement of workers from one parish to another; yet each parish only gave relief to those who could prove that they belonged to it. The rest were not always whipped as vagabonds, but they were certainly harried from parish to parish if they were unlucky enough not to find work. The Poor Law was the price which the English landowner paid for having a readily available pool of labour; but it was a price which was carefully calculated and strictly controlled.

Although most employers were landowners they were not necessarily farmers in the traditional sense of the term. During the first thirty years of the century there was a building boom; and after this came to an end there was a period during which many turnpike trusts were set up to build new roads. Later still there was the canal mania: every landowner in the country seemed to be investing in canals, either for the profits they made or in order to open up new markets for the produce of his estate. Sir Roger Newdigate, reputedly one of the most traditionalist of Oxfordshire country gentlemen, was busily planning canals to link the coal mines on his land with Birmingham.[5] All these activities demanded casual unskilled labour: as well as the stonemasons and the bricklayers, the engineers and the surveyors, there had to be thousands upon thousands of men and women who merely fetched and carried and dug. Those associated with the new canals were known as 'navigators', a word which was later corrupted to 'navvy'. The exploitation of mineral resources also required an increasing labour force. In areas where mining had been carried on for many centuries, such as Cornwall or the Forest of Dean, miners were organized into corporations which resembled the trade guilds and were able to protect the rights and working conditions of their members; but in the north of England and in Scotland those who dug coal were abominably exploited. Most of them had to bind themselves to the colliers for long periods and in Scotland there was a system of serfdom: until the reforming legislation of the 1770s miners' children, as well as miners themselves, could be enslaved for life without any redress.[6]

Ordinary farm work was often hard and even crippling – threshing, in particular, was said to break down the strongest constitution after a few years – but at least it was varied and reasonably healthy. The same could not be said for mining and other work connected with the mineral resources of the land. Even Peter Kalm, who thought on the whole that English labourers did not work very hard, was appalled by what he saw at a limekiln near Gravesend. Women had to carry three enormous baskets of chalk or coal on their heads and shoulders at a time and had to help in the hacking up of the chalk as well. For eightpence a day, he said, 'they mostly labour like slaves'.[7] In Derbyshire whole families of workers lived in caves around the lead mines, the men squirming down narrow shafts to bring up the ore and the women and children washing and preparing it. Nearby, at Bakewell, hundreds of tons of chert were mined every year and sent to potteries in Yorkshire. It was sold for eight shillings a ton, of which the miners got three and the Duke of Rutland, owner of the land, five. In theory the miners were superior to the hired labourers in other industries: they were their own masters, selling in the open market what they produced. But in practice the Duke of Rutland, like most English landowners, had the best of both worlds – the maximum profit with the minimum responsibility.[8]

Industry – or 'the manufactures', as it was usually called – was traditionally the sphere of the skilled worker, the man who had served an apprenticeship and expected proper recognition of his superior status. Sometimes he got it. In 1786 Sophie von la Roche was so impressed by the deference which her coachman paid to the carpenters at Deptford dockyard that she wove for herself an extraordinary fantasy about them:

> They were mostly fine-looking fellows; many of them with the eye of a mathematician, still making calculations. In them I saw embodied the fine English schools, where the citizen's son, like the son of the aristocrat, is taught all kinds of mathematics and really good Latin. I am sure many of them will be reading the papers this evening and talking of the common welfare; watching for the names of the outgoing and incoming vessels, glad to find some among the number on which they have worked . . .[9]

In reality the life of a carpenter was less idyllic. His working conditions made him subject to dangerous occupational diseases – Adam Smith remarked that in London a carpenter did not last 'in his utmost vigour' for more than eight years – and his pay was hardly sufficient to enable him to buy newspapers, let alone exercise the 'really good Latin' which Sophie imagined him to have. In June 1776 the journeymen carpenters throughout the cities of London and Westminster decided to strike in order to get their wages put up from eighteen shillings to one pound per week. The newspapers described this as 'exorbitant' and talked about an 'insurrection', although in fact the carpenters' meetings were extremely orderly. They agreed not to work for less than a pound a week and they further agreed that the first to secure this amount would put aside three shillings of it to support those still out of work. Two weeks later their strike broke down, though they still made a brave show of defying those masters who would only pay them late on Saturday nights in an inn, keeping them waiting until midnight so that they poured their wages in advance into the pockets of the innkeeper who was in league with the master carpenter. There were vague promises of parliamentary action from the justices of the peace, in return for which the carpenters dispersed 'without the least indecent or irregular behaviour'. But nothing was done for them and a few weeks later 240 of their number left London in desperation to see if they could get fairer treatment elsewhere.[10]

The carpenters Sophie saw were in fact part of one of the largest industrial enterprises in the country, for the navy and the ancillary services which supplied it formed an important part of England's construction industry. Throughout the eighteenth century war provided a significant stimulus to the economy and to employment. But the greatest industry of all, after agriculture itself, was the textile industry. Hundreds of thousands of workers were occupied in combing and carding and spinning yarn, while many thousands more wove and dyed and bleached the cloth that was made from it. At the time Peter Kalm visited the country most of this activity went on in the labourers' own homes. 'In the cotton trade,' one historian has remarked, 'the women picked and cleaned the cotton, separating it from the bale and beating it on a riddle with switches, a process that can hardly have contributed to the health of the family, as the sole living room must have been thick with the fluff.'[11] There were already workshops that operated on a large enough scale to be dubbed 'manufactories', later shortened to 'factories'. There were even cotton and silk mills powered by machinery: Edward Cave set up one at Northampton in 1742 and there was another at Leominster at about the same time. Sir Thomas Lombe's silk mill at Derby was one of the wonders of the age, though one of the children who worked there later remarked that he would 'carry to the grave' the marks of the barbarous treatment he received.[12]

During the 1770s, when traditional industries such as the woollen manufacture were severely hit by the disruption of overseas markets during the American revolution, the machines that could turn out cheap cotton textiles really came into their own. More and more workshops were mechanized, with the result that the thousands of men and women who spun or wove at home had either to work as fast and as cheaply as the machines or else give up their independence and become factory workers. Domestic textile working was by no means killed by this so-called 'industrial revolution' of the late eighteenth century – handloom weaving, in particular, persisted until at least 1850 – but in many cases it ceased to provide a living wage. Most domestic textile workers were at the mercy of the clothiers, who sold them their raw materials and bought their finished product, as well as renting them looms and other machinery. If these clothiers started to charge more and pay less there was not much that the spinners and weavers could do about it. Even specialized workers like the framework knitters of the Midlands found it difficult to survive in the new climate: they managed to find spokesmen who would petition Parliament for them and even draw up Bills against the low wages and increased frame rents of which they complained. But the Bills were thrown out, as were many other similar measures designed to protect ordinary people against the catastrophic effects of economic development, and thousands of framework knitters found their livelihood gone.[13]

The results of the economic changes were not always bad. There were areas in which there was more work rather than less, just as there were families that could earn more than they had ever done before as long as every member of the family, however young, was prepared to exchange the informality of domestic labour for the long hours and harsh discipline of the factory or workshop. Even in purely agricultural areas the new enclosures and the advent of large-scale capitalist farming meant new jobs and sometimes even higher pay. But few workers could be sure of finding these benefits locally: in most cases they had to go out and look for them. The great hiring fairs, at which farmers and other employers searched for bargains among the men and women who put themselves up for hire, attracted labourers and maidservants from farther afield. The great industrial centres, which grew up in the North and in the Midlands, were thronged with people looking for jobs. And London, always the most powerful of the magnets which drew men to leave their homes and seek their fortunes, grew more powerful still. Arthur Young was quite scandalized by the effect it had and the ease with which people could get to it. 'A country fellow one hundred miles from London jumps on to a coach-box in the morning,' he wrote, 'and for eight or ten shillings gets to town by night.'[14] And then he went on to tell how the poor country fellow, having left his rural paradise for a stinking city, usually finished up destitute or depraved. It was a fitting reward for the cardinal sin of discontent, but it did not alter the fact – the really terrible fact, in Young's eyes – that some country farmer had been deprived of a potential labourer and might even, if the situation continued, have to pay higher wages in order to get the men he needed.

The central figure in Hogarth's most famous illustration of London's magnetic powers was not a country lad who had jumped on a coach-box but a country lass who had bumped and jolted her way to the wicked city in a waggon, the cheapest and most uncomfortable of all forms of travel. In the first plate of his series *A Harlot's Progress*, published in 1732, she was to be seen getting out of the waggon in an inn yard and being seized upon immediately by a procuress, who would turn her into a professional prostitute in a very short time (Plate 11). Steele had described an almost identical scene in *The Spectator* twenty years earlier;[15] and in 1780 a new series of prints appeared entitled *A Modern Harlot's Progress, or the Adventures of Harriet Heedless*. In this version the intermediary services of the procuress were no longer needed: Harriet went straight to a Statute Hall, the town equivalent of the country hiring fairs, and was engaged on the spot by a gentleman who pretended to be looking for a maidservant although in fact he was looking for a mistress.[16] (See Plate 12.) If Sophie von la Roche saw these prints they must have moderated her enthusiasm for the charms of the hiring fairs, where she had been delighted to see 'maids very cleanly dressed . . . selected on the spot'.[17]

The figure of the country girl who came to London looking for honest work and finished up as a whore was in fact one of the standard archetypes of eighteenth-century England, as familiar in her way as freedom-loving John Bull or the priest-ridden foreigner. She was designed to appeal particularly to parents, for whose benefit John Moir issued in 1787 the dire warning: 'you had better turn your daughter into the street at once, than place her out to service. For ten to one her master shall seduce her, or she shall be made the *confidante* of her mistress's intrigues . . .'[18] There were of course other possibilities: girls apprenticed as domestic servants to Mrs Elizabeth Brownrigg, the wife of a London house-painter, were chained in a cellar and flogged to death.

But in spite of these hazardous extremes, there were many girls for whom domestic service in the great houses of London provided a route which led from humble beginnings to a measure of success. This, after all, was one of the other archetypal myths of English life: Englishmen might be fond of warning parents against letting their children loose on the big city, but they were equally fond of asserting that their society was one in which hard work could raise even the humblest to happiness and prosperity. Corruptible or otherwise, the hopeful country girl and her male counterpart were key figures in the process whereby the English poor were supposed to be able to better themselves. The Reverend John McFarlan, writing in 1782 on the causes of poverty, said that he had 'endeavoured to show that the greatest number of those who are now the objects of charity are either such as have reduced themselves to this situation by sloth or vice, or such as, by a very moderate degree of industry and frugality, might have prevented indigence'.[19] He would no doubt have approved even more highly of those who sought not merely to prevent indigence but to transcend it, by seeking for their sons and daughters an escape from the hopelessness of casual labour in which they themselves were entrapped. Whatever discouragements might be offered by Arthur Young and by the illustrators of the progresses of harlots, there had to be some official endorsement of the theory that England was a land of opportunity as well as freedom.

Hogarth himself provided such an endorsement in his extremely influential series of prints called *Industry and Idleness* (see Plate 13) which

1 Hogarth: detail from *A Harlot's Progress*, Plate 1, 1732. The country lass is ensnared by a procuress.

2 *Harriet Heedless applying to a Statute Hall*, 1780. Detail from the first in a series of prints published under the title of *A Modern Harlot's Progress*.

13 Hogarth: *Industry and Idleness*, Plate 1, 1747. The fellow prentices at their looms

were, as he said himself, 'calculated for the use and instruction of youth'. Published in October 1747, a few months before Peter Kalm observed the drudgery of English casual labourers, they showed how serious and dutiful effort raised men above such drudgery, while idleness and loose living cast them down into something infinitely worse. They told the story of two apprentice boys, one of whom worked industriously at his loom while the other idled his time away. The first went from success to success, marrying his master's daughter and ending up as lord mayor of London; but the idle apprentice sank lower and lower in depravity until he finished up on the gallows at Tyburn. Here was something positive, a tale in which the rewards of virtue counterbalanced the wages of sin. The trouble about *A Harlot's Progress* had been that the good girls in the waggon (if there were any) had been ignored. But now the good was there alongside the bad, so that there was something to emulate as well as something to eschew.

This was very encouraging, but from the point of view of the poor there were certain snags. In the first place, both boys were privileged from the beginning: they were both apprentices, which meant that somebody had been able to pay a premium for them to learn a trade. Their respective fates illustrated some of the difficulties of clambering up from the middle rungs of the social ladder to those nearer the top, but they had nothing to offer those at the bottom for whom even the middle rungs were quite out of reach. Hogarth's idle apprentice was originally a figure of hope rather than desperation, somebody upon whom money had been spent. He had little in common with the poorest in the land, the unskilled labourers who looked in vain for the opportunities he was about to throw away. Nor were the opportunities themselves quite as golden and easy to grasp as might appear at first sight. The success of the industrious apprentice did not come just from hard work but from studied sycophancy and a calculated marriage; and few masters in London had as many daughters as they had apprentices. Hogarth knew something of the subject, since he had married Sir James Thornhill's daughter while he was a student – though scarcely an apprentice – at the Thornhill academy. He also knew that very few apprentices made good, marriage or no marriage, and that even fewer became lord mayor of London. Francis Place, who belonged to a Fleet Street club of apprentices in the 1780s, wrote later that apart from himself there was only one lad who was at all successful – and he had married his master's daughter. It was also in the 1780s that the Solicitor-General, introducing the abortive Bill for a London police force, pointed out that nine out of every ten criminals hanged in London were under the age of twenty-one.[20] The idle apprentice had many successors in real life, the industrious apprentice very few; and the difference between the two categories was as often a matter of luck as of hard work.

The vital part played by marriage in the story of Hogarth's successful apprentice underlines Sir Lewis Namier's remark, made in a very different context, that English history in the eighteenth century was made not by individuals but by families. There were dynasties of merchants and industrialists just as there were dynasties of landowners and politicians. There were even dynasties of scavengers, men and women with no other skills and no other prospects who had established their right to sift over London's rubbish heaps and sell what was saleable. Since they refused to allow their children to marry anyone poorer than themselves and since there was little chance of their marrying anyone richer, they were notoriously inbred. There was less inbreeding among the rich and propertied dynasties, who usually had sound business reasons for making marriage alliances with other families and even with other social groups: one of Hogarth's bitterest satires, *Marriage à la Mode*, showed the disastrous results of a marriage of convenience concluded between the son of a poverty-stricken nobleman and the daughter of an aspiring merchant. Nominally, *Industry and Idleness* was about earning one's living, working hard to achieve success; but in fact it was about 'making one's way in the world', which was rather a different matter. The earning of a living, by means of hard and unremitting toil, was the business of the lower classes; as Arthur Young admitted with such refreshing candour, nobody but an idiot would expect them to work at such a rate unless it *was* their only way of earning their living.* But for those more fortunate people who had a way to make rather than a living to earn there were other factors to be taken into account. They must concern themselves with social connection rather than physical exertion.

Those who came to England from other and more hierarchical countries got a very different impression. French visitors, in particular, were amazed to see how much respect was given to merchants and manufacturers and even to simple farmers, men who in France would have been constantly reminded of their inferior status. ''Tis pity,' wrote the Abbé Leblanc, 'this plenty which the English farmer enjoys should make him so proud and insolent. He does not only dispute the road with those whom the order of society has made his superiors, but sometimes jolts and insults them for his pleasure.'[21] And Vincent de Gournay, one of the most fervent

* See p. 80.

French admirers of England, insisted that France would be a better and more prosperous place if French industrialists would take a pride in their business, as their English counterparts did, instead of scrambling to buy patents of nobility and move into the ranks of the aristocracy.[22] But this was in fact rather a back-handed compliment to the social mobility of which the English were so proud. The point about English merchants and manufacturers was that they were in most cases unable to buy patents of nobility. In France many thousands of financiers and lawyers and merchant capitalists moved from the middle classes into the nobility during the eighteenth century by the simple expedient of buying their way in. This was impossible in England: nobility was not for sale. The seventeenth century had seen a great deal of social mobility, as old families were cast down and new ones raised up, but from 1688 onwards the existing landed families were consolidating their position. As one historian has recently pointed out, there were few counties in England where the proportion of recently ennobled families was as great as it was in many areas of France on the eve of the French revolution.[23]

The moral was that neither hard work nor the wealth which it earned was sufficient to make a commoner into an aristocrat. Ironically enough, the very success of the middle-class capitalists had made things more difficult for them. Their business activities had extended and buttressed the credit structure, with the result that capital was more readily available in England than in most European countries. This in turn meant that landowners seldom had to sell their estates if they wished to avoid doing so: they could always mortgage part of the land in order to raise the capital they needed. The land market was on the whole a sellers' market. Merchants and industrialists who wanted to turn themselves into landed gentlemen found it very difficult to buy the sort of estate which would give them the position they sought. The old landed families had more success in keeping out intruders during the eighteenth century than at any other time in modern history. It was for this reason that the few new men who did manage to force their way into the charmed circle – particularly the 'nabobs', the newly enriched East India Company servants – provoked such violent resentment on the part of their outraged aristocratic neighbours. It was for this reason, also, that rich but non-noble men of substance asserted themselves in ways that offended the Abbé Leblanc, instead of buying their nobility and thus making their assertiveness socially acceptable. The respect paid to the middle ranks in English society was a measure of their distance from the nobility and gentry to which some (though by no means all) of them aspired.[24]

None of this was of much relevance to the poor. There were many success stories in eighteenth-century England, men and women who rose to great wealth from comparatively humble beginnings; but very few of these stories concerned the really poor, the unskilled labourer who could not afford to apprentice his children even to the humblest of trades. For him the existence or otherwise of 'social mobility' was an academic question, however important it might be for the innkeeper or small tradesman or tenant farmer who could afford to give his children some start in life. During the second half of the century the figure of the 'self-made man' began to make his appearance in the mythology of English society, especially in connection with the dramatic new industrial growth that took place in the Midlands and the North. But even these heroic successes were seldom as self-generating as they seemed. Matthew Boulton, one of the central figures in the growth of the Birmingham iron industry and the development of the steam engine, got much of his capital either from his father or from his wife; and John Wilkinson was able to become one of the most successful ironmasters in England largely because he made judicious marriages into the landed families that controlled the existing iron resources of the Severn Valley.[25] Others among the so-called 'new men' of industry were members of old-established Dissenter families (Quakers, in particular, were highly esteemed as businessmen, as industrialists and as model employers), which were certainly not poor, however carefully they might be excluded from the Anglican landowning society which dominated their counties. And finally, of course, there were the aristocratic industrialists – men who did not soil their hands or worry their heads with the actual business of making money, but whose bailiffs and land agents were nevertheless the real promoters of the so-called 'industrial revolution'. The Duke of Rutland, receiving his five shillings on every ton of chert that was dug from his land, was a more significant figure in the new process of economic growth than the mythical 'self-made man'.

Having established the right connections, the next step for the aspiring member of the middle classes was to get the right patronage. At a local level, tradesmen and small manufacturers centred on market towns were almost entirely dependent on the favour of the surrounding landowners. 'The frozen benumbing temperature of the winter does not damp the growth of vegetables more than the poverty of the farmers doth the interests and spirits of tradesmen,' wrote William Allen in 1736.[26] In London the continual search for the patronage and favour of the great was even more intense; and it was not confined to those manufacturers who actually worked in London itself. Even Josiah Wedgwood, the Staffordshire potter who did more than any other man to open up a mass market for domestic crockery, was desperately anxious to bring his wares to the notice of the nobility, the gentry and above all to the members of the Royal Family. Such patronage was equally important for those who offered services rather than goods. When Andrew Cooke advertised himself in the 1770s as 'the oldest Bug-destroyer in England', he remarked angrily that

> a set of people style themselves Bug-destroyers to his Majesty, which serves for no other purpose than to draw in the unwary; please to refer to the Court Calendar for twenty years back. You'll find that no person was ever appointed to that office; if any has a right, it is myself, having worked at sundry apartments in the King's Palace.[27]

The more successfully a man made his way in the world of trade and industry, the more adept he had to be at manipulating patronage and connections. The local tradesman or manufacturer was usually content to buy and sell at prevailing prices and to compete openly both for markets and for supplies of raw materials. But the great mercantile fortunes of the City of London had not been built up in such a naïve fashion. The leading commercial magnates of the realm were not Members of Parliament or governors of the Bank of England for nothing. These positions of power and privilege enabled them to take up government loans at advantageous rates, snap up contracts to supply government departments at exorbitant prices and play an important part in the debates that decided what duties should be charged on what goods. The great manufacturers and industrialists soon found that their interests needed to be guarded with equal vigilance. Matthew Boulton, who was later to be thought of as a member of a frustrated 'new class' that thirsted in vain for the reform of the representative system, was in real life an extremely skilful manipulator of the existing parliamentary structure. He knew the right people and he knew how to use them to the best advantage.[28] Farther north, the needs of the Lancashire textile industry were looked after not only by the gentlemen of the county but also by the traders and shipping magnates of Liverpool, who had much of their own capital sunk in Lancashire industry. Even as early as the 1750s Samuel Touchet, a Lancashire industrialist and a London financier as well, used his contacts with the government of the day to mount campaigns in West Africa designed to give him a corner in some of the materials he used in the manufacture of cloth.[29]

Whatever their original aim may have been, activities of this sort soon became a straightforward matter of investment. Governorships of the Bank of England and of the other influential companies such as the East India Company or the South Sea Company were not always available on the open market, but the blocks of shares that led to them usually were. Seats in Parliament could normally be bought, either by coming to an arrangement with some landowner who had the right to nominate to a closed seat or by buying enough votes in constituencies where the electorate was larger and the contest more open. Capital laid out in this way, like that invested in buildings or machinery, was expected to show a proper return. London merchants made sure that their seats in Parliament paid handsome dividends, just as men like Boulton or Wedgwood, too distant or too busy to sit in the House of Commons themselves, hoped to get good value for the money they spent briefing parliamentary agents and organizing pressure groups.

For the great monied men investment of this kind was an ancillary activity: they invested in political influence in order to make more profitable their basic investment, which was usually in the manufacture or distribution of goods of one sort or another. But for many landed families such investment was the main concern of their lives. Mrs Bate, the wife of an ambitious clergyman in the middle of the century, was connected with the politically powerful family of Stanhope – as a result of which, her tombstone declared proudly, 'She had the merit to obtain for her husband and children, twelve several appointments in church and state'.[30] Clergymen were not normally great landed magnates, so that in this particular case Mrs Bate's services were especially necessary; but even noblemen and gentlemen with extensive estates might well feel the need of such connections if they had a lot of children to provide for. If the estate itself was not to suffer – and with most landed families it was axiomatic that it must not – then younger sons must be found places in the armed forces or the church or government service, while for the daughters honourable marriages must be arranged which did not demand too much of the estate in the form of dowry. These things required influence – influence which because of its practical value was regarded as property, with a value as tangible and sacrosanct as the value of land or merchandise. If a man bought a commission in the army, or if he bought a seat in Parliament in order to put his sons in the way of rich benefices in the church or rich sinecures in some government office, he expected to be properly paid if he was asked to use his influence on behalf of anyone outside his own family. There was nothing mean or corrupt about this: it was as realistic as charging people for the land they bought from you or the goods with which you supplied them. Office and place and influence were all forms of property; and as such they must be properly respected if they were to keep their value.

This did not mean that all transactions in the world of careerist politics took place in cash terms. Men did favours for one another without putting an immediate monetary price on them; but they usually expected an appropriate return in due course – a fact which gave to eighteenth-century political life its own peculiar flavour. It was a world of gentlemen's agreements and self-conscious virtue, a world in which men claimed always to be acting without mercenary motives and then complained bitterly if their disinterested generosity was not properly requited. At its best it produced political groupings based on genuine trust; at its worst it led to vendettas which were as terrible in their consequences as they were trifling in their causes. The violent animosity between Charles Fox and the Earl of Shelburne, a key factor in England's political weakness during the age of the American revolution, had its roots in some vague promises, never clarified and never made explicit, which Shelburne was said to have given to Fox's father and then broken.

To the cynic it might seem that the real line between industry and idleness was that which divided the poor, who had to work in order to earn their living, and the rich, whose livings were assured for them as part of the property which their families had acquired. It was certainly true that the eighteenth century made a sharp distinction between noblemen and gentlemen on the one hand, whose business was to consume, and ordinary people on the other, whose business was to produce. When the silk weavers rioted in London in the spring of 1765 the king's natural reaction was to make sure that the ladies of his court wore expensive silk gowns at his next ball, in order to show that the aristocracy was performing its proper function of providing work for poor weavers.[31] Yet there were other duties which many gentlemen took very seriously indeed. The fact that they had invested in office did not necessarily mean that they were bad officials, any more than investment in land necessarily made them bad landlords.

This was especially true in the armed forces: officers could not afford to be sinecurists simply because they had bought their commissions. Military service to the king had been the original *raison d'être* of noblemen – and therefore of gentlemen too, for the English gentlemen were the equivalent of the lesser noblemen of other countries. The sword was no longer the distinguishing mark of gentle birth in England, as it was in many other countries, but the view of it held even by such a progressive thinker as Lady Mary Wortley Montagu was significant. She once remarked that she thought it as scandalous for a woman not to know how to use a needle as it was for a man not to know how to use a sword.[32] Duelling was still the final resort in quarrels between gentlemen, even though the pistol had come to replace the sword as the favourite weapon. Everyone who had any pretensions to gentility worried about the possibility of a challenge and wondered what he would do if he received one: for the most part men were afraid of fighting but even more afraid of the shame and loss of status which would result from not fighting. When two Irish hairdressers got above themselves and tried to fight a duel in 1774 their seconds filled the pistols with boiled potatoes – something which few seconds would have dared to do, however humanitarian their motives, if the protagonists had been noblemen or gentlemen.[33] One foreign visitor to England in the 1720s had remarked that duelling was going out of fashion and that English gentlemen demeaned themselves by fighting members of the lower classes with their fists – a practice which continued to amaze foreigners throughout the century.[34] Porters and coachmen, who were often noted for their pugnacity and their strength, were among the favourite antagonists picked out by these battling patricians.

When officers went into action against the enemy rather than against their coachmen, physical courage was not always enough. In 1744 the British fleet in the Mediterranean threw away the chance of smashing the combined French and Spanish fleets largely because the Vice-Admiral refused to follow the Admiral when he broke formation in order to engage the enemy. But at the subsequent court martial it was the Admiral who was cashiered, because he had committed the technical offence of 'breaking the line', while his second-in-command was acquitted on the grounds that he could not have brought his ships into action without committing this same offence. One of the officers present at this court martial was George Byng, who when war broke out again in 1756 was sent to defend Minorca against French attack. Remembering the earlier case, he chose to be circumspect rather than brave: he broke no lines and he failed to engage the enemy. Unfortunately for him, Minorca fell to the French and he was court-martialled and shot for neglect of duty. A few years later Lord George Sackville, son of the Duke of Dorset, was court-martialled and dismissed from the army with ignominy for disobeying an order to bring the cavalry into action at the battle of Minden. On this occasion William Pitt, as Secretary of State, ordered that the sentence be read out to every regiment in the army, 'so that officers may be convinced that neither high birth nor great employments can shelter offences of such a nature'.[35]

The Sackville case certainly made a considerable impact: Lord George was shunned by society and it was only after the accession of George III, one of his most unswerving defenders, that he managed to change his name and find his way back into public life. Byng's fate was even more of a jolt for any officers who thought they could take their duties lightly. Byng was undoubtedly guilty of serious neglect of duty, but his sentence might well have been less severe had it not been for the ferocious public outcry, led by the gutter press, which howled for his blood. When Voltaire remarked sardonically that the English shot admirals from time to time in order to encourage the others, he was perhaps revealing his instinctive loyalty to the hierarchical principle which he affected to attack so bitterly. Like most Frenchmen, he was shocked that officers and gentlemen should be hounded down by those who were their social inferiors. But war is part of politics; and in England politics were carried on in the open, with both sides seeking support where they could find it, at all social levels. As a result the English officer class, however indolent and inbred it may have been, could not afford to be utterly incompetent. The king's commission might be a piece of private property, but it nevertheless involved a man in public duties.

Unfortunately this was not the case with most civilian office-holders. John Huggins, a patron of Hogarth and the father of one of his best friends, bought the wardenship of the Fleet prison in 1713 for £5,000 and milked it very successfully for fifteen years, charging all the fees that were permissible and many that were not. When prisoners died – which was fairly often, since Huggins made no attempt to keep the place clean or to deal with outbreaks of disease – he left the bodies unburied for days on end, refusing to let the relatives have them until all outstanding fees were paid. On the other hand, he could be very accommodating if prisoners wanted to escape and had enough money to bribe him to let them do so. In the end he sold his office for what he had paid for it, which on the face of things was not a very good bargain: most office-holders expected capital appreciation as well as dividends. But within a year it became clear that Huggins had been very shrewd to get out when he did: there was a public inquiry into the abuses and atrocities at the Fleet and Thomas Bambridge, the man to whom Huggins had sold his place, was dragged before a committee of the House of Commons and accused of practising diabolical cruelties upon his prisoners. (See Plate 24.) There were serious charges against Huggins as well – indeed, Hogarth's preliminary sketch of the Commons committee in session showed the interrogation of someone labelled 'Huggins the Keeper' – but in due course his associates managed to get the proceedings against him dropped. One of them was Sir James Thornhill, who was said to owe both his knighthood and his post as

Sergeant Painter to Huggins's influence. Hogarth for his part proceeded to marry Thornhill's daughter and to change his picture so that Bambridge was unmistakably the villain – two steps that were perhaps not entirely unconnected. Huggins survived to feature in Hogarth's later work as a respectable patron, while Bambridge's image was fixed for all time as that of 'the inhuman gaoler'.[36] It would be comforting to see this difference as reflecting differing degrees of infamy, but probably more realistic to interpret it in terms of superior political skill and more influential connections.

Similar skill was shown by many men in public life, who bought and sold offices for themselves and their dependants with a keen eye for all the circumstances which might affect the value of these assets. The offices in question tend to figure in the history books as 'sinecures', a misleading word which suggests absence of care, a total disregard of the office itself and a total absorption in the world of pleasure which it made possible. In fact offices could be very worrying things, especially if they yielded less in fees than they should have done or failed to match up to the dignity of the man who held them. All this was a matter for constant attention, for vigilance which was every bit as close as that which a gentleman expected his stockbroker to give to his investments in stocks and shares. If the propertied classes had given as much of their time to earning their living as they gave to making their way in the world – if they had paid attention, that is, to the duties of their offices rather than to the dividends which those offices yielded – the machine of government would have functioned a great deal better. As it was, politics and public life depended almost entirely on the deputies whom the office-holders employed, the army of clerks and scribes who worked long hours for wages which represented only a fraction of the fees received by their principals. Professions which were closely associated with the business of government, such as the church and the law, were organized along very much the same lines and attracted very much the same kind of people. Those who made a career out of public service were highly professional in their approach to careerism itself but they were often amateurs when it came to the actual business of serving the public.

The whole structure of office-holding and career politics was under constant attack from independent gentlemen. The backbenchers in the House of Commons thundered against corruption, ably supported by opposition politicians anxious to discredit present office-holders in order to turn them out and seize their offices. But none of these critics, whether genuine independent or opposition careerist, really believed that efficiency rather than birth should be the criterion of public life. Apart from eccentric radical theorists at the very end of the century, there was nobody in politics who wanted civil servants to be appointed on the results of an examination and promoted according to length and quality of service. Most people believed that the offices of power and influence in the kingdom belonged to the nobility and gentry, each according to his station, as indubitably as the throne belonged to the king. They had the disposal of the honorific capital of the land, just as freeholders and freemen had the disposal of its material wealth. The cause of complaint was not that gentlemen had sinecures, but that the wrong gentlemen had sinecures. Opposition careerists and genuine independents differed only in the extent to which they wanted to open the field: the former only wanted to open it enough to include themselves, while the latter wanted to include everybody – everybody, that is, who had the necessary wealth and position to sustain the office to which he was appointed.

Thomas Bewick the wood-engraver, a man of earnest but somewhat naïve political views, pushed the argument of the independents to its logical conclusion when he suggested that the great offices of state should be undertaken in the same spirit as the office of justice of the peace. Everybody in public life, from the king's chief minister downwards, should perform his duties without payment and without thought of self-advancement, just as the local squire sat on the bench and tried petty criminals without hoping to make a career for himself out of so doing.[37] In 1794 this vision of disinterested probity and purity of intentions was extended by Gisborne in his *Enquiry into the Duties of Men in the Higher and Middle Classes of Society*: he thought that local justices and London ministers alike should go into public life for what they could give rather than for what they could get.* He also thought that they should widen their sphere of operations. The justices of the peace in Lancashire had taken it upon themselves in 1784 to recommend certain precautions which should be taken in industries where there was danger of injury to workers; and this action, which to some people seemed an intolerable interference with the rights of employers, seemed to Gisborne an example which should be followed more and more widely. Men in public life should earn their livings by concerning themselves with the conditions in which lesser men earned theirs. Even the casual labourers, who had seemed so neglected when Kalm considered their situation half a century earlier, were put forward by Gisborne as proper objects for a gentleman's concern. They should have 'a reasonable share of his attention bestowed on the relief of their distresses and the improvement of their morals'.[38] As in so many

* See pp. 56–7, for Gisborne's further comments on justices.

other aspects of English life, there was a moralistic sting in the reformer's tail. Moral tutelage was the price that the labouring classes were expected to pay for an increased sense of responsibility on the part of their superiors.

The new attitude showed itself in a variety of ways. It was clear even by 1780 that the loss of colonial markets in America would mean drastic changes for British industry; and the pamphlets and reports which discussed these changes no longer contented themselves, as they might have done thirty or forty years earlier, with the purely commercial aspects of the problem. Josiah Tucker, the erudite Dean of Gloucester who was also a famous economic theorist, thought that the best answer to the troubles of the woollen industry would be to force the working classes to dress in coarse woollen cloth, as befitted their station in life, instead of tricking themselves out in cottons and silks and fine linens.[39] By the end of the 1780s, however, it looked as though new industries like cotton were as vulnerable as the old ones: there was a serious recession throughout the textile industry, which continued to be affected by financial crises of one sort or another for the rest of the century. Once again the answers proposed for these problems spilled over from the commercial into the social sphere. Joseph Acland's *Plan for Rendering the Poor Independent of Public Contributions*, which came out in 1786, reflected the growing interest in Friendly Societies and in other ways of making the poor more thrifty, so that they should not finish up by becoming paupers and involving their betters in unnecessary expense.

In itself this was not new. Arthur Young had been saying for years that the country's salvation lay in thrift and plain living. Nor had he expected the working classes to be alone in their sacrifices: while suggesting that labourers should deny themselves tea and wheaten bread he had also suggested that farmers should do their bit by denying themselves pianos and post-chaises.* But now there was a new note of urgency in the appeals for working-class thrift. Quite apart from the teething troubles of the new industries, which seemed to involve unpredictable slumps and credit crises, there was the increasingly serious problem of unemployment on the land as well. Capitalist farming and enclosures had not led automatically to higher productivity and higher profits and more jobs, as so many people had hoped. On the contrary, there were farmers all over the country who were having to lay off workers. By the end of the century this agrarian unemployment, combined with an unprecedented rise in the price of food and other essentials, had produced widespread distress. Worse still, from the point of view of the propertied classes, it had produced a frightening

* See p. 73.

rise in the cost of poor relief, which increased three or four times over during the last quarter of the century. Harassed overseers, struggling to keep more and more paupers alive on what money they had, tried to hire out pauper labour at cheap rates. This made matters worse, creating even more paupers as farmers laid off existing workers in order to take advantage of the overseers' bargain offers.

It was clear that problems as vast as these could not be solved by using the poor in order to create demand at home, in the way that Dean Tucker had suggested selling coarse woollens by compulsion. Any appreciable increase in the home market would have to be achieved by an increase in wages, which was quite unthinkable: the emphasis on the need for a plentiful supply of cheap labour was still at the core of all economic thinking. If Britain's economy was to continue to expand – as it must, since her capitalist revolution had now passed the point at which it could be put into reverse – she would have to seek her markets abroad, while holding down living standards at home in order to keep production costs low. The duty of the poor was clear: it was not their business to spend more – that could be left to the foreigners – but to save more. A detailed and properly documented study of the labouring classes was needed, in order to find out just what their needs were and why they failed to adjust their expenditure to their income. By this time respectable Englishmen had convinced themselves that the problem was not poverty but profligacy. Henry Zouch summed it up in 1786, when he wrote:

> Idle and disorderly persons of both sexes and of all descriptions are everywhere to be met with, living many of them in a state of perpetual vagrancy, profligate, diseased and miserable in the extreme; a nuisance and expense to the community and a standing reproach to the government under which they live.[40]

What followed was not so much a debate as a chorus. Some writers attacked drunkenness, some gambling, some sexual excess. Some sought reformation through education (particularly through Sunday schools, which would not interfere with the productivity of the other six days), some through a wider preaching of the gospel, some through legislation and government intervention. But they all agreed on one thing: if the poor were unable to earn a proper living they must concentrate on living more thriftily rather than on seeking higher earnings. Then, in 1797, the detailed and properly documented study which the situation demanded finally appeared, in the shape of Frederick Morton Eden's epoch-making work *The State of the Poor*. For the first time in history the propertied classes of England could see how the poor lived. With icy precision Eden cut through the cant about profligacy and revealed the truth about poverty. He totted up family earnings and family budgets and showed that for the great majority of the labouring classes there was little enough margin for luxury. Such dissipation as the poor could afford, the occasional bout of drunkenness or the flutter on the lottery, might indeed end by precipitating the whole family into the workhouse; but there was no guarantee that abstention from such vices would keep it out of this grim institution. No doubt the moral reformers were doing the country a great service in the theological and political spheres: many people felt that the disasters in America had been God's punishment for past immorality and His warning against future sins, while many more felt that 'idle and disorderly persons' were the cause of the French Revolution and must be rooted out if they were not to lead to similar trouble in England. But the moralists could not claim to have the answer to the country's economic problems. For most people the problem of earning a living remained a problem of what you earned rather than how you lived.

For Thomas Malthus, who published his sombre *Essay on Population* in 1798, it was not so much a problem of how the poor lived as one of how *many* of them lived. He foresaw a world in which the well-meaning efforts of the philanthropists would result in more and more people being kept alive, while the country's food resources would constantly lag behind this rise in population. Instead of increasing the wealth of the country, capitalism was merely increasing its problems. According to traditional morality, men of property were right to provide more jobs for the poor, right to alleviate their distresses, right to encourage them to live more frugally so that they and their children increased and multiplied; but according to the new morality of Malthus all this was misguided. In the end it must lead to a disastrous crisis of over-population. Industrial expansion and moral reform, which the moralists thought had come that men might have life and have it more abundantly, could only lead to death and suffering on an enormous scale.

Undeterred by the dark forebodings of Malthus, the new armies of social reformers continued to devise ways in which the poor might live more thriftily, more happily and more profitably. The years of unconcern were over: it was now as fashionable to have opinions about the condition of the working classes as it had once been to have opinions about art and music and literature. Most of the reformers thought of themselves as liberators, tearing down the old barriers of birth and privilege and chartered rights in the name of free enterprise, free thought and free trade. They wanted to create a society based on contract rather than on status, a world in which a man's only duty would be to his employer. But behind this apparent concern for freedom there was a new and unprecedented interest in direction and regulation. Jeremy Bentham, who was later to be hailed as one of the prophets of nineteenth-century freedom, was particularly fascinated by the problems of the interaction of work and leisure: one of his pet schemes concerned a children's seesaw which would be connected to pumping machinery so that play could be turned to useful purposes. It does not seem to have occurred to him that his invention might presage a world in which play became more like work, rather than one in which work became more like play. Ingenuity of a similar kind had already been applied to animals: since dogs needed exercise and enjoyed running, men had put them in treadmills beside hot fires so that their continual running could turn a spit for roasting. In the end the treadmill was to prove more suitable than the seesaw for human purposes as well, as nineteenth-century prison authorities were to discover. In the meantime Bentham expended his own ingenuity on the problems of contemporary prisons, where his ideas for constant regulation and organization could be applied more effectively than in the world of free men. His orderly mind was offended by the unhygienic bawdiness and unsystematic violence of prison life. As early as 1778 he proposed to replace all this with something much more orderly, a prison in which men and women were to be put to hard labour for 'as many of the four and twenty hours as the demand for meals and sleep leave unengaged'. They were to shed the verminous rags which were standard wear in eighteenth-century jails and put on instead specially designed clothes calculated to humiliate them as much as possible. As a final manifestation of orderly benevolence they were to have their names and the addresses of their jails printed on their faces with indelible chemical washes.[41]

By the end of the century Bentham was becoming obsessed with his plan for a 'Panopticon', a circular building designed in such a way that an overseer stationed in the centre could see all that went on in the segments of the circle. Although the panopticon was particularly suitable for use as a prison, Bentham envisaged it having many other uses as well: factories, schools, workhouses, orphanages and many other institutions could be built in the same way. Wherever there was need for supervision and regulation, whether of work or of leisure, the panopticon would make it easier and more effective. Just as the Christian moralists aimed to make the working classes feel that the eye of God was upon them at all times, so Bentham the rationalist would ensure that the gaze of reason – or at any rate of reason's representative, the overseer – would penetrate to every corner of their lives. By this means, he claimed, it would be possible to gain 'power of mind over mind in a quantity hitherto without example'.[42] And while he designed buildings to supervise particular groups of men and women, Bentham designed codes of law to ensure the supervision of society as a whole. The haphazard and vindictive violence of the old penal system must be replaced by a carefully graduated scale of punishments and rewards. Bad actions must result in exactly the correct amount of pain, good in precisely the correct amount of pleasure. In this way accurately measured stimuli would be bound to produce desired responses in all cases. While other moralists sought a controlled society, Bentham offered something even better: a conditioned society.

As the age of neglect gave way to the age of supervision, the effects were felt within the ranks of the propertied classes as much as among the workers themselves. For an age of supervision meant an age of supervisors. More and more men of property and substance found themselves involved in planning society and in overseeing the actions of other men. A large and important section of the population earned its living by regulating the way in which other people earned theirs. Public office was still a form of private investment, but now it involved duties as well as dividends. Life among the propertied classes was no longer simply a matter of making one's way in the world and then enjoying it once it was made; it was a matter of doing one's duty, of working for work's sake, of filling the unforgiving minute with the performance of worthwhile tasks. Few dared to ask whether the tasks were really worthwhile or whether work was really an automatically ennobling activity. Fewer still dared to examine the concept of duty or question Wordsworth's ringing description of it as the 'stern daughter of the voice of God'. Some felt that the shades of the prison house were closing in on English society, in the way that Wordsworth himself had seen them closing in on children as they grew up. For England too was growing up: in the solemn atmosphere of the 1790s the rumbustious knockabout violence of the eighteenth century seemed like an irresponsible childhood that was being left behind. As the propertied classes became more declamatory about their duties and more discreet about their pleasures, the fashionable world locked itself up in a prison of respectability. But those for whom life in the factories was already prison enough, for whom respectability brought but little return, were not always willing to follow. Fortunately for England's future, those who lived by the sweat of their brows retained a spontaneity and an honesty which was lost to those who lived by the sweat of their consciences.

5 A Paradise for Women

IN THE spring of 1750 a country gentleman, 'fifty-two years of age next July, but of a vigorous, strong and amorous constitution', decided to advertise for a wife. He inserted a paragraph in the *Daily Advertiser* stating his requirements:

> Tall and graceful in her person, more of the fine woman than the pretty one; good teeth, soft lips, sweet breath, with eyes no matter what colour, so they are but expressive; of a healthy complexion, rather inclined to fair than brown; neat in her person, her bosom full, plump, firm and white; a good understanding without being a wit, but cheerful and lively in conversation, polite and delicate of speech, her temper humane and tender, and to look as if she could feel delight where she wishes to give it . . . She must consent to live entirely in the country, which, if she likes the man, she will not be unwilling to comply with; and it is to be hoped she will have a heart above all mercenary views and honest enough not to be ashamed to own she loves the man whom she makes her choice. She must not be more than fourteen years, nor less than seven years, younger than the gentleman.[1]

The fact that he was prepared to accept candidates up to and including the age of forty-five seems to suggest that he was not primarily concerned with the need to breed children, which was often the motive in cases like these. Begetting heirs was a very serious business and for most eighteenth-century gentlemen the need for a son was greater than the need for a wife: it is significant that when Arthur Young really wished to curse one of his enemies he said that he hoped God would punish the man in question by 'interrupting his posterity'.[2] In spite of the strictures of Dr Alexander, who once stated that Englishmen gave more attention to breeding colts and puppies than children and that they would match themselves with 'the most decrepit or the most diseased of the human species',[3] it was on the whole true that those who were concerned with breeding were concerned also with the health and pedigree of the women from whom they bred. The interesting thing about the anonymous gentleman in the *Daily Advertiser* is that he simply wanted a wife for himself and not a dam for his future children. He could afford to think purely in terms of married bliss and to write out his personal prescription for the ideal wife.

It was in its way a masterpiece of compression, a beautifully constructed summary of the things that eighteenth-century Englishmen looked for in a woman. From considerations of personal appearance and social acceptability (a fine woman, tall and graceful to impress guests and tenants, as well as a woman with soft lips for her husband's own use) it moved to more intimate qualities of mind and body. The lady in question must be cheerful and lively without being too intelligent and she must be able to 'feel delight where she wishes to give it' – a charming phrase and one which would soon be made unacceptable by the moralizers and the prudes later in the century. Finally, she must be a lover of the simple country life. Whatever else they disagreed about, almost all men were agreed that towns were the destroyers of feminine virtue. Women were thought to be peculiarly susceptible to the fashionable fripperies and time-wasting amusements of the town: even physicians were advised solemnly to think twice before sending their patient to take the waters, for fear that this should 'please his wife and daughters by sending them to a scene of fashionable amusement'.[4] Only in the country could a man be sure that his wife was his and his alone.

The advertiser did not of course assume that the sort of woman he was after would herself read a newspaper: he merely asked gentlemen readers who knew of such a woman to let him know (letters should be sent to the Smyrna Coffee-house, marked A.B.). Then, presumably, there would be an examination of teeth, lips, breath, bosom and so on, followed by an exchange of vows and the drawing up of the deed for the jointure of £600 a year which was the price offered for this female paragon. No doubt some of the women approached felt themselves slighted. Their price might not be above rubies, but at least it was above £600 a year. If so, they should be careful: England was noted for its old maids and there was no lack of writers to advise women not to pitch their price too high. Oliver Goldsmith's Chinese philosopher was amazed when he was told that in England many women remained unmarried out of choice rather than out of necessity. He told of one who would not marry a poor man simply because her sister had married a rich one: she finished up as governess to her sister's children, 'the drudgery of three servants without receiving the wages of one'. Another was the daughter of a rich pawnbroker and wouldn't settle for a husband poorer than herself, 'without ever considering that she should have made an abatement in her pretensions, from her face being pale and marked with the smallpox'. Then there was Lady

Betty Tempest, who preferred lovers to husbands until finally she became too old for either. Finally there was Sophronia, perhaps the most tragic figure of all: 'She was taught to love Greek and hate men from her very infancy: she has rejected fine gentlemen because they were not pedants and pedants because they were not fine gentlemen.'[5]

The imaginary Chinaman was a useful vehicle for Goldsmith's particular brand of male arrogance. Like most of the writers and artists of eighteenth-century London – including of course Hogarth himself – Goldsmith moved in a predominantly masculine society, discussing in clubs and taverns and coffee-houses the literary and philosophical questions which women were not supposed to know about. His crony Dr Johnson, with whom he founded 'The Club' in 1764, once made a remark about a woman's preaching which some of his associates would have applied to the feminine conversation which was occasionally tolerated in their circle: it was not done well, he said, but one was surprised that it was done at all.[6] One fashionable topic of conversation was the relationship between European society and the very different societies which Europeans were discovering all over the world, from the sophisticated rituals of ancient China to the apparently idyllic simplicity of the South Sea islanders. Most people were confident that the culture of western Europe was superior to these more 'primitive' communities, but there were those who saw nobility in the savage and a deep wisdom in his social arrangements. Some even felt a sneaking admiration for the crude customs of countries which Englishmen had been taught to regard as 'backward'. Goldsmith made his Chinaman outline, obviously with considerable relish, a wedding custom which he said prevailed in Russia: the bride's father beat her with a cudgel before handing both his daughter and his cudgel over to the bridegroom, to whom the bride then curtseyed in token of submission. English women should be grateful, he implied, that they were treated more generously than this.[7] As Dr Alexander remarked in 1779, 'It is the characteristic of the men in every enlightened nation to treat the weaker sex with lenity and indulgence.'[8] And of course England, being the most enlightened of all nations, was also the most lenient and the most indulgent.

This was a very old and well-established belief. As long ago as 1621 Robert Burton had quoted in his *Anatomy of Melancholy* the ancient proverb that England was 'a paradise for women and hell for horses'; and in 1686 an Italian visitor had repeated the same saying, adding that 'if there was a bridge from the island to the continent all the women in Europe would run thither'.[9] These were comments which Englishmen could and did receive with complacent approval; but when their Italian guest went on to say that in England women 'generally wear the breeches', they were considerably less pleased. Seventeenth-century Puritanism – similar, in this and other ways, to the taboo-ridden primitive societies which the eighteenth century was now discussing – had been terrified of feminine domination, which it seemed to link with the sins of the flesh. It was no accident that the book of Revelation, with its lurid images of an enthroned woman as the ultimate evil, made such an impression on the Puritans. They bequeathed to their successors, Anglican as well as Puritan, a heritage of over-anxious masculine authoritarianism. By the beginning of the eighteenth century the henpecked husband, the man who could not keep his wife under proper control, was the most derided of all the stock figures of fun in English life and literature. The original John Bull was such a figure: Mrs Bull, Arbuthnot wrote, was a choleric and domineering woman who constantly nagged her husband for loitering in alehouses and billiard-rooms while his trade was being stolen. She had to be exorcized, along with John Bull's bovine tendency to be led by the nose, before the sturdy archetype of English freedom could emerge at the end of the century. Englishmen were proud of their reputation for treating their womenfolk with 'lenity and indulgence', but they were even more proud of their determination to exclude them from all authority, domestic or otherwise.

This morbid fear of what the English called 'petticoat government' had widespread effects, political as well as social. Whenever Englishmen disliked a particular king or a particular politician they looked for – and usually found, or invented – the woman who was the sinister force behind him. The Stuart despotism which had been overthrown by the revolution of 1688 had been popularly associated with frivolous courts and feminine wiles, with power-crazed mistresses who manipulated their lovers for their own ends. The Hanoverians could hardly be seen in quite the same light: by the time George I became king of England he had already imprisoned his wife for life, an action which must have endeared him to authoritarian English husbands. But the stock stories were still dragged out, of royal mistresses who had politicians in their pocket and court ladies whose lightest caprice was preferred to the combined wisdom of the House of Commons. George II turned out to be a rather vain and self-important king with an extremely able and sagacious queen, so that the satirists and the gossip-mongers had ample opportunities to put about stories (many of which were true, fortunately for the country's stability) of Queen Caroline's political influence. But it was George III's mother, the

Dowager Princess of Wales, who fell victim to the most virulent of all eighteenth-century anti-feminist campaigns. Her supposed transgressions, which ranged from undue influence on her son's reading to illicit love-making with his tutor, were the subjects not only of broadsheets and caricatures and newspaper attacks, but also of violent public demonstrations at which petticoats were symbolically burned.

In fact the amount of power which women could wield was small. Apart from some professional women such as schoolmistresses, writers, actresses and the keepers of bawdy houses, women could only exercise power through their husbands. There were no women justices of the peace, no women councillors or aldermen, no women lawyers or parsons. Women did not sit in the House of Commons and they only appeared in the House of Lords in very exceptional circumstances. Elizabeth Chudleigh, once maid of honour to the Princess of Wales, was summoned there in 1776 in order to establish whether she was the Countess of Bristol or the Duchess of Kingston and whether she was or was not guilty of the crime of bigamy. She was finally found guilty, but her rights as a peeress shielded her from punishment. It was a sensational trial because it placed the lone figure of a woman at the centre of the essentially masculine splendours of the House of Lords; but it did little to enhance either the dignity or the power of the peeresses of England. Like the mistress she had once served, Elizabeth Chudleigh found that for a woman it was a great deal easier to achieve notoriety than power.[10]

Nor was it particularly easy for Englishwomen to exercise authority indirectly, to be the power behind the throne or the bench or the pulpit. During the second half of the century a few exceptional women, such as Mrs Thrale or Fanny Burney or Lady Holland, began to meet men on equal terms as conversationalists; but in most circles John Shebbeare's judgement of 1758 remained true. Woman, he had said, was 'the companion in the hours of reason and conversation' in France, but in England she was only 'the momentary toy of passion'.[11] Really important decisions were taken in men's clubs and above all in that most exclusive of all masculine preserves, the House of Commons. If Englishmen wanted to talk business or politics in their own homes they did so in their studies or over their port, while the ladies were supposedly chattering innocently elsewhere about their frills and their fripperies. Almost every foreign visitor remarked with some surprise upon this English custom of segregating the sexes. The drawing room, that eminently civilized place where in France and in other countries men and women met on equal terms to have serious conversation, was little used in the great houses of England. The very word *salon*, which in French meant not only the drawing room itself but also the discussions and readings that took place there, seemed dangerous to many Englishmen. Thomas Gisborne, who produced in 1797 an *Enquiry into the duties of the female sex* to follow up the success of his earlier enquiry into the whole duty of the gentleman, was very scathing about the word and everything that it stood for. If education encouraged women to copy the *salon* leaders of Paris, he said, then women would be better left uneducated.[12]

To the majority of Englishwomen, unlikely to acquire much education and even less likely to have a *salon* in which to exhibit it, this particular aspect of women's liberation was a matter of profound indifference. For them the proverb comparing the Englishman's treatment of his two traditional beasts of burden, women and horses, probably had some truth in it. Peter Kalm was amazed to see how little work the women did in England:

> I confess that I at first rubbed my eyes several times to make them clear, because I could not believe I saw aright, when I first came here, out in the country, and saw the farmers' houses full of young women, while the men, on the contrary, went out both morning and evening to where the cattle were, milk-pail in hand, sat down to milk, and afterwards carried the milk home . . . when one enters a house and has seen the women cooking, washing floors, plates and dishes, darning a stocking or sewing a chemise, washing and starching linen clothes, he has, in fact, seen all their household economy and all that they do the whole of God's long day, year out and year in . . . They are lucky in having turned the greater part of the burden of responsible management on to the men, so that it is very true what both Englishmen and others write, that England is a paradise for ladies and women.[13]

Kalm's adaptation of the original proverb was significant: whereas earlier writers had been concerned simply with women, he brought in the ladies as well. He admitted himself that much of what he said applied to those who were reasonably comfortably off, rather than to the poor. 'Common servant-girls,' he conceded, 'have to have somewhat more work in them . . . the mistresses and their daughters are in particular those who enjoy perfect freedom from work.'[14] At the Gravesend limekilns a few weeks later he saw women working like slaves for a few pence a day *; and if he had looked more carefully and travelled more extensively he would have found plenty of hard-working women in the English countryside. It was not in fact usual for the men to do the milking: milkmaids were normally expected to get up at three or four o'clock in the morning and

* See p. 82.

begin their working day by milking ten or a dozen cows. There were areas in the North of England where a labourer was only engaged if he agreed to provide the labour of at least one woman – wife, daughter or hireling – as well as his own. Many travellers were shocked to see the kind of work that women had to do: ploughing, reaping, cheese-making, carting dung.[15] The fact that these good people were shocked was of course significant in itself, but it did not alter the fact that women still performed these tasks in some parts of the country. In the towns, too, women did some of the nastiest and least healthy jobs. As well as the thousands of apprentice girls and other domestic servants there were countless women who spent their lives cleaning fish in the markets, picking rags and other refuse on the rubbish tips or scrubbing clothes for long hours on end.

The treatment of apprentice girls, who were often obtained from the parish authorities as a cheap form of domestic labour, does not seem to have improved very much during the course of the century. The case of Elizabeth Brownrigg, who was hanged at Tyburn in 1767 for torturing her apprentices to death, caused a considerable stir: the *Annual Register* collected all the gory details it could in order to shock its readers and it pointed out that such things could easily happen again unless something was done.[16] Nothing was done and domestic servants continued to be subject to terrorization on the one hand and lechery on the other. Traditionally it was the latter that led a girl into a life of crime, but the former could also have the same effect. In 1775, a dozen or so years before Moir uttered his dire warning about seduction being the common fate of serving women* a girl called Martha Latimer was forced by her employer to help him in his operations as a coiner. They were caught and Martha was sentenced to be burned alive. Fortunately for her Lord North, the King's chief minister, heard about the case from his neighbours and wrote to the King. 'As you seem to interest yourself in favour of Martha Latimer,' George III replied somewhat loftily, 'I authorize you to direct Mr Eden to have her respited and the punishment transmuted to transportation.'[17] The streets of London and other cities were full of servant girls who were drifting or had drifted into a life of petty crime, even though their fate was seldom as dramatic as that of Martha Latimer. Most were pickpockets or prostitutes who made an uncertain living by robbing their clients or informing on other criminals: Hogarth's idle apprentice fell into the hands of one of them and was betrayed by her. One or two were more ingenious and more picturesque in their methods. Mary Young, a pickpocket who was convicted and hanged in 1740, had a pair of artificial

* See p. 86.

arms made for her so that she could sit with them folded demurely in her lap at church while her real arms were busily delving into her neighbours' pockets.[18]

Somewhere between the squalor and drudgery of labouring women and the self-destructive aspirations of the would-be lady there lay the paradise that contemporary male writers enthused over. Like the gentleman who advertised his needs in 1750, most men considered that a woman who was rich enough to escape manual labour and sensible enough to avoid the temptations of the town could live an ideally happy life as long as she was married to a good man and took pains to please him. A talent for contentment was, in male eyes at any rate, a woman's greatest gift. Discontent in one form or another was the root of all feminine unhappiness, just as it had proved the undoing of the old maids listed by Goldsmith's Chinese philosopher. They had all wanted more of something – more material possessions, more physical pleasure, more book learning – and they had all been punished as a result. Far happier were the simple farmers' wives described by Kalm. They had handed over the tedious and exhausting tasks to their menfolk or their servants, leaving for their own attention household duties that were varied enough to be interesting and light enough to leave them plenty of leisure so that they could still be, as Kalm noted, 'very handsome and very lively in society'.[19]

Fifty years after Kalm's visit a farmer's wife in Herefordshire wrote down an account of her daily life over a period of some eighteen months, from the beginning of 1796 to the middle of 1797. Her name was Anne Hughes and she certainly possessed a gift for contentment. 'When I doe think back,' she wrote in the final entry in her diary, 'I doe know how verrie luckie I bee ande wythe soe muche toe bee thankful for.' One of the things for which she was most thankful was the fact that her mother had made sure that she was taught 'how toe rite and figger'.[20] Certainly in her case this modest amount of learning did not have the dangerous results feared by the opponents of women's education. She carefully concealed from her husband the fact that she was keeping a diary, but her mother-in-law found out about it and was very tolerant, even giving her a new book to replace the one she had filled up. Lady Susan, wife of the lord of the manor and a great friend of Anne's, assured her that it was a perfectly respectable pursuit and that many of 'the quality' did it. Nevertheless Anne continued to keep her writing a secret from her husband: she told herself that he was a great baby – men, she said, were just like children and as much trouble in many ways – but for all that she could not bear the thought of being laughed at by him if he found out.[21]

Anne was extremely fond of her husband, but she had no illusions about him. He could be harsh and ill-tempered at times, so that she spent a good deal of time protecting the servants from his wrath and conniving at their various tricks to win his favour. When he got drunk she was mightily amused, giving him 'a sounde smacke on hys backe parte', and when he fell into the muck-heap she was even more amused, though on this occasion she tried to conceal it, for he was a man with a great sense of his own dignity. On one occasion a pig bit him in the leg and he became so short-tempered as a result that he tried to dictate how the kitchen should be run and what work the maid should do. At this Anne became so incensed that she threw a lump of bread at him; but she only hit the kitchen door, which he slammed behind him. She then pictured to herself what his face would have been like if she had hit him. This made her laugh so much that she regained her good humour, concluding that 'John doe thynk hee bee such a grett man, butt lord hee bee juste a grete bigge sillie'. Fortunately John's mother knew a recipe for violet pudding which was a good cure for cross husbands and was also useful in cases of 'giddyness of the head'. Fortified by this and other useful hints, Anne learned to manage the fractious John very effectively.[22]

Up at the manor house her friend Lady Susan seemed to have a less pleasant relationship with her husband. On one occasion Anne was scandalized to find 'his lordship' pawing at her and trying to kiss her, upon which she boxed his ears soundly and resolved to keep her maid Sarah out of his way, 'shee bein a prettie wenche'. Like most women of her kind, Anne was deeply suspicious of the idle rich and their immoral ways: she came of a generation that had been influenced directly or indirectly by Hogarth's prints and by Fielding's novels, so that she was ready to assume that noblemen behaved like Hogarth's Viscount Squanderfield when they were in town and like Fielding's Squire Western when they were in the country.* She decided that his lordship cared for nothing but his hounds and his drinking companions. Then Lady Susan fell ill and Anne was a little surprised to see how deeply his lordship was affected. 'Poor fellow,' she wrote, 'hee doe love her muche, in spite of hys ruff wayes.' Lady Susan died after a short illness; and three weeks after her funeral John and Anne were roused from their bed by a knock on the door late at night. It was the lonely widower from the manor house, dressed all in black and come to say goodbye, 'hee bein off toe furrin partes note lykinge thee bigge hous wyth oute Ladie Susan'. He asked Anne if she

* Viscount Squanderfield was the dissolute young nobleman in *Marriage à la Mode*; Squire Western was the peppery fox-hunting country gentleman in Fielding's *Tom Jones*.

would take flowers from time to time from the dead woman's garden and put them on her tomb. With tears in her eyes Anne agreed. She was revising her opinions about married life among the nobility and gentry.[23]

She may well have been misled by her own sentimentality. There were plenty of other men, some of them a good deal more distinguished than Lady Susan's widower, who found out their good fortune only when it was too late. William III behaved badly to his wife while she was alive and then grieved for her when she was dead; and Lord Hervey's story about George II at Queen Caroline's death-bed is justly famous.[24] When she exhorted him to marry again after she was dead, he refused with tears in his eyes and said that he would keep mistresses instead. '*Mon Dieu!*' replied the dying woman, '*Cela n'empêche pas.*'* The truth seems to have been that the upper classes in eighteenth-century England were intensely diffident about married life. A gentleman felt that any open admission of his affection for his wife, at any rate while she was still alive, was almost as unmanly and ill-advised as over-indulgence of his children. On the surface marriage was the subject of endless sneers and jokes and scandals, an arena across which husband and wife faced each other like characters in a comedy of manners. Since nobody was interested in the manners of the country wives and their country husbands, they were left in peace to perpetuate the myth of the simple country life and its beneficial effects on married life. But the fashionable world – and those from the country who were foolish enough to aspire to it – provided inexhaustible material for the gossip-writers. If they were to be believed, most upper-class marriages lurched from one infidelity to another for most of the time. If married women in the labouring classes were made miserable by violence and poverty, those among the aristocracy were made equally miserable by vice and impropriety. Only in the contented ranks of 'the middling sort of people' was the paradise for women to be found.

Popular views of the treatment of women in the upper and lower classes of society were neatly illustrated by some of the prints of the year 1782. In the spring of that year Sir Richard Worsley, colonel of the Hampshire militia, took proceedings against Captain Bisset, one of his officers, for adultery with Lady Worsley. (See Plate 14.) Although the misconduct was proved the colonel only got one shilling damages because it was shown that he had himself connived at the affair, even encouraging Bisset on one occasion to spy on Lady Worsley while she was disporting herself in a bathing establishment at Maidstone. The caricaturists seized on the case with enormous relish: a crop of prints appeared showing Bisset in his rôle

* My God, that won't get in the way.

14 *Sir Richard Worse-than-Sly*, 1782. The press was delighted with the case of Sir Richard Worsley, who encouraged Captain Bisset to peep at his wife's ablutions and then went to law when the two of them committed adultery.

15 *Mr Justice Thumb in the Act of Flagellation*, 1782. A print inspired by John Buller's declaration that it was perfectly legal for a man to beat his wife as long as he used a stick no thicker than his thumb.

of *voyeur* and Worsley acting as pandar for his own wife. In the autumn another batch of prints on the subject of marriage appeared, inspired this time by Judge Buller's declaration that it was perfectly legal for a man to beat his wife as long as he used a stick which was not thicker than his thumb. The print shops had scarcely managed to sell off their stocks of pictures of the Hampshire colonel as pandar before they were swamped with portrayals of the high court judge as pedlar, hawking bundles of regulation-sized rods to enthusiastic husbands. (See Plate 15.) But it was noticeable that all the husbands shown came unmistakably from the lower classes. The women who were being divested of their petticoats and stays in order to receive marital discipline were all slatternly, drab and shrewish creatures. The world of the popular prints was one in which the marriages of labourers disintegrated into violence while those of noblemen degenerated into vice.[25]

There was probably some truth in this picture. The poorer people were, the more they were forced to live close together in a confined space where deception and secret infidelity were pretty well impossible. If they could not live together in love then they had to live together in hatred. Their reactions were probably more instinctive and less premeditated than those of the middle and upper classes, so that they made less attempt to break down the natural relationship between love-making and violence. As Cadogan said so condescendingly in another context, 'they enjoy blessings they feel not and are ignorant of their cause'.* There is no reason to doubt that many marriages were essentially happy ones: just as Anne Hughes dissolved into affectionate laughter after hurling her lump of bread at John, so thousands of other wives may have found satisfaction and even serenity in the midst of their marital squabbles and fights. For the rich it was easier for a tiff to turn into a breach. At the very least there was another room to go to, perhaps another wing of the house or another estate altogether. Angry husbands could take themselves off to town, leaving behind them angry wives who would seek consolation where they could find it. In Fielding's novel *Joseph Andrews* Lady Booby made advances to her footman because her husband had died; but it was generally believed that many other ladies did so as a result of far less permanent and less tragic separations. The advertiser of 1750 insisted that his future wife 'must consent to live entirely in the country', but he did not say whether he intended to do the same himself. Perhaps he felt that the town corrupted women more easily than it corrupted men: certainly the phrase 'man about town' was a markedly more complimentary than 'woman of the

* See p. 59.

town'. But in fact the thing that moralists called corruption was not a peculiarly urban pursuit. It usually resulted from separation, from husbands and wives being rich enough to lead different lives in different places. The rich could afford to be tempted and they could usually afford to yield.

In 1743 Hogarth produced, as the fourth print in his *Marriage à la Mode* series, a picture which summed up all the temptations of fashionable society and the disastrous effects which they were thought to have on married women (Plate 16). He showed the countess lounging at her morning *levée*, surrounded by all the worst denizens of the *beau monde* to which her lover has introduced her: fops and effeminate connoisseurs, pretentious dandies with their hangers-on. Even the pictures on the wall represent lust, while the negro page-boy, himself a symbol of the current fashion for exotic servants, points to the horns which suggest that the countess is making a cuckold of her husband. There was nothing exotic about Hogarth's own servants – the portrait group he painted in the early 1750s showed two menservants, one boy and three serving women, all six of them soberly dressed and clearly kept for use rather than for exhibition – and there was certainly nothing giddy or indecorous about his wife. Jane Hogarth never had any children, but there is no reason to think that her marriage was in any other respects unfulfilled or unsatisfying. She did not seek to enter high society or amuse herself with fashionable gallants while her husband was away. And yet Hogarth himself, like most men of the period, spent a good deal of his time away from home. He frequented taverns where prostitutes were to be had almost as easily as in the brothels which Squanderfield visited in *Marriage à la Mode* and which were in some sense the excuse for the countess' behaviour. The real moral of *Marriage à la Mode* was not that husbands and wives should be content with one another's company but that wives should be content either with loneliness or with the company of their own sex.

By the end of the century this double morality on the subject of marriage had taken on even more sombre and repressive overtones. It was significant that in 1787 Moir's book on the education of girls should be subtitled '*An Address to Mothers*': the English custom of segregating the sexes was hardening into one whereby mothers and daughters and their friends, servants and acquaintances were supposed to form a society within a society, a woman's world where men were the subject only of blushes and giggles. Mrs Cartwright had advised mothers ten years earlier to make companions of their daughters – useful and necessary advice, since it was to become increasingly difficult for married women to find companion-

16 Hogarth: *Marriage à la Mode. The Countess's Levée*, 1745. By aspiring to be a patroness of the arts the Countess has plunged into all those extravagances which eighteenth-century men saw as a woman's undoing.

17 Hogarth: *Marriage a la Mode. The Marriage Contract*, 1745. An impoverished nobleman marries his son to a rich merchant in order to raise money for his building extravagance.

ship anywhere else without endangering their reputation and their peace of mind. As long ago as 1740 Elizabeth Montagu, feminist though she was, had roundly condemned her cousin Lady Mary Wortley Montagu for travelling abroad without her husband.[26] By the 1780s there were many women in London who lived their own lives, rather after the manner of French society ladies, and were known for what they were rather than for what their husbands were; but the price they paid for their temerity was an atmosphere of lubricious scandal and a succession of ribald attacks in the popular press. Gillray, who had inherited many of Hogarth's attitudes of mind but without any of his restraint and self-discipline, made some particularly savage caricatures of these ladies. Dr Alexander had prophesied in 1779 that Englishwomen would never be able to defy the conventions of society as scandalously as their French counterparts did;[27] and by the 1790s it seemed as though he was being proved right. The *salons* of the French revolutionary period shocked English public opinion even more than those of the *ancien régime* had done, so that more and more women were driven back into that unwholesome world of repressed domesticity which Jane Austen was to describe with such telling precision.

It is not easy to decide just how repressed and prudish this world was. Certainly it was not as harmful as it was to become after another hundred years, when a doctor was to tell a group of undergraduates at Oxford that nine out of ten women disliked the sexual act and the tenth was a harlot.[28] But even by 1809 Mrs Mary Cockle had to apologize for discussing seduction in her *Important Studies for the Female Sex*: it was, she admitted, a subject 'from the very mention of which the cheek of youthful purity should turn aside blushing', but she felt 'an almost religious conviction' of the need to talk about it. Unfortunately the remarks that followed this portentous preamble were of very little value. Instead of giving some practical hints on dealing with seducers, she retreated to the rather optimistic view that virtue was its own defence. It seemed to be a curiously self-generating quality which would grow more steadily and operate more effectively if women hugged it to themselves. There was much talk later in Mrs Cockle's book of Englishmen placing their 'domestic happiness, honour, virtue and all their mild and graceful attributes' under the 'gentle guardianship' of their wives and mothers and sisters and daughters. Quite what it was that was contained in this domestic tabernacle guarded so closely by the ladies was difficult to determine; but one of its characteristics seemed to be a self-imposed ignorance, a refusal to face the physical realities of the relations between men and women.[29] The popular medical handbooks of the 1790s were full of dark tales of the results of masturbation among girls: it was said to lead to barrenness and to a 'frigid relish for genuine love'. One unfortunate young lady in Birmingham was said to be 'in a decline because of self-pollution'.[30] But there was little attempt to break into the cloistered world of mothers and daughters and get at the real causes of such distress – the guilt and fear which were begotten of ignorance and false modesty.

There were honourable exceptions. Samuel Solomon, in his *Guide to health, or advice to both sexes*, took mothers to task for not explaining the mysteries of menstruation to their daughters. He also included in his book a detailed description of the act of love, refreshingly free both from prurience and from euphemism.[31] But there were many thousands of households in which a woman discovered reading such a book would have been made to feel that she was obscene and polluted, a monster who had betrayed the high standards of ignorance expected from her sex.

The moral revolution of the late eighteenth century was something which affected society as a whole and not merely women, married or otherwise. Both its causes and its results were involved with politics, with attitudes to money and worldly success, and even with international affairs, as well as with attitudes to the family and to the physical side of love-making. These wider implications will be discussed in due course, but at this stage it is important to remember that women were almost entirely defenceless against those aspects of the moral revolution that affected them and their position in society. By demanding of them modesty above all things, even above honesty and sincerity, the new attitude automatically condemned in advance any woman immodest enough to resist the masculine attempt to scale her down to the level of a mere 'gentle guardian of domestic happiness'. Even the redoubtable Mary Wollstonecraft, author of *A vindication of the rights of women*, published in 1792, came dangerously near accepting the very constraints against which she should have been arguing. She wrote in the dedication of her book:

> The personal reserve and sacred respect for cleanliness and delicacy in domestic life, which French women almost despise, are the graceful pillars of modesty; but, far from despising them, if the pure flame of patriotism have reached their bosoms, they should labour to improve the morals of their fellow-citizens, by teaching men not only to respect modesty in women, but to acquire it themselves, as the only way to merit their esteem.[32]

This vision of woman as the reformer and saviour of society was in fact shared by the French, whose republic was eventually to adopt as its national symbol the figure of a woman. She was to be represented over and over again by the artists of the next half-century, her flowing garments streaming out behind her as she led the crusade against the male tyrannies and corruption of the *ancien régime*. Mary herself had been a crusader against such tyrannies from an early age, as her husband William Godwin later recounted:

> Her father was a man of quick, impetuous disposition, subject to alternate fits of kindness and cruelty. In his family he was a despot, and his wife appears to have been the first and most submissive of his subjects . . . When that was the case, Mary would often throw herself between the despot and his victim, with the purpose to receive upon her own person the blows that might be directed against her mother. She has even laid whole nights upon the landing-place near their chamber door, when, mistakenly or with reason, she apprehended that her father might break out into paroxysms of violence . . . Her childhood, as she often said, had known few of the endearments which constitute the principal happiness of childhood. The temper of her father had early given to her mind a severe cast of thought and substituted the inflexibility of resistance for the confidence of affection.[33]

The inflexibility of Mary Wollstonecraft's resistance was commendable and necessary; but it had more in common with the cramping conventions of the new morality, with their insistence on the closeted and inbred nature of feminine virtue, than she may have realized. The truth was that married women had been so successfully caged for so long that they now had the illusion of escape when in fact they were only bolting themselves into a prison within a prison, a stuffy citadel of self-conscious modesty which was farther than ever from the fresh air.

For some fortunate or intrepid individuals there had always been the possibility of real escape. Miss Mary Edwards, who married the son of the Duke of Hamilton in 1731, realized within a few years that he was interested in nothing but her money – she had an enormous fortune of her own – and so she decided to end her marriage. She was lucky, in that her wedding had been one of those clandestine transactions within the precincts of the Fleet prison which were so notorious during the first half of the century. Such marriages were dangerously easy to contract and this made them seem traps rather than escape-hatches for women: a lady who wrote to the *Gentleman's Magazine* in 1735, signing herself 'Virtuous', complained bitterly of the 'drunken swearing parsons with their myrmidons that wear black coats and pretend to be Clerks and Registers to the Fleet, plying about Ludgate Hill, pulling and forcing people to some peddling Alehouse or Brandyshop to be married'.[34] But that which was easily done could sometimes be easily undone, given enough money to pay the right lawyers and enough determination to use them properly. Mary Edwards had both money and determination. By 1734 she was a single woman again, her marriage having been declared null. Her family, of which Hogarth had already painted a group portrait, was broken up and her year-old son – the subject of another and very charming picture by Hogarth – was now a bastard instead of a scion of the ducal house of Hamilton.[35]

Few of those who were married in this clandestine fashion were either willing or able to pay such a high price for their freedom. Many of them were probably brought to agree with Walter Wyatt, one of the Fleet parsons, who wrote remorsefully in his pocket book: 'The fear of the Lord is the beginning of wisdom. The marrying in the Fleet is the beginning of eternal woe . . . May God forgive me what is past and give me grace to forsake such a wicked place, where truth and virtue can't take place unless you are resolved to starve.'[36] But the trade in such marriages continued to thrive for another twenty years after Mary Edwards had annulled her own. Fortune hunters of either sex were glad of a procedure which gave partners no time to reflect and parents no time to intervene. Nor was it only in London that such things were possible: the Reverend Sweetapple of Fledborough in Nottinghamshire did a roaring trade in hasty weddings for couples from far and wide, while the tiny parish of Rowner in Hampshire saw eighty-three marriages, over half of them irregular, in the ten years between 1743 and 1753. Then during the next twenty years, after the new Marriage Act had come into force, the number dropped to twenty-eight – a yearly average of only 1.4, one-sixth of the average before the Act.[37]

The experience of Rowner illustrated some of the arguments put forward when the Act was debated in Parliament. Its opponents had said then that ordinary people would not be able to go through all the new rigmarole of having banns called and getting a licence, so that the measure would make 'common whoring as frequent among the lower sort of people as it is now among those of the better sort; and multitudes of wenches in all parts of the country, when they find they cannot get husbands according to law, will set up the trade, so that the Bill ought really to be called a bill for the increase of fornication in this kingdom'.[38] And as even the regular marriages in the parish of Rowner (that is, marriages in which one or other party resided in the parish) fell to one-third of the previous level, there may have been some truth in this contention. Certainly the Marriage Act of 1753 did not make things any easier for the many thousands of girls who had to get married in a hurry when they found they were pregnant. After they had gone through the business of having the banns called, their wedding, when it finally took place, was likely to resemble the one described by George Crabbe:

> By long rent cloak, hung loosely, strove the bride,
> From every eye, what all perceived, to hide.[39]

It was also alleged that the Act would make things worse for women of property and substance, since their seducers would now have legitimate excuses for putting off marriage and thus for persuading them to surrender their maidenhood in advance of the wedding day. And it would limit their choice: parents would now be able to exercise an effective veto on matches that displeased them, so that heiresses would wither away waiting for a suitable mate to be found for them. One speaker even envisaged the House of Lords being enabled, as a result of the Act, to close its ranks against all intermarriage with commoners and thus in the end to overthrow the balance of the constitution.[40] These fears proved exaggerated: the dynastic matchmakers and marriage-brokers of propertied England were not really affected one way or the other by the provisions of the Act. The disastrous and mercenary marriage of convenience illustrated in Hogarth's *Marriage à la Mode* was arranged a full ten years before the passing of the Act, and similar marriages continued to dispose of daughters like pieces of property for the rest of the century. Goldsmith's imaginary Chinese philosopher attacked the Marriage Act vigorously, saying that those who married for the right reasons – genuine love, consuming passion, youthful zest – did so spontaneously and would never marry at all if their ardour was given time to cool down while banns were called. Only the calculating and the mercenary – which in his view meant the old and the ugly – would get married. The children of such people, he concluded gloomily, 'will probably be an ill-favoured race like themselves'.[41] Yet he went on in a subsequent letter to list soured spinsters who had been left on the shelf because no suitable arrangements could be made about their money.* The Act did not seem to have helped these particular members of the calculating and mercenary classes.

Whatever its effects may have been on the social structure of the country and on the fluidity of the marriage market, the Marriage Act of 1753 seems to have had only marginal effects on the lives and the happiness of individual women. Some of them may have had slightly more freedom of action as a result of it: parents no longer had to fear that their daughter would be carried off by an unscrupulous fortune hunter as soon

* See p. 104.

as they let her out of their sight.* Others, mostly from the poorer classes, may have been tempted to dispense with marriage altogether now that it had been made more difficult. Waggoners and bargemen and other itinerant workers may have found it hard to comply with the Act, as one speaker in 1753 had pointed out.[42] Soldiers and sailors were in a similar position, so that their womenfolk may have found it more difficult to get themselves turned from mistresses into wives, if that was what they wanted. Justices of the peace, who had been accustomed to enforcing marriage upon men accused of being the fathers of illegitimate children, may have been hard put to it to do so now that the process took several months. But it is almost impossible to be certain about such things: it is clear that thousands of couples lived together without bothering to get married, but it is by no means clear how far this was the result of the Marriage Act.

One thing that is certain is that the particular loophole through which Miss Edwards escaped had now been closed. The only way to dissolve a marriage that had been legally contracted and properly consummated was to obtain a private Act of Parliament. The number of these Acts increased steadily – there were sixty between 1715 and 1775, but no less than seventy-four during the remaining twenty-five years of the century – but they were still extremely rare and they were almost invariably passed at the instigation of the husband rather than the wife. It was infinitely easier for a man to rid himself of a wife who committed adultery on a single occasion than it was for a woman to escape from a husband who was habitually unfaithful to her. This was equally true at the bottom of the social scale, where the colourful but unpleasant custom of selling wives still persisted in some places. In 1796 John Lees, a steel burner in Sheffield, sold his wife to Samuel Hall, a fellmonger, for sixpence. Mrs Lees was handed over to her new owner with a halter round her neck; but since the clerk of the market took fourpence for toll it is hardly likely that the purpose of this offensive pantomime was monetary gain.[43] This was in fact the labourer's equivalent of divorce by Act of Parliament. Only in the middle ranks of society, where people were too poor to obtain Acts of Parliament but too proud to sell their wives in the market place, was there no escape at all. It was no wonder that middle-class wives had a reputation for contentment: they had no choice. In most cases their contentment was rewarded with a measure of security, if not of happiness; and their virtues were recognized and listed on their tombstones, sometimes at great length, even if they

* Until 1856 it was still possible for determined elopers to marry without parental consent at Gretna Green, just over the Scottish border. Under Scots law a declaration before witnesses constituted legal marriage.

had previously been passed over in silence. Sometimes disconsolate widowers found even more grandiose ways of expressing their gratitude and their affection. In the spring of 1775 a London tooth-drawer had his dead wife embalmed by a famous anatomist and placed in a glass case in his drawing room. 'Though she has been dead three months she looks as well as when alive', another wife told her husband in some wonderment.[44]

However unpleasant marriage might have been for many women, it was at least a destination, a state of definite arrival rather than an indefinite period of waiting. Whether matrimony was heaven or hell, there was little doubt in the minds of most males that spinsterdom was a limbo from which women should be only too glad to escape. There was constant talk of the immorality of the times and of the consequent decline of marriage as an institution, but most people saw this as a one-sided development, a misfortune for the poor spinsters who were disappointed and a merry romp for the gay bachelors who had been clever enough to fight them off. It does not seem to have occurred to anyone that it might have given the spinsters a chance to live fuller and happier lives. Lady Mary Wortley Montagu, who did her best to combine the advantages of marriage with the independence of a single woman, came nearer than most to this realization; but even she could not repress entirely her disapproval of those young ladies who saw the single state as an opportunity rather than a penance. 'I am very sorry for the forlorn state of matrimony,' she wrote rather tartly in 1723, 'which is as much ridiculed by our young ladies as it used to be by young fellows; in short, both sexes have found the inconveniences of it and the appellation of Rake is as genteel in a woman as a man of quality.'[45] It was only a step from this somewhat prim comment – written, incidentally, when Lady Mary was only thirty-five – to the sweeping verdict pronounced by an anonymous writer some fifteen years later on women who defied convention: 'When a woman once declares that she does not care what the world says of her, I give her up for gone; and I take it for granted that if she is not a prostitute already she intends to be so.'[46] Male arrogance assumed that if a woman did not want to be the property of one man she must automatically be destined to become the property of all men.

There were of course many women of whom this was true. When a fashionable whore put a thousand-pound banknote into a sandwich and ate it, as Kitty Fisher was said to have done on one occasion, she was clearly asserting her own superiority over men, over the conventions they tried to lay down and over the paltry sums with which they sought to buy her.[47] Elizabeth Chudleigh seems to have held in contempt the society which she was able to shock so easily: she turned up to a masquerade in Ranelagh Gardens in 1749 dressed in a costume which showed more of her than of itself. 'Miss Chudleigh's dress or rather undress was remarkable,' wrote Elizabeth Montagu. 'She was Iphigenia for the sacrifice, but so naked, the High Priest might easily inspect the entrails of the victim. The Maids of Honour, not of maids the strictest, were so offended they would not speak to her.'[48] The King himself showed less scruples: he was said to be infatuated with her, as were many members of his court at one time or another. Even after she got married, finding herself in the end with too many husbands rather than too few, this impressive woman continued to show the same nonchalant disregard for convention as when she was single. For a few fortunate women promiscuity was a way of life, and a successful and rewarding one at that. By not caring what the world said of them they managed to daunt it into reluctant admiration; and by refusing to become the property of an individual they greatly enhanced their market value.

Such women formed a privileged minority. Even Lady Betty Tempest, the fictitious tart described by Goldsmith's Chinaman, was fortunate in that after a lifetime spent rushing from one lover to the next she was able to spend her declining years as a respectable spinster. Farther down the social scale a single lover – or at any rate a single pregnancy – was usually enough to consign a woman to a far less pleasant fate. In 1731 a doctor wrote to the *Universal Spectator* about those who came to him 'on the venereal account' and in particular about 'the woman of the town, who, if not quite abandoned, gives a loose to her passion on such occasions. The consideration of her past, present and future state fills her with distraction and involves her in endless evils from which only death can deliver her'. As far as he was concerned the real villains were the men, 'who first seduce the poor young creatures from their innocence and then triumph in their wickedness'.[49] Fifty years later Sophie von la Roche saw the poor young creatures in rather a different light, when she went to Sadler's Wells, 'the playhouse dedicated to the small middle class':

> The box next to ours was occupied by eight so-called light girls, all with fine blooming figures, well dressed and true to their name, the most obvious gaiety in their eyes and faces. Not one of them looked older than twenty, and every one so made that the best father or husband would be proud of having a virtuous daughter or wife with such stature and good features. We were sorry to think that Mr Archenholz had counted fifty thousand of these surely unhappy creatures.[50]

The two different impressions, one of utter degradation and the other of apparent gaiety, resulted partly from the fact that Sophie saw the girls when they were on duty and on sale, whereas the doctor did not. But it also resulted from the increasing organization and stratification of the business in which the 'surely unhappy creatures' were engaged. The Mr Archenholz mentioned by Sophie was an observer and an amateur statistician, an authority in Germany on the manners and morals of the English, rather than an indefatigable fornicator: his count of 50,000 was an estimate and not a boast. Had he in fact been concerned with personal sampling rather than detached observation he would have found tremendous differences within the ranks of the 50,000, who ranged from fashionable courtesans down to common streetwalkers like the 'monstrous big whore' who showed Boswell 'all the parts of her enormous carcass' in 1763.[51] At about the same time Casanova claimed to have sent away twelve women who were produced one after another for his delectation at the Star tavern: none of them was sufficiently attractive to excite him and so each was dismissed with a shilling.[52] Prostitutes of this sort, waiting in their lodgings for a call to one of the taverns at which they were retained, had not changed much since Hogarth had depicted them and their world in his *A Harlot's Progress* in 1731–2. The women who enlisted them and organized them and exploited them had learned, however, to be more discreet. Mother Needham, the real-life original of the bawd who turned country girls into whores in Hogarth's series, died in May 1731 after being viciously pelted in the pillory by the very people whom she had served so well. Her successors profited from her example and took care to secure influential patronage and protection, turning their bawdy houses into *bagnios* or *seraglios* and getting them mentioned in *Henry's List of Covent Garden Ladies*, the standard directory for the brothels of eighteenth-century London.

While the moralists lamented over the prostitutes with a mixture of pious sympathy and righteous indignation, the majority of Englishmen reserved their sharpest censures for women who were single because they were not feminine enough rather than because they were too overtly so. 'When either man or woman deviates from what is more peculiar to their own sex and approaches in anything too near the other,' declared a writer in the *Universal Spectator* in 1738, 'they must consequently become less amiable and pleasing to one another, the farther they have departed from their respective qualities and characters ... courage and magnanimity, such noble accomplishments in man, do very much depress and debase the character of a woman'.[53] This may have been true of the upper-class woman, but among the labouring classes courage was as much respected in a woman as in a man. In 1728 Cesar de Saussure saw two women fighting with swords in a public arena, watched by a distinguished crowd of noblemen and gentlemen who wagered large sums of money on the outcome of the combat. One of the women was thrown shillings and half-crowns when she managed to give her opponent a serious cut across the forehead. This was sewn up and the wounded woman returned to the fray after fortifying herself with a large glass of spirits; but she soon received another wound, which was also sewn up on stage while the successful combatant was again rewarded with coins. A third wound, this time right across the neck and throat, decided the fight, by which time both women were covered with sweat and the loser with blood as well.[54]

Courage of a similar sort was required of those exceptional women who decided to masquerade as men. Christian Davies, an Irishwoman who enlisted as a soldier in 1693 under the name of Christopher Welsh, served for more than a dozen years before her sex was finally revealed as the result of a wound received at the battle of Ramillies in 1706.[55] Half a century later there appeared *The Female Soldier, or the surprising life and adventures of Hannah Snell*: Hannah claimed to have served both in the army and in the marines and to have received five hundred lashes and several wounds, mainly in her legs and groin, without her sex being discovered. She successfully petitioned the military authorities for a pension of a shilling a day and she secured several engagements to appear on the stage and sing martial songs in soldier's uniform.[56] It was perhaps not entirely coincidental that Charlotte Charke's narrative of her life, which appeared five years after the success of *The Female Soldier*, should have contained several episodes in which the heroine dressed up as a man, on one occasion even planning to marry for her money a young girl who fell in love with her while she was so disguised. While these stories were accepted for the fictions that they probably were, there was more credence given to the adventures of Mary Anne Talbot, first published in 1804. Her colourful exploits, which included service both in the army and in the navy, were vouched for her by her employer and were therefore somewhat more respectable than the sagas of Hannah Snell and Charlotte Charke. Since Mary Anne Talbot died in 1808, only four years after her employer had published her story for his own profit, she did not have the chance to confirm or deny very much.[57]

There was one faculty, however, which the writer of 1738 was even more concerned to reserve for the use of men only. The thing that really offended him, even more than feminine courage or feminine magnanimity, was feminine intelligence and erudition. Women who strove to improve their minds were a danger to society in general and to their families in particular:

> Learning itself is no ornament, but lessens our value of those charms which must be unavoidably either obscured or tarnished by it . . . The most beautiful woman in the world would not be half so beautiful if she was as great a mathematician as Sir Isaac Newton . . . While she was contemplating the regularity of the motions of the heavenly bodies, very irregular would be the proceedings of her children and servants.[58]

He was fighting a losing battle. Elizabeth Carter was already publishing poems and writing for the *Gentleman's Magazine*; soon she would produce some impressive and scholarly translations from French, Italian and Greek. Elizabeth Elstob had published her editions and translations of important Anglo-Saxon texts some thirty years earlier and was still alive, a venerable figure in the world of scholarship. During the second half of the century the number of women authors increased steadily; and they were not all sentimental novelists, as male arrogance liked to think. Mrs Catherine Macaulay, whose weighty and impressive *History of England* appeared between 1763 and 1783, was a spirited controversialist as well as a woman of considerable scholarship. When Burke published his *Thoughts on the Causes of the Present Discontents* in 1770 she was one of the few writers who had the courage to reveal the partisan prejudices which lay beneath his apparently liberal sentiments; and her consistent advocacy of democratic principles riled Dr Johnson so much that he threatened to go to dinner with her and ask if her footman could join the company.[59]

On another occasion the sycophantic Boswell, presumably hoping for an amusing tirade from Johnson, told him that Mrs Macaulay was said to sit for hours at her toilet and even to put on rouge. Johnson merely replied that 'it was better she should be reddening her own cheeks than blackening other people's characters';[60] but the very fact that this trifling bit of gossip should be going the rounds, and that Boswell should think it worthy of repetition, was illustrative of the dilemma women writers were in. Whenever they did anything feminine it was used to detract from their dignity as writers; whenever they said or wrote anything intelligent it was used to detract from their charms as women. Shortly after this Mrs Macaulay married a second husband, a certain William Graham whose brother had invented a device called the Celestial Bed, in which those who had lost their sexual vigour could regain it for a charge of £100 a night. This was altogether too much for the gossips and the satirists, particularly since her new husband was more than twenty years younger than she was. Poor Mrs Macaulay Graham, as she now called herself, remained a figure of fun for the rest of her life.[61]

Other women were more successful at combining the pleasures of authorship with those of femininity. Some, like Fanny Burney, did it by limiting their writing to fairly light fiction and adopting a slightly deferential attitude to the more intellectual achievements of their male counterparts. Others went to the opposite extreme, publishing ponderous books and living blameless lives. Mrs Margaret Bryan, whose *Compendious System of Astronomy* appeared in 1797, was a much-respected schoolmistress, first in Blackheath and than at an extremely fashionable address near Hyde Park Corner. Many other schoolmistresses wrote successful textbooks on a variety of subjects, though there were some who were less respectable academically than they were socially. Miss Sophia Lee, proprietress of a fashionable girls' school in Bath, wrote historical novels of quite staggering inaccuracy.[62]

One problem had not changed with the changing attitude to women and to their intellectual achievements. Whatever form masculine condescension might take, whether indignation at the chaos of a lady mathematician's household or amusement at Mrs Macaulay's presumed cut-price visits to the Celestial Bed, it still assumed that marriage and motherhood should be the ultimate goals of all feminine endeavour. However distinguished a woman's career might be, it could never provide a recognized alternative to the honourable estate of matrimony. The underlying attitude of most Englishmen was the same as that of Goldsmith's imaginary Chinaman: men remained single from choice, women did so out of necessity. One of the less-publicized results of the Protestant reformation was the fact that Englishwomen no longer had any refuge other than marriage. Freeborn Englishmen might boast of their triumph over the dark forces of popery, but for the single woman there was loss as well as gain. In Catholic countries the convent often provided a genuine haven for the single woman, a place where she could escape not only from loneliness but also from the contempt and ridicule with which she was all too often treated in the world outside. Not all religious orders demanded a complete renunciation of the world: in some nunneries women who could afford it could be housed in comfortable quarters, rather like lay sisters or permanent visitors. As early as 1694 Mary Astell, one of the earliest advocates of education for women, had suggested in her *Serious Proposal to Ladies* that women should establish their own centres of education and culture, institutions which would be rather like secularized nunneries.[63] If Oxford and Cambridge existed for the convenience of scholarly and celibate men, there was no reason why similar foundations should not be endowed for the convenience of scholarly and celibate women.

In fact, it seemed, there was every reason. Men were quite prepared to tolerate secularized monasteries, even though it was clear that they sheltered many who were running away from ordinary life into alcoholism or homosexuality.[64] They were even prepared to tolerate the licensed sadism of the celibate schoolmaster. But they felt obscurely threatened by the idea that women might form self-sufficient communities: for the eighteenth-century male the whole point about a woman was that she was *not* self-sufficient. After all, even Catholic nunneries had to have priests as confessors – a fact which had always occupied a central place in Englishmen's lewd jokes about popery and was now coming to occupy an equally important position in the erotic 'Gothic' novels which were very popular towards the end of the century. Meanwhile Sir Francis Dashwood and his friends were said to be acting out similar fantasies in real life, dressing up as monks and keeping prostitutes in the cells of a ruined Cistercian abbey near Marlow. In 1785 William Hayley revived the idea of a secularized convent in his three-volume *Essay on Old Maids*. It was received with derision and indignation: reviewers who were reasonably polite about the earlier sections of his book, in which he praised the achievements of single women, were appalled when he went on to envisage 'a sisterly community of elderly virgins'. This, they said, was 'mingling sacred subjects with those of a lighter nature'.[65] And the really sad thing was that it seemed to be the supremacy of a male God which was sacred, while the difficulties and distresses of single women were assumed to be 'of a lighter nature'. Englishwomen in search of their paradise, whether in heaven or on earth, were expected to look for it in a place prepared for them by a man. In their fathers' and husbands' houses there were indeed many mansions; but few of them were really comfortable if they were furnished only with a single bed.

6 Making a Home

IT WAS Sir Edward Coke, the almost legendary champion of English liberties in the early seventeenth century, who once declared that in England 'a man's house is his castle'. Throughout the eighteenth century this doctrine continued to comfort and sustain freeborn Englishmen, including many who would never have the chance to own a house of their own. Shakespeare's John of Gaunt had seen England itself as a home, surrounded by a moat to protect it against 'the envy of less happier lands'; and most Englishmen liked to imagine their own homes in much the same way. When William Thornton threatened to throw census officials into a horse-pond * he was reverting instinctively to the image of the moat as the freeholder's proper answer to the incursions of the central government. Water in one shape or another, almost magical in its protective embrace, cropped up even in less belligerent dreams of the ideal home:

> I often wish'd that I had clear,
> For life, six hundred pounds a-year,
> A handsome house to lodge a friend,
> A river at my garden's end,
> A terrace walk, and half a rood
> Of land, set out to plant a wood.[1]

Perhaps because they had rejected the mother image so vigorously at a conscious level, Englishmen were deeply influenced by those echoes of it that rose from their unconscious: while despising as idolators the papists who prayed to Mary the mother of God, they were able to nestle happily into their own private dreams of womb-like homes ringed by gardens and woods and lapping water.

For most of the century the importance of these dreams was primarily political. In 1733 and 1763, when governments sought to levy excise duties first on wine and tobacco and then on cider, the opposition to the proposals centred on the charge that the new army of excise inspectors

* See p. 33.

would be empowered to invade the Englishman's home in their search for goods that had not paid the excise. Those who formed the excise mobs during those years usually lived in tenements or hovels where there were few of the comforts of home and few of the consolations of privacy. If they were householders at all their rights were the limited rights of copy-holders or leaseholders or tenants at will, rather than the splendidly self-sufficient rights of the freeholder. For many of them water was something that seeped up through the mud floors of their cottages instead of staying in a conveniently protective ring around them. Nevertheless, they shouted and rioted for the sanctity of the English home and they were successful: in both cases the proposals were either withdrawn or repealed.

By the 1780s things were changing. The younger Pitt was consolidating and extending the powers of the excise inspectors without any serious opposition: the propertied classes had decided that excise mobs were more of a threat than a support to their own domestic comfort. Embattled figures like William Thornton, gathering the members of his household around him in order to repel government officials, had come to look slightly ridiculous. Men of property now tended to gather their house-holds together in prayer rather than in battle. The home was still thought of as a bastion, but now it was a bastion of domestic piety against the wicked world of the homeless and the unsettled and the unprincipled. Mrs Cockle, with her picture of domestic happiness and virtue under the 'gentle guardianship' of good women, summed up the new view of the English home.* The emphasis was no longer on thick walls and on gates barred against excise inspectors but on united families whose members were 'bound each to each by natural piety' rather like the days of the poet Wordsworth.

Since Hogarth intended his pictures to hang on the walls of English homes he did his best to convey in visual terms the values for which those homes were supposed to stand. Some of his early portrait groups, such as the painting of the Wollaston family in 1730 or that of the Cholmon-deley family two years later, reflected the stability and security of family life among the upper classes. *Industry and Idleness* sought to show, among other things, that home life was the reward of the industrious and home-lessness the fate of the idle. While the idle apprentice cowers under threatening skies or in squalid lodgings, the industrious one is safely ensconced within solid walls. And yet there is something a little unreal about the splendid houses and halls through which the industrious ap-prentice moves: he seems to be acting out his edifying story against a

* See p. 115.

background of stage sets. In *Marriage à la Mode* the passion for building ever more elaborate houses, in which most of the eighteenth-century nobility indulged, is at the root of the whole sad story. Hogarth abominated the Italianate Palladian style of architecture, popularized in England by his hated rival William Kent under the patronage of the Earl of Burlington, and so he made it the scapegoat in his moral fable. Lord Squander marries his son to the merchant's daughter in order to raise more funds for the monstrous Palladian building which can be seen under construction in the first print; then the doomed young couple whom he has sacrificed act out the tragedy of their empty marriage in enormous and pretentious rooms which are also Italianate, decorated by the hated hand of William Kent. If the story of the idle apprentice shows the fate of one who cared too little about making a home, *Marriage à la Mode* shows the results of caring too much about building a house. If its moral was really to be brought home it needed something to balance it out, in the way that the success of the industrious apprentice balanced out the misery of the idle one. It needed a companion piece showing the simple joys of a happy marriage and a real home life.

Hogarth tried to provide such a companion piece in his *Happy Marriage* series, undertaken even before the publication of *Marriage à la Mode* was complete. But this second series was never finished: the artist was unable to devise a string of incidents which would dramatize contentment in the way that the first series had dramatized ambition and greed and discontent.[2] And he never made another attempt. In the whole of Hogarth's published work, in all the prints that were to hang on the walls of so many homes, there was scarcely a single representation of genuine domestic happiness. Almost all his characters, with the dubious exception of the stiffly virtuous hero of *Industry and Idleness*, were restless and rootless, moving uneasily from one folly to the next and valuing their homes, if they valued them at all, purely as symbols of their wealth and their power. However successful he may have been in reflecting the movement of eighteenth-century England, the shifting crowds and the thrusting social change, Hogarth never produced a convincing picture of the stillness that was supposed to be at the centre of all this movement, the self-sufficient home life which was the declared aim of social ambition.

In the autumn of 1749, while he was still struggling with the *Happy Marriage* series, Hogarth settled at long last in a country house of his own at Chiswick, a Thames-side village a few miles to the west of London. Lord Burlington's Palladian villa, Chiswick House, was not far away, though it certainly could not be seen from Hogarth's windows after the manner of the first print in *Marriage à la Mode*. Indeed, very little could be seen from Hogarth's windows except his own garden. The house was surrounded by a brick wall and it looked entirely inwards, the outside walls being almost completely blank. It had none of the arrogance of the moated manor house which was the object of so many Englishmen's dreams, but it was in its way just as self-sufficient, just as ready to enfold its owners and cut them off from the outside world. The sort of home life which it represented and made possible was very different from the home life that Hogarth had known in his childhood. His father had kept a coffee-house at St John's Gate in the City of London, where he had claimed to be 'always ready to entertain gentlemen in the Latin tongue'. This combination of business and scholarship had failed and Hogarth's father had spent four years in a debtors' prison while his wife peddled Gripe Ointment and other home remedies to keep the family alive.[3] Hogarth's childhood had been public rather than private, closely involved with the crowded streets of London and with those who earned their livings there. Now that he had grown rich by depicting these people and their bustling, almost communal, way of life he could afford to make his own life more private and more detached.

Hogarth's own progress was a vindication both of *Industry and Idleness* and of *Marriage à la Mode*: he moved from the rootless world of tenements and lodging houses into the secure world of the country house, but he rejected the corrupting splendours of Kent's Palladian extravagance. His house was too imposing to be dismissed as one of the 'suburban villas, highway-side retreats'[4] which successful London tradesmen were building all round the fringes of the city and which were a favourite target for the satirists; yet it was not grand enough to tempt him into aping the country gentleman or embarking upon expensive improvements or extensions. He is said to have given the village children mulberries each year from the tree in his garden, but that was the nearest he got to behaving like an imitation country squire.[5] If he had had a son he might well have been more ambitious: it was the prospect of the continuing and growing dignity of their families that led so many propertied men into buying large estates and building enormous houses. But the house at Chiswick was never intended to be the seat of a future line of Hogarths. It was simply a place where he and his wife and sister – Anne Hogarth, who had been living with her brother and sister-in-law for the past seven years, helping with the business side of things – could live out their days in peace and quiet. And this they seem to have done: very little is known about Hogarth's home life, but there is no reason to doubt that its very uneventfulness was the product of happiness and stability. It was perhaps for this reason that Hogarth abandoned in the end his attempt to apply his satirical and anecdotal art to the subject of domestic happiness.

This progress from the penury of a London apprentice to the prosperity which was denoted by a substantial house in the country was not of course typical: Hogarth was an exceptionally successful artist and he was also an astute businessman, always on the look-out for new ways to profit from his work and to protect it from being pirated. His way of making a home was as careful as his way of turning his art to profit: he saved up his money until he was in the position to buy a house in an area where he was reasonably sure of being welcome and in a state which would permit almost immediate occupation. This apparently straightforward procedure was not always easy, especially in the country. The villagers around London were used to seeing rich tradesmen and artists and actors and writers settling among them, but in the more hierarchical atmosphere of the counties and the small market towns there was more resistance and more resentment.

In spite of all the froth and bustle of London and the big cities, England was still essentially a static community, one in which most people lived where their fathers had lived and accepted whatever station in life their fathers had bequeathed to them. And the houses of England, from the great palaces of the aristocracy down to the cottages of the poor, formed the outward and visible sign of this settled society. The social unit was not the individual but the family or the household, a fact which gave great importance to the actual houses in which these units were contained. The possession of a hearth, traditionally the centre and focus not only of the house but also of the people who lived in it, was the thing that defined a man's position and gave him a place in society. When these pieces of masonry changed hands, or when new ones were built, society itself could be seen to be changing or expanding; and that was something which many people viewed with dismay.

Every parish in England was supposed to appoint each year one of its parishioners as constable; and one of the constable's duties was to see that no new cottages were built in the village without due authority. In many places ancient custom decreed that a man might build himself a home on the village waste land provided he completed it in one night. This was still being done all over the country, but as the enclosure movement gathered impetus it became increasingly difficult for the owners of these home-made shacks to assert their rights. The squatter was always present at the fringes of rural society, especially in moorland and forest areas; but his position became increasingly precarious, until he eventually became identified with the migrant labourer, the gypsy and other rootless and masterless men. In 1748 Kalm was amazed to find that gypsies, 'this useless folk' as he called them, were tolerated at all in England – though in fact, as his nineteenth-century editor pointed out, the treatment of gypsies in the eighteenth century was often very harsh indeed.[6] Wandering folk of all kinds tended to inspire fear in people who were more settled and respectable, though this fear did not always find expression in harshness. In 1796 Anne Hughes heard that the villagers were convinced that there was a ghost in a disused cottage called Gun's Cott. Her husband and the other men made brave noises about going to investigate, but they never went – 'All men bee just babies att harte', commented Anne – so that in the end she and two other women plucked up their courage and banged on the door of Gun's Cott:

> Mye legges didde shake muche and mye teethe didde rattel wythe fere. Noe anser cummen, Mistress Livvy didde saye toe oppen thee dore, wyche Mistress Prue didde, I feelinge verrier skeert theratt. Noeboddie sayinge nay, wee all inside, ande, la there was naute toe fere, itt bein onlie a pore gipsie boddie there for sheltere, and hys wiffe who was lyinge sicke on sum rubbishie sacks in a corner. Mistress Prue didde saye what were they doinge ande thee man didde saye theye were verrie pore, ande no home, ande seeinge thee cott emptie theye in itt one wet nite and hadd stopt there . . . I doe saye can wee doe anythinge toe helpe ande thee man doe saye iff hee can gette toe hys brothers plase hee sure off sum worke there.[7]

It would seem that these sad people were not in fact gypsies but labouring people down on their luck, vagrants out of necessity rather than choice, who had somewhere a relative who might get them work. Anne and her friends looked after the woman while the man went off to seek work at his brother's house, but they had to do so in secret: Anne paid her maid's sister a penny a day, plus food and firewood, to nurse the woman in her cottage. Earlier in the century such precautions would not have been necessary, as agriculture was comparatively prosperous and the poor rates yielded enough to enable overseers to be generous. Cases are recorded in which vagrants were given help by the authorities instead of being whipped from parish to parish as the law demanded. But by 1796 there was widespread agrarian unemployment, which put a terrible strain on the Poor Law system. Poor rates rose to unprecedented heights, with the result that less prosperous farmers had to employ still fewer men in order to pay their poor rates. This vicious spiral produced an increasingly harsh attitude to vagrants, not only on the part of the Poor Law authorities but also on the part of the settled villagers who were themselves living on the edge of starvation and in the shadow of the workhouse. The homeless were no longer a reproach but a threat. If Anne Hughes was rich enough to afford pity, that was her good fortune; but she must be careful to bestow it in secret.

It was not easy for labouring people to be sure of getting themselves somewhere to live and thus avoiding the miseries of homelessness. If they were patient they might get one of the village's existing cottages: as old men and old women died or were moved to the workhouse younger people had their chance. The men of property who had cottages to rent to their workpeople usually looked with approval on patience of this kind, since it meant that the poor did not get married until there was a cottage for them to live in. This in its turn meant that the numbers of the poor were kept in check, always an important consideration with the rich. And in many cases the rewards of patience were very substantial: by the latter years of the century it was becoming fashionable for farmers to build model cottages on their estates, sometimes with an upper storey and with proper wooden or flagged floors. Gilbert White claimed proudly in 1788 that in his village of Selborne in Hampshire there were no longer any mud cottages. All the villagers, however poor, had comfortable stone or brick cottages with glass in the windows and upstairs bedrooms.[8] When Arthur Young went to France he commented scornfully on the sacking or horn which had to do instead of glass windows in the cottages of the peasants there.[9] John Byng, travelling round England in the 1780s and 1790s, saw many labourers' cottages that appalled him – 'mud without and wretchedness within' was his comment on one occasion[10] – but it must be remembered that he was by nature a prophet of gloom, always ready to pick out the worst examples he could find in order to show that the new capitalist landowners were neglecting their duties.

Impatient couples, or those who had to get married in a hurry because of an unwanted pregnancy, might sometimes to be able to live with parents or other relatives. If not, they might have to go farther afield in their search for a home. At the hiring fair the husband might be lucky enough to find an employer who was offering a job with a cottage attached, in which case a move to another village, with new certificates of settlement for poor law purposes, might have to be arranged; but it was much more likely that the search would lead them in the end to London or some other great city. Here the parish authorities would be less worried about increasing numbers being packed into existing accommodation. For most of the century, until the price rises at the very end of the 1790s, it was possible to get a tenement of some sort in London for about half a crown a week.[11] Conditions were often appalling: houses which were already closely packed would be sub-divided and then divided again for the sake of more profits. Sanitation was non-existent and there were frequent fires, which resulted in loss of life as serious as that caused by the collapse of the houses themselves, which was by no means uncommon. But in spite of all these difficulties and dangers, ordinary men and women might find it easier to get a roof over their heads in London than in the country parishes in which they had been born. Country gentlemen complained continually of the unsettling effects of London, but they seldom stopped to think that their desire for stability and a settled society was driving thousands of labourers and their wives every year to seek in London the settled home they could not find in the country.

While the labouring classes struggled to find cottages or tenements, their immediate superiors in the social hierarchy had rather different problems. These were the tradesmen and the artisans, ranging from innkeepers and shopkeepers and brothelkeepers to masons and artists and bookbinders. In their case their place of work was usually their home as well, at any rate until they became prosperous enough to buy a house out of town, as Hogarth did at Chiswick in 1749. Whereas cottagers and tenement dwellers had merely to find their home and then find the rent that was asked for it, shopkeepers and workshop owners were involved with leases and purchases and contracts. This was the level of society at which the lawyer, perhaps the most universally hated and despised figure of the eighteenth century, began his depredations. In *Marriage à la Mode* it is Silvertongue, the lawyer responsible for drawing up the disastrous marriage contract, who is later the countess' seducer and her guide in the treacherous world of connoisseurs and fops; but most satires on lawyers were more direct and concerned plain dishonesty rather than lechery. *The Beggar's Opera* launched a sustained attack on the villainy of the legal as well as the criminal classes; and the barrister in Samuel Foote's play *The Lame Lover* was made to declare that his job was to wrest land from its owners and thieves from the gallows.[12] Householders in London complained continually about the thieves but they were even more worried about the land, which seemed to require constant protection against the machinations of one set of lawyers by means of high fees paid to another set.

The line between lawyers on the one hand and land agents or stewards on the other was not always very clear, especially at the beginning of the century. For several hundred years the propertied classes in England had been obsessed with the law, which they saw both as a friend and as an enemy. They were immensely proud of the Common Law of England, with its provisions broadening down from precedent to precedent in the law courts themselves instead of being handed down from above by an absolutist king; but they were also intensely suspicious of those who practised in these courts. Most landed families tried to ensure that at least one member of the family in each generation was educated in the law, taking his dinners at one of the Inns of Court after he had come down from Oxford or Cambridge. In addition, men of property often employed agents or 'men of business' who had some sort of legal training. In the midst of all these amateur or semi-amateur lawyers the man who was actually called to the bar and pleaded before judges could easily be distinguished, but the humbler figure of the attorney was less clearly defined. In 1739, when the attorneys formed a 'Society of Gentlemen Practitioners in the Courts of Law and Equity', they began to move towards the proper recognition which they would eventually secure under the new name of 'solicitors'; but there was still some doubt as to where their loyalty lay. When a great landowner employed an attorney he often expected him to be as partial and as unswerving as a steward or an agent: the lawyer was there to run the legal side of the estate, just as the steward was there to run the financial side. The law was a battle-ground for great men, whose ferocious and complicated quarrels with one another rolled on for year after year. One of the most notorious, a dispute between the Duke of Portland and Sir James Lowther over the leasing of some land in Cumberland, led in 1768 and 1769 to a political crisis and to special legislation in Parliament.

It was this all-pervading influence of great men, rather than plain dishonesty among attorneys, that created difficulties for the smaller proprietors. The ordinary householder who ran into trouble could not be sure of finding an impartial lawyer, since he had neither the means nor the need to retain one permanently; and lawyers, like everybody else, had their way to make in the world. They must attach themselves to some great patron and serve his interests. If other work came their way they must make such profit from it as they could, but they must still make sure that the interests of their patron did not suffer. In Bloomsbury, for instance, the influence of the Russell family, Dukes of Bedford, was paramount: as early as 1702 building speculators and the lawyers associated with them were clinching important deals for land development in the Covent Garden area with the then Duke of Bedford.[13] On the whole the Russells seem to have been good landlords, often renewing leases without any increase in rent; but their total receipts from their Bloomsbury property nevertheless rose from £3700 in 1732 to £8000 in 1771.[14] Any tradesman or craftsman or innkeeper in Bloomsbury whose property raised legal problems might well find it difficult to get an attorney who would cross swords with the Bedford interest. Even an apparently convincing clash in the law courts might conceal a private arrangement between lawyers who did not want to ruin their careers by offending important people. Similar conditions existed in other parts of London, where landowners had extensive interests; and in the country the influence of the great was even more pervasive. Encouraged by the satirists, the public saw the attorneys as plain villains, agreeing behind their clients' backs on a division of the spoils. But often it was as important to divide the danger as it was to divide the spoils.

The other class of person with whom the property owner must sooner or later have dealings was the builder. 'This is the third day you have been from my work,' wrote Henry Purefoy angrily to Charles Parker the stonemason in September 1738, 'I think you are a very unworthy man to neglect it so this fine weather.' He threatened to give the work to somebody else if Parker did not turn up immediately; but there may have been a certain desperation in this threat, for he had already tried another mason, William Gunn, a couple of years earlier and had found him dilatory and forgetful. Then there was the problem of co-ordination. Even when he had prodded William Gunn into building a wall floor-high he could not get John Jones the carpenter to come and put in the floor at the right time.[15] Purefoy was a bachelor and he had no political or social ambitions, so that the running of his estate at Shalstone in Buckinghamshire occupied most of his time. Having no posterity to glorify, his building plans were comparatively straightforward – his tussle with William Gunn and John Jones over the synchronization of walls and floor concerned nothing more ambitious than a new servants' hall – and he had no need of agents or contractors. But those who were really bent on 'improvements' on the grand and fashionable scale soon found that there was a whole network of traders and factors waiting to serve their needs. While owning a house merely involved a man with lawyers and builders, improving a house involved him with a new and rapidly expanding industry.

Some surprising people were affected by the mania for 'improvements'. William Pitt the elder spent most of his political life proclaiming his dislike for the great families of England and their pretensions; and he did this so successfully that a sturdy country gentleman called Sir William Pynsent, whom he had never met, decided to leave all his property to this champion of the simple life. As soon as Sir William was dead and the estate of Burton Pynsent was in Pitt's hands, the schemes for improvement and extension started to be worked out. Within a very short time Pitt had called in Lancelot Brown, the landscape gardener who specialized in harmonizing a house and its gardens with the surrounding countryside. While formal gardens in the French style challenged the natural settings in which they were placed, creating nothing but tension and discord, Brown claimed to be able to make gardens which blended with the landscape and brought out its potentialities (or its 'capabilities', to use the term that gave him his nickname). His methods were sometimes very drastic, involving the diversion of rivers and even the moving of small hills from one place to another; but Burton Pynsent was perched high on an escarpment overlooking the Bristol Channel, so that there was not really much scope for undulating expanses or artificial lakes or new contours. But what could not be moved could at least be bought up: within a few months Pitt was looking round for opportunities to extend his property, while his brother-in-law Earl Temple was flattering him on his 'estates in Somersetshire'. In July 1766, eighteen months after Sir William Pynsent's death, Pitt decided to accept a peerage and become Earl of Chatham. It was a decision that was to have very considerable political repercussions, but historians have perhaps been wrong to think that for this reason it can be explained in purely political terms. The dreams of grandeur which Burton Pynsent fostered may well have played their part in turning the Great Commoner into a would-be great nobleman. The house created the man as surely as the man created the house.[16]

Landowners whose houses were in positions less precipitous than Burton Pynsent were able to make more extensive use of Capability Brown and of the many other gardeners who copied his methods. The contents of the garden received no less attention than its contours: Philip Miller, gardener at the Chelsea Botanical Gardens, made important advances in the cultivation and propagation of rare plants, while masons and architects produced books of designs for the many structural features with which gardens could be embellished, from fountains and fish-ponds to colonnades and classical temples. Later in the century the classical taste gave way to the Gothic, so that reminders of the Middle Ages such as hermits' cells or imitation ruins were put up alongside the reminders of ancient Greece and Rome. And in the midst of all this historical pageantry and geographical metamorphosis the great houses of England did their best to merge with the diversified landscape that had been created for them. New wings or new fronts were added, sometimes with the original fabric of the house left standing behind the neo-clasicals façades. Whatever Hogarth may have thought about William Kent's imitations of Palladio, they were at least consistent: Kent was a landscape gardener as well as an architect and designer, so that the houses he built blended with the settings he devised for them and the furnishings he put into them. The same could not always be said for the houses whose owners struggled to keep up with changing fashions by building a piece here and a piece there, as and when they could afford it. As they saw their efforts outstripped and outmoded by the arbiters of taste, they were tempted to imitate Lord Squander and embark on something entirely new, whatever the cost.

Interior decoration was less expensive: even the cautious Mr Purefoy decided in October 1739 that he would go along with fashion to the extent of ordering a new mantelpiece in 'handsome red and white marble', together with a black marble slab for another of his fireplaces. The marble was bought from a stonecutter in Bedford Row in London; and when it finally arrived, after nearly three months' delay, it turned out to be the wrong size and to have 'bits of something put into it artificially' because it had been cracked. After receiving reassurances on these points, Purefoy finally paid the stonecutter's bill, which amounted to twelve pounds seventeen shillings. But his troubles were not over. It took another two months to get somebody to put the marble in place and then there was an awkward period during which they could not have fires in the best parlour because the marble had been fixed wrongly and was exposed to the fire.

By now it was the end of February but it was still very cold: the winter of 1739–40 was one of the most severe in the whole of the century. Since the parlour was now unusable Purefoy decided to have it painted and the floor planed, which took another four months. Meanwhile the mason who had put the fireplace in wrongly seems to have refused to do anything further about it, for in June 1740 a rather pathetic letter was sent to another mason asking him to come over forthwith if he was prepared to 'polish and lay and set up marble mantelpieces'. Then after a few months it became clear that the marble slab sent with the mantelpiece was a fake: it blistered and cracked off in a thin shell, revealing coarse stone beneath. The stonecutter sent another, after a three-month delay, but Purefoy's friends assured him gloomily that it was as bad as the last and would peel and crack in time. Meanwhile there was the heavy cost of sending marble slabs back and forth between Buckinghamshire and London, quite apart from the increasing damage to the newly planed floor as slabs were laid and then prised out again. In June 1741, when the correspondence about the matter comes to an end, the parlour was still out of use as yet another slab had to go back to the stonecutter because it was found to be bound together with iron to stop it falling to pieces. Eventually the story must have had a happy ending, as the fireplace was still in place in the 1930s; but there is no knowing how long it took.[17]

Country gentlemen like Purefoy were particularly liable to troubles of this sort, since they were neither poor enough to ignore the dictates of fashion nor rich enough to move to another house while agents and contractors dealt with things for them. Simple farmers and tradesmen contented themselves with brick or stone fireplaces and they stained their floors with soot or beer to hide the dirt, rather than bothering to have them planed. Where floors were of flagstones or of earth (which was mixed with bullocks' blood and then beaten hard) they were usually strewn with rushes and fragrant herbs to conceal the mess and the stench. But in spite of this apparently unsanitary custom, most foreigners commented on the cleanliness of English homes. 'English women generally have the character of keeping floors, steps and such things very clean,' wrote Peter Kalm. 'They are not particularly pleased if anyone comes in with dirty shoes and soils their clean floors, but he ought first to rub his shoes and feet very clean, if he would be at peace with them in other things.'[18]

In most homes the walls and ceilings were treated with the same simplicity and economy: plaster was whitewashed and wooden beams and panels were painted with paint which was usually mixed on the spot by the painter, the householder having purchased the necessary pigments and linseed oil from the colour merchants in advance. By the middle of the century carpets were becoming less of a rarity because some of them were now woven at home instead of being imported. Both the Wilton and the Axminster carpet industries were established within a decade of Henry Purefoy's adventures with the mantelpiece. Wallpaper was also becoming fashionable, though the range of designs available was limited. Perhaps the greatest revolution of all was in the design and manufacture of furniture, which during the first part of the century was still made locally by craftsmen whose methods and designs changed only very slowly. When new beds had to be ordered it was necessary to get in touch with a draper, an upholsterer and a joiner and then attempt to co-ordinate their work. The same applied to armchairs, which were now more plentiful and more comfortable than ever before, although items such as dining chairs and tables could be made up by a cabinet-maker or joiner without outside help.

Most of those who desired such things were content to accept standard traditional designs, but the desire to follow the latest London fashion was beginning to play its part here as in most other aspects of home life. In 1754 Thomas Chippendale published his *Gentleman's and Cabinet Maker's Directory*, which enabled any gentleman who bought a copy to show his cabinet-maker just what he wanted and just how it was to be made. Within a comparatively short time even the most conservative local cabinet-maker was forced to buy books of designs for himself and keep abreast of the standards of elegance laid down by Chippendale, Hepplewhite and many other lesser-known manufacturers. Although these men did not themselves mass-produce furniture, they made possible a standardization of design and technique which was to form the basis for the age of mass production. When the new industries arrived later in the century they simply fitted into the pattern: the hardware of Birmingham and the pottery of Staffordshire were sold by means of design books and catalogues similar to those of the furniture makers.

While men of moderate means wrote angry letters to stonecutters or pored over books of designs in the workshops of their local cabinet-makers, the rich summoned a small army of craftsmen and designers and contractors to wait upon them. The nobleman who wanted his house improved might first have to put up with it being invaded, as the whole hierarchy of the improvement industry moved in on him. The agents and men of business who discussed his plans with him had themselves been bombarded and solicited by architects and landscape gardeners and interior designers, who were in their turn importuned by contractors and masons and artists. And so it went on, right down to the stonecutters with their marble (although in fact carved wooden fireplaces were now coming into fashion). Some of these men came in daily from the neighbouring countryside, but a large number of them had to be put up in the house itself for long periods. It was like an extended version of the countess' *levée* in *Marriage à la Mode*, as painters and sculptors took their places alongside the resident musicians and scholarly librarians who already formed part of the great man's cultural retinue. In *The Rake's Progress*, as in *Marriage à la Mode*, Hogarth portrayed these people as dangerous parasites: it is the artists and musicians and pretentious connoisseurs who first set the rake on the downward path by tempting him into senseless extravagance. Only then do the taverns and gambling dens and brothels take over and complete his ruin. Hogarth's comment was the product of professional jealousy as well as moral fervour: the world of the self-styled art expert and the 'man of taste' was for him a commercial threat. Even so, he did not dare to suggest that great noblemen should not patronize it. It is only the upstarts like the rake and the countess (both of whom are people of comparatively humble origin seeking to ape their betters) who make themselves first ridiculous and then pathetic. Bitter though it is, Hogarth's attack on the connoisseur and all he stands for is made within the context of a hierarchical society. He does not dispute the right of the genuinely great and high-born to bestow their patronage on whom they please.

Patronage on this scale and at this level affected not merely the house but the household. When great men improved their homes they extended their households, demonstrating their refinement and their munificence as much by the individuals they maintained as by the objects they accumulated. Just as in earlier days the man who built a minstrels' gallery had to have minstrels, so now the man who built libraries and aviaries and galleries had to have librarians and birdkeepers and art experts and perhaps even orchestras. When he remodelled his gardens he might involve himself in the need for horticultural experts who would irritate his gardeners as surely as the connoisseurs and musicians irritated his indoor servants. Sometimes there were even more bizarre additions to the household: though most landowners contented themselves with stuffed hermits when hermitages came into fashion, there was at least one case of a real live hermit being employed to grace the park with his melancholy presence.[19] Meanwhile the fashion for 'improvement', combined with the increasingly business-like exploitation of noblemen's estates, brought important changes within the hierarchy of existing servants, as stewards became more gentlemanly under the name of land agents and as valets and ladies' maids were transformed into secretaries and companions. Some masters and mistresses were determined to preserve the traditional domestic hierarchies: John Spencer of Cannon Hall insisted that his new housekeeper should not have a room of her own but should sleep in the same room with the other servants so that she would have 'a proper awe and command over them'.[20]

When Gregory King had reckoned up the population of England in the year 1688 he had calculated not in terms of individuals but in terms of families – by which term he had really meant households. 'Temporal lords' had come at the head of his list, with an average of forty persons per household, followed by 'spiritual lords' with an average of twenty.[21] By the middle of the eighteenth century, although there were still many people alive who remembered him, King's view of society had come to seem very archaic. He had made no attempt to list domestic servants as a separate category of workers, even though they formed one of the largest occupational groups in the country; but by the 1750s the domestic servant class was clearly defined. There was a great deal more movement from one family to another – Peter Kalm noted with disapproval in 1748 that the English seemed to prefer daily domestic help to living-in servants – and there was less certainty and less security within the servants' hierarchy itself. Employers complained because servants no longer knew their places, but they seldom stopped to think that they themselves had made those places less recognizable by breaking up the old pattern of the household and substituting new patterns that changed with changing fashions. In 1759 James Townley's comedy *High Life Below Stairs* caused a riot when it was first staged because the footmen in the gallery resented its portrayal of servants as unprincipled rogues who aped their masters and mistresses.[22] As the gentry in the fashionable seats laughed and applauded and the menials up above them hissed, the new and hardening line between employer and servant was clear for all to see. The family, in the sense that King had used the word, existed no longer. Even the household, the unit made up of the employer's family and those who lived with them in order to serve them, was losing its identity as capitalism and fashion between them changed the way of life of propertied families. The new frontier was a horizontal one, between those who employed and those who were employed, rather than a vertical one between one household and the next.

Changing attitudes brought a new and different way of life. While country gentlemen like Henry Purefoy built servants' halls to house their domestics, families living in town rearranged their houses so that the servants lived 'below stairs' – a phrase which in real life as in Townley's play was a good deal more divisive than the more traditional phrase 'below the salt'. There had been a time when the whole household had eaten together at one table, the master and his family at one end above the salt cellars and the servants at the other end below them. In some houses this still happened, even if only on special occasions like Christmas or a harvest supper, but in most cases there were separate tables or more often separate rooms, the family eating in the dining room and the servants in the kitchen. The French fashion (see Plate 18) dictated that there should even be different food for the servants: France's reputation for delicious soups was based on the fact that meat from which all the goodness had been extracted in the process of making soup could then be fed to the servants. English servants resisted this custom sturdily, though in Scotland

Lady Grizel Baillie fed her domestics on a separate diet, consisting mainly of broth and herrings, as late as 1743.[23]

However much fashion might change the structure of the household, importing Negro page-boys or imitation hermits or French dancing masters, there were certain unchanging rituals which had to be performed and which automatically kept the old hierarchy in being. Since most households had to keep stocks of essential food and drink of all sorts there had to be innumerable cupboards and cellars and icehouses and store-rooms in order to provide exactly the right conditions for the storage of each commodity. The housekeeper with her imposing bunch of keys was the living epitome of this labyrinth of storage space. The still-room, which was the centre of her domain, was no longer regularly used for its original purpose of distilling cordials and medicines and aromatic essences from flowers and herbs. These things were usually bought from the nearest apothecary, but beer and cheese and honey and all kinds of pickles and preserves were made at home, particularly in the country. Usually this entailed special responsibilities and special rooms: Johnson's fictitious Lady Bustle, who turned the cheese herself every morning, was almost certainly the exception rather than the rule. In most great houses the mistress expected the steward and the housekeeper to look after such things, a fact which tended to check the transformation of these functionaries into men or women of business.

In more modest homes these ritual tasks brought mistress and servants together in bouts of frenzied activity. When her husband killed some pigs Anne Hughes assembled all the help she could get, the carter's wife and the farm servants as well as her own maid, and got them up very early in the morning in order to put on the pots in which the animals' insides had to boil for three days. Then the offal had to be cleaned – 'a messie jobb that I doe mislyke, butte they bee verrie goode when cooked' – and the flitches rubbed with a mixture of salt, black sugar, saltpetre and soda. In the midst of all the soaking and boiling and cutting and cleaning John Hughes cut his thumb, while 'sillie olde Joe Tombes didde slipp and sitt in thee pan off boyling watter, and didd youpe about because itt didde goe hott toe his britches'. The following day they were up equally early in order to make the lard, after which Anne cut up the animals' tongues, hearts, lungs and livers and baked the mixture in the oven with sweet herbs and onion. Six months later, when they made the honey, it was the turn of the carter's wife to slip and sit down unintentionally, this time in a hive of bees. She ran off in agony, 'holdeinge uppe her gowne wile jumpeinge over thee cabbidges', and came back 'wythe a mitie bigge nose were a bee hadd satt upp on itt'. But most of the bees were dead by this time, having been killed by sulphur papers burned under their hives, and the combs of honey could be taken back to the house. There the clear honey was strained off, while honey wine was made with the comb wax and the rest of the wax was clarified for use in polishing and harness cleaning.[24]

The end product of all this laborious preparation of food and drink was the English dinner, a magnificent and protracted affair which was an object of wonderment for most foreign visitors. Originally it had been a midday meal but during the course of the eighteenth century it became steadily later and later: to dine late was a sign of sophistication. Boswell knew of a London mercer who had settled in Durham and impressed the locals by dining at two or three o'clock in the afternoon instead of at one. 'How little and how poor he would seem,' commented Boswell, 'to a fashionable man in London who dines between four and five.'[25] By the end of the century dinner had finally become an evening meal in fashionable circles in London, but in the depths of the country people still dined in the middle of the day. Early in February 1796 John and Anne Hughes had visitors one Sunday and served dinner as soon as they came back from morning service. Even though there was a two-hour gap between dinner and tea it was still possible for their guests to leave after tea before it got dark.[26] In and around the provincial towns people tended to dine in the middle of the afternoon: when Catherine Hutton went to dinner with the rector of Aston near Birmingham in 1779 the meal was served at three o'clock and ended at five. The ladies then withdrew to the drawing room for an hour, after which they ordered tea and sent for the men to finish off their drinking and come and join them.[27] But when the men dined on their own, in all-male clubs, they drank longer and deeper. The Lunar Society of Birmingham, which was flourishing at this time, consisted of serious-minded scientists and manufacturers and philosophers who took the precaution of having their convivial evenings on the night of the full moon so that they could see their way home.[28]

The fare provided varied as much as the hour. While London hostesses vied with one another to pile their tables with elaborate pies and roasted game birds and such fashionable dishes as salmagundi (a salad of meat eggs and fish dressed with vinegar, herbs and onions), Anne Hughes gave her guests a roast leg of mutton and then worried in case they ate too much and there would not be enough left for the next day's cold meal. The meal provided by the rector of Aston consisted of pigeon pie, roast veal and a dish of salmon with fennel sauce and lemon pickle. These were accompanied by peas and kidney beans, after which there was chicken and ham and then a currant tart. Finally, after the tablecloth had been removed, there were gooseberries and currants and melon for dessert, accompanied by wines and cider. It was not a particularly elaborate meal and it was reasonably expeditious, taking only two hours from start to finish. In high society and in the great houses of the English countryside dinner would proceed on its stately way for hours on end, leaving exhausted foreign visitors with the feeling that they were experiencing eternity rather than hospitality. Sophie von la Roche was rather shocked by the amount of food that was put before her in England, but she consoled herself with the reflection that 'England knows nothing of separate cooking for the servants, who partake of all the courses sampled by the masters, the latter having first choice and the servants what remains – hence the large dishes and portions are explained'.[29] In some houses the servants did indeed whip the dishes away before the guests had had the chance to eat very much, but in others there was leisure for enough 'sampling' to be done to make the servants' privilege of eating their master's food a rather doubtful one.

As dinner moved into the afternoon, breakfast naturally grew in importance. Kalm noticed in 1748 that breakfast, which was a rare and scanty meal in his own country, was in England 'almost everywhere partaken of by those more comfortably off'. It consisted of tea and toast, the latter being an English invention which almost always delighted foreign visitors: it was still a novelty for Pastor Moritz when he came to England from Germany more than thirty years later. Kalm thought that it must be because English houses were so cold in the winter, and the butter therefore so hard, that they had hit on this idea of toasting the bread to make spreading easier.[30] Chocolate was sometimes taken instead of tea, though coffee was not very often made, at any rate at home. In London the men might go to the coffee-houses while the ladies had their tea or chocolate served to them in bed; and even in the provinces this new and more genteel type of breakfast was becoming popular. Charles Deering wrote that in Nottingham in the 1750s 'even a common washerwoman thinks she has not had a proper breakfast without tea and hot buttered white bread'.[31] In the country the more traditional breakfast of bread and cheese, with beer or cider according to the part of the country you were in, persisted right to the end of the century. This was what Anne Hughes served, even on special occasions when guests were present, as late as 1796. And one of the few snippets of information we have about Hogarth's home life is that he liked a bit of cheese for his breakfast.[32]

18 *The Duke of Newcastle and his French cook*, 1745. The royal proclamation against Catholic aliens gave the satirists a chance to mock Newcastle's supposed dependence on his French cook Chloe.

19 Hogarth: *Night*, 1738. A satire on Thomas de Veil and also a comment on some of the hazards to be met with in London streets after dark.

While dinner was sacred and breakfast quite acceptable, other meals had a much more dubious status. Those who dined late might take a snack some time between their breakfast and their dinner, a habit which was eventually to be known as luncheon. It was generally regarded as time-wasting, since breakfast itself was a mid-morning meal, taken around ten o'clock, rather than a literal breaking of the fast upon rising. Afternoon tea, originally a way of rounding off dinner, began to be a social occasion in its own right in some homes once dinner had moved into the evening. Supper was associated with high society and with balls and assemblies that went on into the small hours, although in most homes some kind of cold collation was laid out before the food was finally locked up for the night in the larder. On special occasions, however, even the most modest household would give an evening party, with elaborate dishes set out on the sideboard and the floor cleared for dancing. Hogarth showed such an occasion in his unfinished sketch called *The Country Dance*, one of the most charming pictures he ever painted. It may have been intended to form part of the *Happy Marriage* series; and it is indeed a very happy picture. Fifty years later John and Anne Hughes were throwing much the same sort of party, though on a less ambitious scale than the clearly very prosperous household depicted by Hogarth. While John hired the fiddlers for the dancing, Anne prepared a round of beef, a stuffed ham, a chine of some unspecified meat, three fowls and some roasted hares. Her mother-in-law showed her how to make a pudding with apples, eggs, cream and breadcrumbs soaked in brandy, as well as a honey pie and various tarts and cakes. This was accompanied by a special drink made of Anne's home-made primrose wine mixed up with honey, brandy and white of egg. Then, to round the evening off, there was steaming hot punch.[33]

And so to bed, after much barring of doors and closing of shutters. This particular party was in January of 1797, so that it was cold and very dark outside. In the sixty years since Hogarth had painted his picture of London at night (Plate 19), with Thomas de Veil picking his way through the darkened streets with a lantern, street lighting on a scale which amazed foreign visitors had been introduced in London and other big towns; but in the countryside the nights were still pitch dark unless there was a moon. Cottagers gathered reeds and soaked them in coarse fat to make rushlights, while in the houses of the middle and upper classes there were candles. Once the candles were snuffed out the darkness inside the house could be as frightening as that outside, particularly as it was often difficult to light the candles again quickly in an emergency with clumsy and unreliable tinder-boxes. Anne Hughes had to leave her bed on several occasions during the eighteen months or so that she kept her diary, when either human or animal marauders broke into the house at times when John was away; but as long as there was silence she was only too glad to stay under the blankets.

The great solid beds of the eighteenth century, with their curtains and canopies and their piles of blankets and pillows (sometimes so high that the night commode was designed to convert into steps for the sleeper to reach his bed), provided a comforting refuge from the cold and the darkness. Children and servants, who normally slept on low wooden bedsteads without curtains, might find the night chillier and more frightening, especially as most of them were fervent believers in ghosts and witches. And travellers who slept away from home might find other hazards as well as the ever-present fear of bed-bugs. When Hogarth and his four friends put up at an inn in Kent in May 1732 they could only get three beds between them and the sheets were so damp that after an hour they had to get up and put their clothes on again, sleeping fully dressed for the rest of the night. At three in the morning they woke to find their lips and eyes and hands swollen with gnat bites, but they managed nevertheless to get back to sleep again until six. The following night one of them found a small boy asleep in his bed, while another stalked out of their lodging house because he was expected to sleep in a flock bed without curtains.[34]

Almost as important as the bed itself was the chamber pot beneath it, perhaps the most necessary of all utensils in an age which had as yet no proper drainage or sanitation. Hogarth himself was not particularly scrupulous in his personal habits: on one occasion he pulled down his breeches and squatted down over a grave, at which his companion slashed at his bare rump with a bunch of stinging nettles and 'Hogarth finished his business against the church door'.[35] In his picture of London by night he showed the unpopular Thomas de Veil receiving the contents of a chamber pot on his head, traditionally one of the hazards of town life but in fact probably rarer than the humorists would have us believe. Peter Kalm in 1748 was impressed with the care with which Londoners gathered up night soil and sold it, rather than flinging it at one another in a coprophilic orgy. 'Those who sell this dirt are said to derive large incomes from it in the course of a year,' he wrote, 'and a farmer does not think much of paying a few pence for every load he takes on the return journey home in an otherwise empty wagon.'[36] In 1775 Alexander Cummings, a watchmaker in Bond Street, took out a patent for a water-closet and three years later Joseph Bramah invented a new and more effective model, though it was some years before there were proper pans and proper traps to prevent the spread of foul gases.[37]

Baths, like water-closets, were the prerogative of the rich until well into the nineteenth century. The Hughes do not seem to have possessed even a bath-tub: when John Hughes fell into the muck-heap he merely went into the back scullery and 'didd strippe off all hys cloes, and washe verrie harde toe gett ridd off thee stinke'.[38] Celia Fiennes had seen a marble bath with hot and cold running water at Chatsworth at the end of the seventeenth century, but it was a great rarity and one of the wonders of the country.[39] By the middle of the eighteenth century the Duke of Bedford had hot baths both at Bedford House (where the New River Company supplied him with running water for seven pounds sixteen shillings a year) and at his country home at Woburn Abbey.[40] More modest homes had bath-tubs which were placed before the bedroom fire and filled with water carted upstairs by the servants. Those who lived in cottages where the well or spring was some distance away, or in tenements where water had to be fetched from a communal tap in the street, probably shared the old-fashioned view of Thomas Turner, a Sussex grocer of the 1750s who thought that a bath should be taken every spring, along with the annual blood-letting.[41] But the homes of the upper and middle classes were coming to be centres of cleanliness in a sewerless and stinking country. The picture which the moralists drew, of the family unit as a haven of decency and purity in a corrupt world, had at any rate that much truth in it. Family bibles and family prayers may not have made the middle classes more virtuous than the masses, but family baths and family privies probably made most of them a good deal cleaner. For William Thornton in the 1750s home had been a bastion against governmental tyranny, but for the fastidious families of the 1790s it was primarily a retreat from the world of the unwashed.

In changing its nature the concept of home had become much more exclusive. The majority of the population had always lived in homes that were cold in the winter, damp in rainy weather, dark at night and unhealthy most of the time. By the end of the century there were probably more such homes rather than less: the undoubted improvements that had taken place in working-class housing in the countryside had been more than outweighed by increased overcrowding in the towns and by the rows of jerry-built hovels that were going up in the new industrial areas. What was more serious was the fact that more and more of the people who lived in such homes were completely cut off from anything better. They were not part of their employers' households in the way that previous generations of workers had been. From the classes above them they received condescension rather than genuine contact: the squire's lady would appear at cottage doors with gifts and homilies, but the squire himself no longer held harvest suppers or Christmas feasts in his own home. In the 1740s Gray had been saddened by the thought of the isolation of the dead, 'each in his narrow cell for ever laid'; if he had been alive in the 1790s he might have found the isolation of the living even more depressing. Each in his narrow home, the workmen of England were expected to achieve a cheerful domesticity which was undermined by the conditions in which they lived, the hours they had to work and the attitude of society towards them. The miracle was that so many of them succeeded.

7 The World of Pleasure

HOGARTH was a hardworking man whose pleasures were for the most part simple ones. He enjoyed eating and drinking and brawling: when he and his friends went on a jaunt into Kent in 1732 they spent a great deal of their time throwing dung at one another, ending up with 'a battle royal with sticks, pebbles and hog's dung'. When he got to Rochester he insisted on playing at hop-scotch under the colonnades of the town hall, while at Sheerness he sat down and cut his toe nails outside the fort.[1] A few years earlier de Saussure had been shocked to find that the 'pastimes of the people' in England including beating cockerels to death with clubs and throwing dead dogs and cats at one another on certain festival days. He was particularly alarmed by the national game of football: 'In cold weather you sometimes see a score of rascals in the streets kicking at a ball, and they will break panes of glass and smash the windows of coaches, and also knock you down without the slightest compunction; on the contrary, they will roar with laughter.'[2] The English seemed to have a genius for enjoying themselves in ways that were violent, cruel, destructive or uncouth, while being profoundly bored by more elegant and properly organized pleasures. At the pleasure gardens of Ranelagh and Vauxhall the traveller would find people as grave as if they were in church, while at Chelsea and Greenwich, where he expected to find the army and navy pensioners nodding away their days in dignified retirement, he would encounter scenes of wild excitement as the old men organized races between the lice they picked off their bodies.[3]

Like most foreigners, de Saussure considered that the pleasures of the English were cruel, ferocious and 'very rude'. He was disgusted by the prize fights which he saw and he was disturbed by the fact that whenever members of 'the lower populace' had a quarrel they stripped to the waist and started fighting, the bystanders meanwhile gathering round and placing bets instead of trying to separate the combatants.[4] He was sickened by those sports that involved cruelty to animals, though he would undoubtedly have been even more appalled if he had travelled around the country and seen some of the bull-baiting and bear-baiting that was sanctioned by local custom and ancient traditions in various places. Liverpool had an annual bull-baiting festival, while at Stamford a bull was ceremonially hunted to death through the streets of the town every November. At Tutbury in Staffordshire an even more brutal form of bull-running was put down by the local landowner in 1778, but attempts to abolish the Stamford custom ten years later were sturdily resisted by the townspeople, who managed to continue their annual bull-running until 1839.[5] Although he never seems to have seen a bull baited, de Saussure did know all about the fights to the death which were staged between the savage dogs trained for bull-baiting and other purposes. He considered this a very uncivilized form of amusment, but cock-fighting on the other hand fascinated him. For some reason his squeamishness completely left him when he came to discuss the merits of the birds and the finer points of the sport:

> When the bets are made, one of the cocks is placed on either end of the stage; they are armed with silver spurs and immediately rush at each other and fight furiously. It is surprising to see the ardour, the strength and the courage of these little animals, for they rarely give up till one of them is dead . . . Sometimes a cock will be seen vanquishing his opponent and, thinking he is dead (if cocks can think), jump on the body of the bird and crow noisily with triumph, when the fallen bird will unexpectedly revive and slay the victor. Of course, such cases are very rare, but their possibility makes the fight very exciting.[6]

Hogarth's comments on cock-fighting are less enthusiastic. In the first plate of his *Four Stages of Cruelty* (Plate 20) some of the boys are trying to organize an impromptu cock-fight, but their efforts receive much less attention than other and more brutal amusements. Even the boy who is driving an arrow up the anus of a dog is not drawing as big a crowd as those who have hung two cats up by their tails in order to watch them fight. The cat-fight is for the street urchins what the cock-fight is for their elders: a violent and ferocious combat upon which bets can be laid. At the very core of the English idea of pleasure lay a fight to the death combined with the chance to gamble. When Hogarth came to illustrate the cockpit itself, as he did at the end of his life, he put the emphasis not so much upon the violence as upon the gambling. The central figure in his engraving (Plate 21) is the blind Lord Albemarle Bertie, who stakes money he cannot control on the outcome of a fight he cannot see. Many of those around him are more concerned with tricking him and stealing from him than they are with the cocks themselves. It is a sombre and even frightening picture because of its portrayal of human folly and degradation rather

20 Hogarth: *The First Stage of Cruelty*, 1751. Hogarth later noted with some satisfaction that this print had 'checked the diabolical spirit of barbarity to the brute creation, which, I am sorry to say, was once so prevalent in this country'.

21 Hogarth: *The Cockpit*, 1759. The blind Lord Albemarle Bertie is in the centre of the engraving.

than because of its representation of animal suffering. And there is an obvious echo of the *Four Stages of Cruelty*, in the last of which the central figure, who started off as a boy torturing the dog in the first print, lies upon the circular anatomy table in Surgeon's Hall, his body having been given over for dissection after being cut down from the gallows. (See Plate 22.) A figure as impassive and yet as concentrated as the blind nobleman presides over and directs the operations, while the circular composition of the whole design anticipates that of the cockpit. Both in subject matter and in composition Hogarth's comment on cock-fighting in particular refers back to his earlier homily on cruelty in general; but it also links up with his many condemnations of gambling. It was these two things, the love of cruelty and the love of gambling, which in his opinion degraded the Englishman's pleasures into vices.

More than thirty years later Samuel Romilly attacked the popular amusements of England in very much the same terms. There was an added urgency in his strictures, for he was writing in the first flush of his enthusiasm for the French Revolution. He was convinced that it would bring about the regeneration of mankind and he was terrified lest the English should prove too corrupted by their degrading pleasures to be worthy of the French example. He took the government to task for encouraging the gambling fever by promoting lotteries: 'It is hardly possible to imagine any institution better calculated than they are to check industry and corrupt honesty . . . by the help of lotteries the most amiable qualities of the human mind are converted into instruments of its corruption.' There followed a sustained attack on the blood sports of the countryside and upon other forms of cruelty to animals, most of which seemed in Romilly's eyes to be attributable to the malign influence of the ruling classes. A man of high rank was said to travel with 'such extraordinary expedition as frequently to kill some of the horses in his service', while the landowning classes in general were condemned for their addiction to shooting and hunting. The latter, in particular, was said to involve sickening refinements of cruelty.[7] Hogarth had merely portrayed an urban population brutalized by the life of the streets and a feckless nobility preyed upon by the rogues of the gambling world; but Romilly's picture was of a whole nation, rural as well as urban, sunk in degrading pleasures because of the deliberate policies of its government and the irresponsibility of its great men.

Like most people brought up in the town, Romilly did not understand the countryside and its pleasures. Any cottager's boy in the land was probably capable of inflicting as much suffering with his sling and his home-made snares and his primitive fishing tackle as the high-born huntsmen Romilly condemned. The great majority of Englishmen were not only countrymen but also hunters of one sort or another. The hunt was ritualized and made more exclusive by laws which forbade such 'inferior persons' as stockbrokers, attorneys and surgeons to kill game, but this did not mean that only the rich took pleasure in blood sports. Poaching was widespread, in spite of the ferocious laws against it and the man-traps which many landlords and gamekeepers set. Killing animals and birds was a necessity for many country-dwellers, either for food or in order to protect crops; and even those who might be squeamish about the kill itself still took pleasures in the stalking or tracking that led up to it. Farmers who shot foxes might find themselves in difficulties – in October 1792, just after Romilly's book was published, one landlord told his bailiff that he was determined to discriminate against tenants who 'interrupted gentlemen's diversions' in this way[8] – but countless other animals could be killed for pleasure without fear of the consequences. Even the harmless hedgehog was almost universally suspected of sucking cows' udders and spoiling the milk, so that churchwardens paid good money for dead hedgehogs. Sometimes it was the gentry themselves who checked the slaughter, particularly of birds. Addison had once remarked that he was prepared to protect blackbirds in return for the pleasure their song gave him, while Kalm noticed that gentlemen in England often regarded the rooks who nested in their trees as being under their protection.[9]

Although it was certainly true that the 1780s and 1790s saw a mania for fast driving, Englishmen were seldom stupid enough to kill the horses upon which they had expended a good deal of money and a good deal of care: in spite of the old proverb, the treatment of horses in England was probably better than in many other countries. Even Dr Johnson, who was not noted as a fast young thing, had once said that if he had no duties and no worries about the future he would spend his time driving briskly in a post-chaise.[10] In 1781 the Prince of Wales boasted that he had driven a phaeton and four twenty-two miles in two hours at the trot, 'which is reckoned pretty good driving'; and in the same year a caricature appeared of Agnes Townshend, one of the incrèasing number of women who shocked conservative opinion by joining in the driving craze.[11] Horse racing had long been one of the greatest of national sports, renowned among foreign visitors for the way in which it brought together rich and poor, and the driving mania was a variant which had been made possible by the tremendous improvement which had taken place in English roads between the 1750s and the 1780s. Turnpike trusts had sprung up all over the country, employing pioneer constructors like blind John Metcalfe, who was said to have built nearly 200 miles of turnpike road by the time he retired in 1792. While the fashionable young speed addicts used the new roads in order to realize Dr Johnson's dream, shrewd businessmen saw the money that was to be made in improving stage-coach services, which now began to drive through the night instead of travelling by daily stages and putting their passengers up in inns. Improvements in the design of vehicles, especially the substitution of steel springs for leather straps, made these night journeys tolerable and sometimes even enjoyable. Thomas Pennant, an inveterate traveller, grumbled in 1782 that whereas he and his friends had had to rough it in their youth, 'their enervated posterity sleep away their rapid passage in easy chaises fitted for the conveyance of the soft inhabitants of Sybaris'. Travel itself was becoming a pleasure rather than an adventure.[12]

The English horse, upon whose strength and endurance all these fashionable pursuits ultimately depended, was the admiration of the world. Even foreign writers who set out deliberately to belittle the English had to admit that their horses were superb. Fougeret de Monbron, after listing all the vices and the follies and the delusions of the English in his *Preservative against Anglomania*, ended up by confessing that they nevertheless had 'excellent horses, very good hounds and complete freedom from monks and wolves'.[13] There were race meetings all over the country – even Purefoy's tiny village in Buckinghamshire had one in 1739[14] – but the real centre of English racing was Newmarket in Cambridgeshire. 'The horses there are generally finer than elsewhere,' wrote de Saussure in 1728, 'and all the noblemen and persons of distinction who take an interest in this amusement go there with their horses. Last month the King attended these races for the first time and nothing was spared to make them successful.'[15] By the middle of the century the Jockey Club had been founded to frame rules for the racing at Newmarket, rules which were eventually to govern racing throughout the country; and the sport enjoyed the royal patronage of George II's younger son, the Duke of Cumberland. It was in his stables that Eclipse, the most famous racehorse of the time, was bred and trained. The nobility's passion for horse racing often exasperated those few noblemen who did not share it: 'These Newmarket gentlemen are so much engaged in their business there,' wrote Newcastle angrily to Pitt in 1763, 'that they hardly give themselves time to write upon any other business in a way to be understood.'[16] His efforts to persuade Cumberland to put politics before racing were not particularly successful: two years later the Duke insisted on holding an important political meeting in the stables at Newmarket. He was dragged reluctantly back to London some days after this, only to disappear to Newmarket again in the middle of a vital debate in the House of Lords.[17]

The other sport that traditionally brought together the highest and the lowest in the land was cricket. De Saussure in 1728 was not quite sure how it worked – all that he knew was that 'they go into a large open field and knock a small ball about with a piece of wood' and that it was far too complicated for him to understand or explain.[18] In 1744 the rules of the game were laid down, although foreigners continued to find it all rather puzzling. In 1769 the Duke of Dorset fielded an eleven which included five of his gardeners, some of his indoor servants and himself as captain. 'His Grace for bowling cannot yield, To none but Lumpey in the field,' wrote an admiring versifier.[19] The games played on the Sevenoaks cricket ground, near the duke's country house of Knole, soon became county matches. In August 1774 there was a great match for one thousand guineas between Kent, captained by the Duke of Dorset, and Hampshire. Kent won 'with great ease' and in the following year took on an All England team. This time the 'Kent people' seem to have consisted of 'the Duke of Dorset, Lord Cholmondeley and about twelve more noblemen and gentlemen' and they did not do so well: they scored thirty-five 'notches', which was the contemporary term for runs, but Small, the England opening batsman, got 'what is almost incredible, seventy-five notches, and was at last bowled out just before eight o'clock'. There followed a great battle among the spectators, in which several people were seriously injured.[20]

In spite of the injuries, it was probably the brawl that provided the real excitement of the occasion for many of the participants. Hogarth was not the only Englishman of his time who enjoyed 'a battle royal with sticks, pebbles and hog's dung'. Quite apart from cricket and electioneering and the other great national sports of this nature, there were countless village festivals and carnivals which provided an excuse for violence and high spirits. When the people of Stamford rallied to the defence of their bull-running in 1788 they were not simply demonstrating their collective cruelty. The furry dance at Helston, the horned dance at Abbots Bromley in Staffordshire and many other pagan rituals would have been defended with equal fervour, although in these cases there was no question of cruelty to animals. The thing which made ordinary people cherish these customs was the thing that made seventeenth-century Puritans and eighteenth-century moralists distrust them: they stood for the ancient tradition of carnival or saturnalia, the few days in the year when the barriers erected by the conscious mind were dropped and people abandoned themselves to

22 Hogarth: *The Reward of Cruelty*, 1751. The boy who tortured a dog in *The First Stage of Cruelty* has grown up a thief and a murderer: after execution his body is given over for dissection.

23 Hogarth: *Southwark Fair*, 1733. The excitements – and the hazards – of an eighteenth-century fairground.

the irresponsible violence which lay in their unconscious. Earlier ages had seen this as sin; later ages were to see it as therapy. The eighteenth century Englishman avoided both these extremes. All he knew was that it was a part of his traditional freedom and that it was extremely pleasurable.

There had been a time when festivities of this sort had been closely associated with open-handed hospitality on the part of the landowning classes. While the Lord of Misrule presided over the carnival, the lord of the manor provided baked meats and plentiful supplies of ale. There were still gentlemen who kept Christmas in the old way, feasting their retainers and observing ancient rituals, but there were very few who did anything more. When James Pye of Faringdon entertained the populace to breakfast on the occasion of his marriage in 1766, providing flags and music and cavalcades and great quantities of food and liquor, it was reported in the local press as a pleasing anachronism, 'a survival of old English hospitality'.[21] The Duke of Dorset, providing the locals with village cricket and discreet refreshments at Sevenoaks, was on to an altogether safer and more economical wicket. The tradition which he thus established was to spread steadily during the next century or so, substituting a quieter and more gentlemanly form of condescension for the old saturnalia.

The thing which saved the tradition of saturnalia from extinction was the fair. All over the country hucksters and mountebanks and acrobats attached themselves to traditional festivities, establishing an annual round of engagements which soon came to include many of the great race-meetings and other sporting fixtures. At Sherborne in Dorset the high point of the year was Pack Monday in October, when the townspeople formed a midnight procession in order to bang tin lids and other utensils in a riot of noise said to commemorate the completion of the town's abbey some centuries earlier. Although a less attractive form of carnival than the picturesque pagan dances of other towns and villages, this rather strange custom nevertheless survived because of the fair which grew up around it and brought both pleasure and profit to the town. Hogarth himself was deeply influenced by fairs: he spent his boyhood within sight and sound of the greatest of them all, Bartholomew Fair in Smithfield in the City of London, and he said later that the shows he had seen there had given him 'uncommon pleasure'.[22] There was a great deal more to Bartholomew Fair than shows: for several weeks every summer it turned Smithfield into a vast network of stalls and booths of every kind in which there were freaks to be seen, tumblers and tricksters to be watched, prizes to be won, merchandise of every kind to be bought. It was a place to buy and sell, to fight and make love, to cheat and be cheated. But for the young Hogarth it was above all else a place to stand and wonder and gape at the strolling players and the marvellous stories they promised to enact.

In October 1733 Hogarth announced in the *Daily Advertiser* that he was 'now engraving nine copper plates from pictures of his own painting, one of which represents the Humours of a Fair, the other eight the progress of a Rake'.[23] There was more to this than the typical salesman's bargain offer, throwing in an additional and disparate item just for good measure. There was a logical connection, a kind of ironical antithesis, between the single picture of the simple fun of the fair and the series which showed the more sophisticated and infinitely more destructive pleasures of the fashionable world. Though the picture of the fair (Plate 23) is full of people being cheated and bullied and even threatened with a violent death as a scaffolding collapses about their heads, none of them is destroyed as completely and as horrifyingly as the rake is destroyed by his pleasures. Moreover, there is a sense of community in the first picture which is totally lacking in the eight pictures of *The Rake's Progress* which followed it. The hucksters and the mountebanks at the fair are as vulnerable as those they cheat: everyone is part of the same hilarious and yet pathetic predicament. In *The Rake's Progress*, on the other hand, there is a clear division between the hunter and the hunted, between the parasitical predators of the world of pleasure and the willing victim whom they destroy. The whole series of nine pictures forms Hogarth's comment on the pleasures of his time, the uncouth pleasures of the poor and the empty pleasures of the rich.

The fair which Hogarth chose to portray was not Bartholomew Fair but Southwark Fair on the other side of the river, to the south of London Bridge. There are hucksters and strolling musicians in the foreground, while in the background there is a tightrope walker and an even more ambitious performer who seems to be plummeting to his death from the tower of St George's Church. This last figure is based on a 'flying man' who had recently caused a sensation by flying from a church in Cambridge with the help of a rope, only to be killed in a subsequent attempt on Greenwich Church. There is even a waxworks to one side of the picture, in which apparently 'the whole Court of France' is to be seen. But it is the booths of the strolling players that really dominate the picture. The crowd can choose between *The Siege of Troy* (which had not in fact been given at Southwark Fair for some time, although it had been played at Bartholomew Fair in Hogarth's boyhood),[24] *Punch's Opera* and *The Fall of Bajazet*. The story of Adam and Eve also seems to be on the bill, along with a piece called *The Stage Mutiny* which is clearly based on the scandals associated with John Highmore's take-over of Drury Lane Theatre from Theophilus Cibber and his company. Although advertised as a picture of 'the Humours of a Fair', this is above all else a picture of the theatre of the people, the 'shows of all sorts' which fascinated Hogarth the artist as much as they had once fascinated Hogarth the boy. Other aspects of the fair, just as suitable as subjects for illustration and for moralizing, are thrust into the background. The morbid preoccupation with freaks, the frenzied obsession with gambling, the constant eruption into violence – all these 'humours of a fair' are subordinated to the fascination of the theatre. Others might have seen the fair as the place where people were lifted out of themselves by the excitement of violence and the hazards of gaming, but for Hogarth it was a place where people could escape from humdrum reality into the marvellous magic of the showman's world.

This was a very important distinction, particularly for those members of the propertied classes who concerned themselves with 'the pastimes of the people'. The Puritans of the previous century had seen nothing to choose between sport on the one hand and theatre on the other: both were equally sinful because they encouraged man to waste his time and escape from his real duties in life. But the two escape routes were in fact very different. A man who acted out his fantasies aggressively, proving himself at violent sports or games of chance and then picking quarrels and breaking heads, was a great deal more dangerous than somebody who would sit quietly in his seat and participate in fantasies provided for him by other people. For Hogarth, who was concerned to use his art in order to reform 'the vices peculiar to the lower class of people', this was a consideration of some importance. While some of his contemporaries would have liked to deny the poor any form of escape from the misery and boredom of their daily lives, he was prepared to judge between one form and another. And there can be little doubt that in his opinion the theatre was the most innocent form of all: he might well have said of it what Dr Johnson once said about music, that it was 'the only sensual pleasure without vice'.[25] Of its sensual nature he clearly had no doubt. For him it worked on all the senses, including those slightly disreputable ones which Johnson was thinking of when he made his remark. Hogarth's work is full not only of constant references to the comedies and dramas of his own time but also of references to the nature of theatre itself, to the stage that seems to become the world and to the world that seems at times to be nothing but a stage. The booth in *Southwark Fair* that falls to the ground even as its occupants are preparing to enact *The Fall of Bajazet* is only one symbol among many. The Duke of Bolton, eyeing from his box on the stage the actress in *The Beggar's Opera* who is in fact his mistress, is another and perhaps even more significant one. Hogarth knew perfectly well that the theatre dealt in all the human passions and that it could have a devastating effect on the lives of those who were involved in it. He seems nevertheless to have believed that this influence was much less harmful than that of most other pleasures of the time.

Whatever Hogarth may have thought about the social importance of the theatre, there was no doubt about its political importance. Plays containing thinly veiled satires on politicians were becoming more and more popular not only in the theatres of London, but also in the booths of the strolling players. It was a travelling showman called Penkethman who was responsible for showing *Wat Tyler or Jack Straw*, one of the most vicious of recent attacks on Sir Robert Walpole's administration. By the time *Southwark Fair* appeared at the beginning of 1734 Henry Fielding was emerging as the playwright who was the bitterest critic of politics – not only the politics of the ministry but those of the opposition as well. His ballad opera *The Welsh Opera, or the Grey Mare the Better Horse*, which he put on at the Haymarket Theatre in 1731, flayed the government and its opponents alike. The leaders of the opposition tried to enlist Fielding as a paid propagandist, but without much success: he continued to write and stage pieces which ridiculed the whole political scene. In March 1736 *Pasquin* was produced at the Haymarket and a year later it was followed by *The Historical Register for the Year 1736*, which showed opposition members accepting bribes to vote for the ministry. This was too much: within a matter of weeks the politicians had their revenge. A Bill to forbid all plays not licensed by the Lord Chamberlain was introduced into a thinning House of Commons on 24 May, after many of the independent members had already gone back to their counties. Outside the world of politics there was a violent reaction. One foreign visitor said that there was 'a universal murmur in the nation . . . it was treated as an unjust law and manifestly contrary to the liberties of the people of England'. But in Parliament itself there was little more than shadow boxing and the Bill received the Royal Assent on 21 June. Even the newspapers contained comparatively little criticism of this measure which was supposed to have caused such furious protestation in all the coffee-houses of London. The theatrical world itself was divided, since the licensees of the two royal theatres of Drury Lane and Covent Garden saw their own monopolistic position safeguarded rather than threatened by the new Act.[26]

25 (*Above*) Hogarth: *A Rake's Progress*, Plate 1, 1735. The Rake taking possession.

24 (*Overleaf*) Hogarth: *The Beggar's Opera*, 1729. The world as a stage and the stage as a world: Lavinia Fenton gazes past her stage lover Macheath to her actual lover the Duke of Bolton.

Unlicensed playhouses were closed as soon as the Act came into force, but it was not long before most of the London theatre managers had got the necessary patronage and protection to allow them to resume operations under the new system. Fielding himself was forced out of business and had to turn to other forms of writing, but the London stage as a whole was certainly not killed by the Act of 1737. It was a different matter for the companies of strolling players who worked the fairgrounds and market-places of the country. In some places the justices of the peace, angry at the way in which the Act had been pushed through, refused to enforce it effectively; but few players could depend on finding sufficient complaisant authorities of this sort to make up a circuit which would keep them going for a whole year. Some companies died slowly, but none the less surely. Hogarth commemorated their passing in the print called *Strolling Actresses in a Barn*, published in 1738. (See Plate 7.) Like all his pictures it operates at many different levels. The grouping of these mortals dressed as gods and goddesses is a deliberate parody of the classical paintings peddled by the connoisseurs whom he hated so cordially, and it is also yet another symbol of the relationship between illusion and reality. But under all the carefully worked-out allusions and references there is the sadness of a way of life that is about to disappear: as their playbill says, these slatternly players and their tawdry costumes and props are assembled together for 'the last time of acting before the Act commences'. Whatever might happen to the theatres of fashionable London, the theatre of the people was in for a very thin time for the next half-century. The collapsing and disintegrating players' booth in *Southwark Fair* had proved to be strangely prophetic.

It very soon became clear that if the provinces could not have strolling players they must have licensed theatres. Older towns such as Bristol already had theatres which could be licensed under the Act, but as the new industrial centres became more and more populous they had to secure special Acts of Parliament of their own to allow them to establish theatres. In Birmingham in the 1770s local clergymen and other earnest persons mounted a formidable campaign against the proposal to license a theatre. They gathered figures to show that 1,468 out of 2,449 ratepayers were against the idea of a playhouse and they pointed out that in Manchester and Liverpool, where there were already theatres, 'masters on the solicitations of their correspondents force tickets on their workers instead of money, which they are obliged to sell at a half or less price to buy bread'.[27] The Lord Privy Seal, the Earl of Dartmouth, was a supporter of the Wesleyan movement and of the revived Puritanism which it tended to bring with it: he lent his aid to the campaign against the Birmingham theatre, with the result that the Bill was defeated. Other members of the propertied classes took a different view, one closer to Hogarth's. The Earl of Carlisle said during the debates on the Manchester theatre Bill that playhouses provided 'cheerful, rational amusements' which would serve to counteract the 'dark, odious, ridiculous enthusiasm' of the Wesleyans. Edmund Burke declared roundly that 'of the various means which idleness will take for its amusement, in truth I believe the theatre is the most innocent'.[28] Moralists like Gisborne continued to worry about the effect that playhouses might have upon 'the lowest orders of the people, mutable, uninformed and passionately addicted to spectacles of amusement';* but the English provincial theatre continued to prosper and was by the end of the century firmly established in most of the larger cities and towns of the kingdom.

Even if *Southwark Fair* was outdated within a few years of its appearance, so that it was left to commemorate the strolling players rather than reflect them, the same could not be said about the eight prints that followed it. These pictures, which made up the series known as *The Rake's Progress*, were among the most successful and influential Hogarth ever produced. Whatever they might think about the first print they received, the subscribers to the 1733 offer would soon have good cause to congratulate themselves on their possession of the remaining eight, which were to become almost as fashionable as the modish pleasures they attacked. In these successive episodes in young Tom Rakewell's progress, from hopeful young heir to raving madman, the cautious and inhibited and the sober-minded could study in detail the fashionable world which both frightened and fascinated them. The gorgeous pleasure domes of London, which had long been condemned by those who lacked the cash or the confidence to enter them, were now revealed as constituting a dark and dangerous labyrinth where terrible engines of destruction waited around every corner, ready to drain a man's substance and suck out his soul.

The first of these was a tape measure. In the opening picture of the series Tom stands in his modest but comfortable family home being measured for a new suit of clothes (Plate 25). It is clear that everything else is about to be renewed as well: now that he has come into his inheritance the old servants will be dismissed and the old home sold up in order to pay for his new pretensions and the parasites who encourage

* See p. 74.

them. But the tape measure is the central symbol, the thing that dominates the composition and serves as an introduction to all the other signs of upheaval. For Hogarth, as for most of those who distrusted the fashionable pleasures of the rich, an exaggerated and ostentatious interest in dress was the first step on the downward path. Once a man abandoned the styles that had been good enough for his father and sought instead to keep up with the butterfly world of London fashion, then he was doomed. This was the first and greatest temptation.

Disapproval of this sort was based on the feeling that a concern for fashion was something essentially effeminate. Englishmen had by this time given up their attempt to stop their wives taking an interest in new fashions. Foreign visitors assured them that it was a laudable and discriminating thing and that the way even maidservants and milkmaids followed the fashions was a sign of the progressive nature of English society. There were always satirists ready to mock the latest fashions, but their grumbling, like that of the crusty country gentlemen they appealed to, had something rather cosy and even affectionate about it. Goldsmith's imaginary Chinaman seemed more amused than infuriated when he reported that he dare not undertake a description of the current fashions, 'lest the sex should undergo some new revolution before it was finished'.[29] The enormous piled-up hair-styles of the 1770s provoked outraged comments, but this was because they were clearly impracticable. Sleeping in them was acutely uncomfortable and parading about a room in them might be dangerous if they caught in the candelabra. Even so they had their supporters: in April 1776, in the midst of all the hostile criticisms and the satirical prints of women unable to move a step because of their superstructures, Boswell wrote that he found the fashion 'more beautiful than what I had ever seen before'. Three years later Dr Alexander gently reproved those who declaimed constantly against the fripperies of fashion. He pointed out that in the course of the century the waistline had gone in and out and up and down several times, each change being greeted by the diehards as a fall from grace to corruption. 'The revolutions of the breasts and shoulders have not been less conspicuous than those of the waist,' he continued, 'the naked breasts and shoulders begin again to appear.'[30] Englishmen bore this particular revelation with some fortitude, though they were rather more disturbed by the fashion for false buttocks (See Plate 26) and for a pad or cushion on the stomach to simulate pregnancy. On the other hand rouge, which had apparently so scandalized Boswell in 1776,* was going out of fashion by the mid 1780s. At the very end of the century a

* See p. 125.

new note of more solemn disapproval crept into male discussion of female fashion, largely because the new fashions usually came from revolutionary France and therefore seemed to be harbingers of atheism and social collapse and nameless immoralities. In the depths of Herefordshire, however, Anne Hughes continued to 'showe off mye best cloes' and to overawe a conceited neighbour with 'mye black sylk wyth thee wyte spottes, what John didd buy for mee ande wiche I hadd nott putt on'. 'This', she concluded triumphantly, 'didde ende her bounce.'[31]

It was not finery and display in themselves that were forbidden to the male of the species. The men of Hogarth's generation dressed colourfully and even at the end of the century, when changing moral attitudes were beginning to make men's clothes more sober, John Hughes went to a party dressed in 'hys purpel velvitt smalle cloes, ande sylke weskett wythe thee gold flowers, ande a velvitt top coat, ande hys best whyte sylke stocke collar all trimmed wythe lace, hys sylke stockens and silver buckled shoes. Hee didd looke verrie grande'.[32] Even the straitlaced moralists of the 1790s would not have condemned a country farmer who liked to look 'verrie grande' once in a while. Nor would Hogarth have done so in his time: Tom Rakewell's father probably looked every bit as grand as John Hughes on occasion. The dangerous thing was not sartorial splendour but craven submission to the dictates of fashion. In the second print of the *Rake* series, Tom appears in clothes which are not only fashionable in themselves but fashioned for a particular modish fashion purpose – the morning *levée*, in which the central figure appears in elaborately negligent clothes in order to underline the studied intimacy of the occasion. He is surrounded by modish people, self-appointed arbiters of taste whose gestures, like his own, are intended to show that they belong to an infinitely desirable but highly exclusive world. This is an initiation rite. It is now clear that the purpose of the tape measure in the first picture was not to make Tom grand but to make him acceptable.

This scene is the real turning point in Tom Rakewell's life. The prints that follow show him carousing in a tavern, being arrested for debt, marrying a rich heiress, gambling to retrieve his fortunes and finally being incarcerated first in a prison and then in a madhouse. At first sight this is the traditional moral fable of a man ruined by his sensual appetites; but Tom seems to have no sensual appetites. In the tavern, glassily drunk and pawed by harlots, he looks the picture of misery. The only thing that matters to him, the only thing that ever has mattered to him, is that he should be taken for a man of taste and fashion, a man of the world. Like a famous character in Colman and Garrick's play *The Clandestine Marriage*

ABEL
Cantata del Principe Ghigi
in occasione dell apertura
del Pantheon
Colla di Parm
Cantata per
il Benefizi

27 (*Above*) Hogarth: *The Laughing Audience*, 1733. Among those who are enjoying the play and those who are enjoying the whores only one face is joyless – that of the would-be connoisseur who must show his superiority by looking bored.

26 (*Overleaf*) An untitled print of 1780 showing the Italian composer Colla fitting his wife with false buttocks. Foreigners in London, and the extravagant fashions they brought with them, provided a favourite target for the satirists.

(which was itself suggested by Hogarth's *Marriage à la Mode*), he is sure that he was 'born to move in the sphere of the Great World'. This Great World is in truth pitiably small, its haughty pretensions neatly pinpointed by Fielding's remark that for the languid man of fashion the word 'nobody' means 'all the people in Great Britain except about twelve hundred'.[33] Tom has not been accepted by the noble twelve hundred and he never will be. The shoddy charlatans whom he took for high priests and gatekeepers to the Great World have already deserted him and are snickering and posturing around some other poor fool. This is not a progress from one heady pleasure to the next but from one central delusion to its inevitable moment of disillusionment.

As if to emphasize the unity of his 1733 offering, the single picture of popular enjoyment and the eight pictures of fashionable emptiness, Hogarth did another drawing which was to act as a subscription ticket and receipt. It was issued on payment of the initial half-guinea and it entitled the holder to receive the first print. It has come to be known as *The Laughing Audience* (Plate 27), although in fact it is a study in contrast, the contrast between those members of a theatre audience who are laughing and those who are not. At the bottom are three members of the orchestra, who are too busy playing their instruments to enjoy the comedy, while at the top are two lecherous and fashionably dressed gentlemen who have come to see the orange-sellers and other women rather than the play. In the middle is the laughing audience itself, relaxed and obviously enjoying the piece. There is only one man who turns aside in disdain, yet this one bored face is more important in the composition of the picture than all the laughing ones. The lines that move up from the three musicians converge upon it, while those that link the audience below with the orange-sellers and their patrons above spring from it. Once noticed, this face cannot easily be ignored. Nor does it want to be ignored. It is not just a bored face but a face desperately anxious that everyone (or at any rate, everyone who is anyone) should see that it is bored. It is the one self-conscious face in the midst of an audience which has lost itself in the enjoyment of a play. In this small corner of a London theatre two worlds meet – the elegant and unnatural world of fashionable pleasure, where sophisticated people parade up and down in order to be noticed, and the simple world of straightforward enjoyment. No better introduction could have been devised to the juxtaposed images of *Southwark Fair* and *The Rake's Progress*.

Where Hogarth led others followed. 'The imitating of every station above our own seems to be the first principle of the *Genteel Mania*', wrote one newspaper in 1756, 'and operates with equal efficacy upon the tenth cousin of a woman of quality and her acquaintance who retails *Gentility* among her neighbours in the Borough.'[34] On all sides the satirists and the moralists condemned the giddy pleasures of the town and the way in which they tempted people to live beyond their means and forget their station in life. The secret of the fashionable world's fatal attraction lay in the simple fact that pleasure and the proper enjoyment and appreciation of pleasure was the thing that most clearly indicated a person's status in society. When the Earl of Chesterfield wrote his famous letters to his illegitimate son, the letters which Dr Johnson later said taught 'the morals of a whore and the manners of a dancing master', he was not concerned to tell the boy how to be a good husband or a good landlord or even a good politician. He was above all concerned that the child should acquire 'the air, the address, the graces and the manners of a man of fashion'. And these airs and graces were to be learned and displayed at balls and assemblies and gaming houses rather than in the course of a day's work. The letters were begun in 1737, when the son was five years old and *The Laughing Audience* a year younger. Whoever else may have taken Hogarth's moralizing to heart, Chesterfield was superbly indifferent to it. 'In my mind there is nothing so illiberal and so ill-bred,' he wrote, 'as audible laughter.'[35] People of fashion were much too busy registering correct degrees of pleasure to indulge in anything so gross as enjoyment.

For the men of Hogarth's and Chesterfield's generation (they were born within three years of each other) this choice between coarse merriment and empty etiquette may indeed have been a real one. Early eighteenth-century England was unsure of itself in many ways, acutely conscious of the long shadow of France and French culture. The magnificent court of the French king at Versailles had dominated Europe for so long that the English could scarcely believe that they had really managed to defy it and win for themselves a chance to develop a culture of their own. Most Englishmen felt a little awkward and self-conscious in the presence of the polished suavity of the French; and they usually reacted either by copying it slavishly, as Chesterfield did, or by becoming even more English and earthy, as Hogarth did. As the world of honest enjoyment became more and more defiantly English, the world of fashionable pleasure became more and more French. But by the middle of the century the continued success of British arms and the continued expansion of British trade had brought a new self-confidence. The Grand Tour, that rather curious custom whereby rich young Englishmen spent several years travelling around Europe after they left school or university, had also done much to improve matters. By 1749, when the publication of Thomas Nugent's *The Grand Tour* in four volumes enabled even those of modest means to know what should be visited and how things should be arranged, the propertied classes of England had learned to look an elegant Frenchman in the face without feeling that they must either imitate him or hold him up to ridicule.

Even though sturdy countrymen continued to thunder against the corruption of the Frenchified world of pleasure, London itself had become a more relaxed place by the time Hogarth died in 1764. The foreign influences which he had attacked so bitterly forty years earlier in *Masquerades and Operas*, perhaps his first really successful print, were far less divisive than they had once been. At Carlisle House in Soho Square the extraordinary Mrs Cornelys, a singer of German extraction who had come to England from Italy by way of the Netherlands, gathered the whole of London society to the balls which she gave at two guineas a head. There were also cheaper ones for the middle classes. The pleasure gardens at Vauxhall were less fashionable than they had been in the 1740s and 1750s when Horace Walpole and many others had given extravagant supper parties there: in *High Life Below Stairs* one of the characters declared that Vauxhall was full of 'filthy citizens' and that the newer establishment at Ranelagh was the only place for people of quality to go. But according to the *London Magazine* in 1774 'the people of the true *ton*' only went to Ranelagh for half an hour or so, in order to stare about them and ridicule what they saw, before trailing off to take supper elsewhere at half-past eleven or midnight. The citizens, meanwhile, gaped about them and looked for fashionable manners to copy: 'The sight of great folks is what they came to see, and how they are dressed, and how they walk, and how they talk.'[36]

Foreign fashions were still mocked, but with an air of easy and relaxed amusement which was very different from the desperate and defensive ferocity of Hogarth's *Masquerades and Operas*. In the early 1770s Matthew Darly, who came nearer to being a successor to Hogarth than anyone else before the rise of Gillray, concentrated almost exclusively on prints which ridiculed those rich young men who got themselves the name of 'Macaronis' by imitating the more extravagant aspects of Italian dress. And French fashions, as well as Italian ones, had now come to be regarded with a contempt which sprang from security rather than with a hatred which betrayed secret inferiority feelings. The umbrella, a French fashion popularized in England by Jonas Hanway, caused much innocent mirth. 'Our Bill's getting a walking stick with petticoats on it', cried Enoch Trickett of Sheffield when his brother William appeared with one.[37]

Those who adopted the outlandish fashions, like those who ridiculed them, were less intense than they had been in Hogarth's early days. In 1771 Lady Leicester of Holkham offered her great-nephew and heir, Thomas Coke, £500 a year if he could agree to travel abroad instead of attending one of 'those schools of vice, the universities'.[38] Few of the rich young men who went to Oxford or Cambridge bothered to do very much studying: a university education, like foreign travel, was regarded as a way of fitting a young man for the world of fashionable pleasures. Although some would have agreed with Lady Leicester in seeing the two as alternatives, the universities teaching the vicious pleasures of drinking and gambling while travel taught good manners and good taste, most people thought of them as complementary. Thomas Coke took advantage of his great-aunt's offer, spending three years on the Continent, but he took it all in his stride and reverted to the habits of an English country gentleman after his return. Even Charles Fox, one of the leaders of the Macaronis who had mixed university education with foreign travel in a bewildering fashion during his teens, was amused rather than captivated by what he saw and heard in Paris and other cities. His father had taken him away from Eton at the age of fourteen in order to introduce him to French gambling and whoring, but Charles had insisted on returning to the school for a final term and then going up to Oxford for just twelve months before being dragged off to France and Italy again for another couple of years. When he finally returned to England in 1768 he was indeed a man of pleasure and a man of fashion, shocking the diehards with his blue hair-powder and his red-heeled shoes and his Italianate clothes; but it was not long before he showed that he was also a man of business and a budding politician. Above all, he was capable of genuine enjoyment as well as fashionable pleasure.[39] For the anxious posturers in Hogarth's prints the elegance of the Continent had been something to be pursued with grim and almost professional determination, but by the second half of the century it was beginning to be absorbed with ease and nonchalance into the genial amateurism of the English gentleman.

Importations from the Continent were not restricted to elaborate hair-styles and fancy clothes. When Hogarth surrounded the aspiring Tom Rakewell with expensive pictures as well as posturing dancing masters he was concerned to attack the cult of the 'Old Master', the fashion for sixteenth- and seventeenth-century paintings and sculptures, mainly from Italy, which made possible the rise of the antique dealer and the professional faker. Naturally enough, Hogarth was infuriated by a fashion which took patronage away from living English artists and gave it to the unscrupulous imitators of dead Italians. Of all the pleasures which fashion ruled with so arbitrary a sway, the pleasure of acquisition and collection was perhaps the most corrupted. It was also the most difficult for the satirist to influence: once the fashion for a particular style had gathered momentum the sheer amount of capital invested in that style made change difficult. But even here there was a gradual process of fusion and interaction which was to lead by the end of the century to the emergence of a style of painting which managed to be both English and grand at the same time. This was largely the achievement of Joshua Reynolds, who once remarked rather scathingly that Hogarth was 'one of the painters who have applied themselves more particularly to low and vulgar characters'. For his part Reynolds applied himself first to the Old Masters of Italy, whom he studied for three years in their own country, and then to fashionable London society, which he painted for very high fees. By the time Hogarth died in 1764 Reynolds was charging £150 for a full-length portrait. Four years later he was chosen as the first president of the Royal Academy, an institution dedicated to the official recognition and encouragement of British artists. As a mark of the new status which he had brought to the profession he was himself knighted the following year.

The success of Reynolds and the failure of Hogarth – if indeed it was a failure – sums up the changing fortunes of the world of fashion in the eighteenth century. To a large extent it was the result of differing abilities and temperaments. There can be no doubt that much of Hogarth's resentment of the so-called 'grand style' of the Italian Old Masters was caused by his own inability to match it. And if he had been less ready to dismiss foreign culture as 'all gilt and beshit', less liable to throw hog's dung when he should have been making bows to fashionable people, he might have ended up with honours and successes similar to those achieved by Reynolds. But Hogarth had very little patience either with the Italian masters themselves – one certainly cannot imagine him devoting three years to their study as Reynolds did – or with the fashionable world of pleasure that worshipped them. His appeal to the public at large seemed to be a deliberate gesture, a rejection of the values of high society in the name of the simpler, more honest and above all more English values of ordinary people. He brought comfort to thousands of Englishmen by reassuring them that their own simple pleasures were in the end more worthwhile than the apparently tasteful and modish pleasures of the few. But by the time he died times were changing. The English were no longer an insecure and truculent island race, resisting foreign culture as though it were a wooden horse from which dangerous enemies would pour sooner or later. London, at any rate, had learned to enjoy itself without worrying too much about the source from which its pleasures came. Reynolds merely came to terms with a society which had itself come to terms with Europe. In their day Hogarth's chauvinistic warnings had been necessary, but now they were beginning to look a little old-fashioned.

It was different in the provinces. There Hogarth's values lasted long enough to come back into fashion again before they had ever really been out. During the 1790s the fear of the French Revolution shattered the new confidence in Europe and things European that had been building up since the middle of the century. The old truculence and insularity returned, intensified by the revulsion of the English propertied classes against the anarchy and atheism with which the Revolution seemed to be infecting the whole of Europe. Once again the Continental became a weak and foppish character, too obsessed with frivolities and trivialities to stand up to the forces of the ungodly in the way that the sturdy English did. Those leaders of London society who copied him were as effeminate and enfeebled as he was himself. Hannah More's *Thoughts on the importance of the manners of the great to general society*, published in 1799, presented much the same picture that Hogarth had painted nearly seventy years before. England's green and pleasant land was a reservoir of virtue which was in danger of being poisoned by the foul effluents from the Frenchified high society of London. Hannah More herself did not use that particular metaphor, for her generation found dung rather less acceptable and less amusing than Hogarth had done. His comment that 'the excrement upon Jack Hall will be made of chewed gingerbread to prevent offence', which had formed part of the caption to one of his prints in 1724, could no longer have been published in the 1790s.[40] That much at any rate had changed: the natural functions of the human body no longer seemed a fit subject for humour.

The same applied to its natural pleasures. In Hogarth's world fornication had been accepted as something which went on all the time and which was generally fairly amusing in a squalid kind of way. It was only when other things were at stake – the breaking of a marriage, the spread of venereal disease, the iniquities of the bawds and pimps – that his satire took on its full and sombre force. But by the 1790s it seemed that fornication, perhaps even sexual pleasure itself, was something which was always to be deplored and never to be made fun of. Malthus' attitude to the means of family planning among the poor made it quite clear that he thought they would be better off without the pleasures of making love – as indeed they would probably be better off without any pleasures at all. And if anyone in England was so depraved as to want sexual orgies, then he would have to go to the wicked city of London in order to find them. There were brothels in many other places as well as London, but it was only there that they managed to be really fashionable and acceptable. Bath had been regarded as an immoral place by many people ever since Beau Nash had established himself there early in the century and had laid down his own codes of etiquette for the balls and assemblies and gaming sessions that went on there. But even its sternest critics could not really say that Bath was the scene of orgies, or that professional whores could make much of a career there. It was simply a place for wasting time and money in an elegant and amusing way. The same was true of the increasing number of provincial towns which now had their own assembly rooms. The citizens of Newcastle had built theirs as early as 1736, and forty years later they provided themselves with a new building which was considered to be 'the most elegant and commodious edifice of the kind in the kingdom, except the House of Assembly in Bath'.[41] Even county towns and small market towns, which could not run to assembly rooms, held regular balls which were not always dull and decorous. Mrs Sherwood later remembered dances in the 1780s at which the ladies would sit in rows on a tablecloth laid upon the stairs. The gentlemen would then pull the cloth 'to the utter confusion of all order and extinction of all decorum'.[42]

What really offended the provincial moralists was that in London vice itself seemed to have its own perverted decorum. Back in 1731 a young lady of fifteen had written to the *Universal Spectator* to ask if it was wise for a lady to entertain several lovers at the same time. She was advised that 'such a licence might be granted if nothing was designed by it but the choosing of the most deserving for a husband', but that on the whole it was undesirable and would 'necessarily be attended by inconveniences'.[43] It was not long after this that Pope delivered his famous judgement on the morals of the two sexes:

> Men, some to business, some to pleasure take;
> But every woman is at heart a rake.[44]

Gentlemen in the country who read such things concluded that they reflected the etiquette of the boudoir, the modish but abandoned code of behaviour which London society had substituted for proper and decent relations between men and women. Dr Alexander was not so sure: he understood that even in the country 'the vulgar of both sexes' drew lots on St Valentine's day to see who would be their sweetheart for the coming year.[45] On St Valentine's day 1796 Anne Hughes's maid Sarah came in from milking 'looking all redd about thee cheke ande her cap ari'; but it seemed that all that had happened was that Carter True's son had said she was his Valentine and she had giggled. Anne was anxious, but only lest Sarah should be so busy 'wysperinge and kissen' that she would neglect the calves and the pigs and the hens. Four months later, at midsummer, Anne saw Sarah stealing off to the stable yard at twelve o'clock at night:

> I didde dress and followe to see whats adoe, to the stabel were shee didd stoppe, ande mee standinge bye thee strawe stacke didde here her saye 'Hempseede I soe, and hee thats mye true love cum toe mee nowe'. Then I didde see what thee sillie wenche were doinge; shee soeing thee seede were thee carters ladd doe walke, ande hys bigge feete crumpinge itt thee smeel there off woulde reache hys nose ande soe make hym toe turne toe her from all thee other wenches. Mee knoeing thee sillie wench was safe, backe toe bed, when I didde here her crepe in later. Thys sett mee toe thynkinge off howe I didde doe thee same thynge before I didde marrie John, mee bein sillie lykewise; ande thee nexte daye didde aske mee too wedd. Butt I didd finde oute later hee didd nott goe neare were I didd strewe thee hempen seede, soe I doubte mee iff Sarah's charme will worke.[46]

In London it was not so much the etiquette of the boudoir as the protocol of the men's clubs that provided the real contrast with these harmless country courting habits. Even in Hogarth's day the coffee-houses, supposedly places for learned conversation and genial good fellowship, were turning into agencies for call girls. Tom King's Coffee-House, shown in the print *Morning* which Hogarth produced in 1738, had in fact long been a brothel under the direction of Tom's widow, Moll King. Other establishments in the Covent Garden area were becoming fashionable and even quite exclusive: the third print in *The Rake's Progress* shows Tom in a room in the Rose Tavern, next to Drury Lane Theatre, which was patronized by men of the highest rank. In the sixth print he is seen gaming at White's Chocolate House, in a room known as Hell which was the favourite resort of fashionable gamblers. At the end of April 1733 a fire started in this room and burned down the whole premises, which were rebuilt as White's Club in St James's Street. Some years later William Almack made a similar progress to respectability, running first a tavern and then a gaming club before he opened his splendid new assembly rooms in King Street, St James's, in February 1765. The Duke of Cumberland graced the occasion with his royal presence, although his corpulence and breathlessness caused some anxious moments. Horace Walpole, though not present himself, sent the details to his friends:

> They tell me the ceilings were dropping with wet, but can you believe me when I assure you the Duke of Cumberland was there? – Nay, had had a levee in the morning and went to the Opera before the Assembly! There is a vast flight of steps and he was forced to rest two or three times. If he dies of it – and how should he not? – it will sound very silly when Hercules or Theseus ask him what he died of, to reply, 'I caught my death on a damp staircase at a new club-room.'[47]

It was largely for the convenience of members of the men's clubs and their guests that *Henry's List of Covent Garden Ladies* and its counterpart, *The Man of Pleasure's Kalendar for the Year*, were published. London brothels became more numerous and more luxurious. By the end of the century they were also becoming more specialized: Mrs Collet ran an establishment in Tavistock Court for those who liked to be whipped and there were also flagellation clubs in Jermyn Street. Hogarth's harlot had kept a bundle of birch twigs by her bed in case of need, but now the arrangements made to satisfy this particular appetite were more elaborate and a good deal more profitable. Those who wanted to make love with members of their own sex were less well provided for. *Satan's Harvest Home*, an anonymous catchpenny publication of the year 1749, claimed that London was full of homosexual clubs, both for men and for women; but there is no really reliable evidence from which these charges can be substantiated. Descriptions of phallic devices, or *bijoux indiscrets*, make it clear that there was a certain amount of lesbianism. A few unusually candid diarists, notably Dudley Ryder at the beginning of the century, make mention of male homosexuality; but for the most part this seems to have been a matter of furtive sodomy, combined with some sensational scandals at the universities, rather than regular commercial exploitation.[48]

This did not mean that there were no deep and lasting emotional relationships between men. On the contrary, the love of one man for another was almost universally recognized as the highest and noblest of human passions. When the dying Nelson begged Captain Hardy to kiss him he caused neither surprise nor embarrassment to those around him. While the poor were regarded as carnal creatures, incapable of feelings deeper than those aroused by mere physical coupling, gentlemen showed their depth of soul and generosity of spirit in their friendship for one another. When they embraced each other and spoke of their love for each other, as they constantly did, they were not indulging in mere politeness. It was in the segregated world of men's clubs, men's conversations and drinking sessions, men's political associations, that the average eighteenth-century male expected to find emotional fulfilment. The effect which this expectation had upon overt physical homosexuality is a matter for conjecture, but there can be no doubt of its central importance in all those human activities, from business and politics to carousing and gaming, in which loyalty and comradeship between men played a fundamental and almost sanctified part.

Perhaps this is the real reason for the sadness and emptiness and final despair of Hogarth's rake. He is able to find mistresses and men of business and dancing masters easily enough, but he finds no friends. Even in the gaming scene, which comes closer than any of the other prints to representing the male comradeship the eighteenth century valued so highly, he is alone and friendless. No doubt there were other lonely men later in the century, moving joylessly through the fashionable rooms of Almack's and White's and the other clubs as the close-knit groups of gamblers gathered round the tables in their conical caps (to shade their eyes) and their enormous greatcoats (to be turned inside out for luck). The world of pleasure was a strange place. For those who already had money and poise and confidence and that elusive quality which Dr Johnson called 'clubbability', it provided happiness of a rare kind. For others it produced nothing but misery, a downward spiral of dejection as their inability to enjoy themselves proved their clumsiness and lack of gentility, while their consciousness of these failings inhibited still further their capacity for enjoyment. And while the world of pleasure went about its purposeful business, weeding out the vulgar aspirants from the real men of fashion, the less purposeful pleasures of the world continued to provide enjoyment impartially for the fashionable and the unfashionable. But by the 1790s the racing of lice and the throwing of dung were less often included among these simple pursuits of the unsophisticated. The concept of pleasure was itself changing, more rapidly even than the world which was nominally dedicated to it, as respectability settled upon the land.

8 The Vale of Tears

'THERE is no nation in Europe, perhaps,' wrote George Cheyne in 1742, 'where great and opulent families sooner become extinct, or change lineage so quickly, as they do in England.'[1] The fortunes of the family of Stuart, once the highest in the land, seemed to prove his point. The eighteenth century had opened with a personal and political tragedy for this family, when the eleven-year-old Duke of Gloucester, only surviving child of Queen Anne, had died on 30 July 1700. Had he lived, this child might in due time have succeeded as undisputed Protestant monarch of England, Scotland and Ireland: his death meant that the country had to choose between violating the hereditary principle and endangering the Protestant supremacy. Parliament chose to do the former, settling the crown on the house of Hanover at the cost of increasingly bitter political conflict. Then at the end of the century the country was again divided because of tragedy within the royal family. George III had a severe bout of mental illness at the end of the year 1788 and even when he recovered in the following spring opposition leaders still made dark references to fathers who had apparently been cured of madness but had subsequently killed their own sons. The stability of the whole country, as well as the happiness of every individual in it, seemed to be at the mercy of a malign fate which struck down even the most innocent of children and even the most virtuous of kings.

There were those who took some comfort from believing that there was a certain divine justice in it all, that although God might visit the sins of the fathers upon the children there were at least sins to be visited. The little girl in leg irons, lifted up to kiss her dying mother in the final print of *Marriage à la Mode* (Plate 28), epitomizes this belief. Her father and her mother and her paternal grandfather have all paid the penalty of their sins; only her mother's father is left to contemplate her tiny crippled body, tainted with inherited disease, which is all that remains of the ambitious marriage he arranged. He is of course far too busy pulling off his daughter's rings (if they are still on when she stiffens they will be forfeit as the property of a suicide) to meditate on the nature of divine punishment. But other and more pious men took this view of hereditary illnesses, not always very justifiably or very charitably. In the 1760s the Dowager Princess of Wales' many enemies whispered, when George III first fell ill, that it was she who had passed on to him some appalling taint. George himself believed that his terrifying bouts of illness, which involved great physical agony as well as mental delirium, were part of God's retribution for his own sins. One of the things which he thought would bring down further punishment upon him was a breach of his coronation oath, such as would be involved in granting independence to the American colonists or interfering with the Anglican supremacy by giving toleration to Catholics or Dissenters. When his ministers urged measures of this sort on him at the end of the century his fears of further illness became one of the central factors in British politics. It now seems, however, that both he and his opponents were wrong and that his disease was a metabolic disorder inherited from his father.[2]

But the English did not have a monopoly of suffering and sadness. All over the world men and women faced disease and disability without effective pain-killers and without proper treatment. It was now sixteen centuries since the physician Galen had declared that 'the life of many men is involved in the business of their occupations and it is inevitable that they should be harmed by what they do'; and little had changed. Men still worked long hours amid damp and toxic fumes and dangerous particles of one sort or another. If their lungs and other internal organs survived these conditions, their limbs often suffered terrible injuries which might in their turn lead to agonizing amputations and to a lifetime spent without even the simplest of artificial limbs. Child-bearing, woman's chief concern, was even more dangerous; and being a child was the most dangerous of all, for more human beings died in childhood than at any other time. And whereas in England individuals died of starvation or caught smallpox or were drafted into the armed forces, on the Continent whole villages and even towns were wiped out by famine or pestilence or were scattered by advancing armies which burned and looted as they came. If life was a vale of tears the shadows were no darker in England than elsewhere.

And yet the tears were a good deal more bitter. All over Europe England was known as the home of gloom and despair. 'A kind of melancholy reigns there,' reported a French agent to his government in 1756, 'a sombre and taciturn humour.'[3] The words he used were not simply metaphors: many people still thought of the human mind as being governed by the four 'humours' of blood, yellow choler, black choler and phlegm which were present in the body in varying proportions. The first two produced positive effects, making a man cheerful at best and angry at worst, but the second two had very sad and serious results if they were present in too great quantities, as they seemed to be in Englishmen. Whereas blood and yellow choler had been associated by the ancients with the volatile elements of air and fire, black choler and phlegm had affinities with all that was dead and cold and dank. Black choler, or melan choler to students of Greek, represented the earth, while phlegm was a watery humour associated with the seas and mists with which the English were surrounded. Admirers of the phlegmatic temperament thought it calm and self-possessed, just as lovers of melancholy stressed its contemplative and even mystical attractions; but livelier races, especially the French and the Italians, thought of both as cold and miserable. At best the English were a nation of contemplative stoics, at worst a collection of melancholic depressives, peering through their fogs at one another to see which of them would commit suicide next.

Visitors from Europe were amazed and appalled at the prevalence of suicide in England. By the second half of the century it had come to be something of a joke. In 1755 the *Gentleman's Magazine* carried an advertisement recommending 'noblemen, gentlemen and others who . . . have incurred such reflections as render life intolerable' to try a new preparation called Stygian Spirit, only one guinea a phial and free to deserving cases, which would enable them to commit suicide even while in company without distressing or inconveniencing those around them.[4] Some thirty years later the Earl of Pembroke told one of his friends ironically about a French Jesuit who had caught the 'English disease' after spending some years in Salisbury and had finished up by hanging himself *à l'anglaise*.[5] Earlier in the century the 'English disease' had been viewed with less amusement. One foreign writer whose treatise was published in *Fog's Journal* in 1737 pointed out that if it went unchecked it would destroy society itself: men were only to be restrained from crime by the commandments of their religion and by the fear of death, so that if both these had lost their force, as they obviously had for the suicide, all manner of violence and rapine would inevitably follow.[6] When Montesquieu's classic work *De l'Esprit des Lois* appeared in 1748 it contained a great deal of praise of English institutions and English liberty, but it also contained a special chapter on the English habit of suicide and the difficulties of framing laws to deal with it.[7]

When de Saussure was in England in the late 1720s he was as puzzled as any other foreign traveller by the suicide mania, until he himself had an unpleasant insight into it:

> I was much surprised at the light-hearted way in which men of this country commit suicide. I could not understand this mania, which astonished me as greatly as it does other foreigners, but it no longer does so, and I must tell you the reason why. Shortly after writing my last letter I fell very ill, and I cannot describe to you all the horrors of this terrible malady. Little by little I lost my appetite and my sleep; I suffered from great anxiety and uneasiness, and that without any reason. Finally I fell into the deepest and blackest melancholy, and suffered untold misery. My friends, full of pity for me, did their best to amuse me, but they gave me more pain than pleasure. Everything made me sad and anxious; I could no longer sleep, and my food disgusted me. Had I been an Englishman I should certainly have put myself out of misery: but I am persuaded that it is a crime to commit suicide, and that there is a life hereafter where we shall have to account for our actions. The desire and thought of putting an end to my sorrows by a speedy death was ever in my thoughts, and it required all my strength of mind to resist its deadly attraction.[8]

Fortunately he was persuaded to leave London for the country village of Islington, where a course of fresh air and fresh milk straight from the cow put him right in a fortnight. He had learned three important lessons about the English disease. The first was that suicide was not the disease itself but its symptom, or perhaps its desperate remedy; the second was that the malady was caused by environment and not by inherited temperament, since he had himself proved as vulnerable to it as the English; and the third was that the ultimate deterrent and defence was the religious conviction which he possessed but which the English seemed to lack.

The fact that suicidal tendencies represented only the tip of the iceberg, the extreme and outward expression of a melancholy malady that went far deeper, had been known to English physicians for a long time. George Cheyne had devoted much of his life to the treatment of mental illnesses, specializing in those that involved the kind of black depression that de Saussure had experienced. His treatise on *The Natural Method of Curing the Diseases of the Body and the Disorders of the Mind Depending on the Body*, in which he made the remark about English families becoming extinct, appeared at the very end of his life when he was already widely accepted as an authority on melancholy, which had been very fully explored in his *The English Malady, or a Treatise of Nervous Diseases of All Kinds*, published in 1733. Like those who advised de Saussure, he was a great believer in milk, which was the basis of the 'natural method' which he thought would cure all bodily ills and therefore all the mental disturbances resulting from them. He vigorously opposed the idea that melancholy could be cured by rushing to the opposite extreme and indulging in riotous living. On the contrary, it was these things that produced it. The mock advertisement of 1755 for an instant suicide preparation was addressed principally to those who 'in the polite world are distinguished by the name of *men of pleasure*, who have by *fast living*, now commonly called *sporting*, formerly stigmatized by the names of *whoring* and *drunkenness*, brought upon themselves at the age of forty all the pains, aches and infirmities of fourscore'.[9] And Hogarth's rake was of course the archetype of the 'man of pleasure' whose pleasures reduced him in the end to hopeless vacant melancholy. When Sophie von la Roche visited Bedlam, more than half a century after Hogarth had consigned the rake to its narrow cells and noisy galleries, she instinctively ascribed the madness which it housed, melancholic as well as manic, to the malign influence of London and its fiercely competitive society. She was even more convinced of this when she heard that there were 300 private lunatic asylums in London in addition to Bedlam itself. 'This mass of asylums is a humiliating counter-balance,' she commented sadly, 'to the reflective qualities and philosophic disposition which distinguish the English nation; and I should only like to know whether these institutes are as necessary in provincial towns and in the country as in the capital, where passion is nurtured and stimulated.'[10]

In spite of the doctors and the moralists, in spite of Hogarth and Sophie, most people still clung to the old idea of the humours and of the polarity between good cheer on the one hand and ascetic melancholy on the other. Dr Johnson, who was a deeply religious man and something of a connoisseur of melancholy, felt nevertheless the need for the stimulation which London offered and which Sophie thought might prove so dangerous. While the doctors of medicine advised their patients to leave London for the countryside if they wished to shake off the desire to end their lives, this doctor of laws laid it down that 'when a man is tired of London, he is tired of life; for there is in London all that life can afford'.[11] He probably valued London life for the companionship and intellectual stimulation it provided, but there were others – and Hogarth in his less moralistic moods was one of them – who valued it for grosser pleasures and who thought that roast beef and good ale and tavern smoke offered a better cure for melancholy than cow's milk and country air. There were after all two statues and not one over the gates of Bedlam: on the one side there was raging madness, the madness of the man who had too much blood and too much yellow choler and whose route to insanity lay through over-indulgence and apoplexy, while on the other there was dark melancholy, the end product of self-denial and self-righteousness and anaemia. If the journey had to be taken most Englishmen knew which route they would prefer. While foreigners pointed out the connection between melancholy and scurvy, the disease which came from eating too much meat and too few vegetables, the English continued to think that the eating of beef was the clearest demonstration of a man's love of life and liberty. And while de Saussure did not expect every Englishman to follow him in drinking milk, he was amazed to find that no water was drunk in London, in spite of the fact that the city had a far better water supply than most continental towns.[12] The lack of fresh water, which was the original reason for Englishmen and Englishwomen and even English children quenching their thirst with beer, continued to be remedied throughout the century; but beer remained the national drink. Just as the symbol of English freedom was for Hogarth a haunch of beef, so his picture of an ideally happy English community was entitled *Beer Street*. If life was indeed a vale of tears, then the best way to forget the fact was to eat, drink and be merry.

There were religious reasons, as well as political and social ones, for this identification of gluttony with the good life. Most Englishmen believed that the Catholic tyranny of Continental countries meant fat priests and monks imposing upon ordinary people a degree of self-denial which they would never dream of practising themselves. Popish foreigners had to starve themselves in Lent and eat fish on Fridays, which was in itself a sufficient reason for freeborn Englishmen to eat good red meat whenever they could. And melancholy, which foreigners and even some Englishmen had the impertinence to call 'the English malady', was on the contrary the product of the black superstition which popery encouraged. It was nurtured by the sinister discipline of the confessional, by the dark austerities and morbid celibacy of monks and nuns, by penitential processions and sacred images which revealed in vivid detail the sufferings of Christ and his martyrs. Englishmen seldom stopped to think that these things might in fact serve to relieve the guilt feelings that lay at the root of melancholy. Nor did they realize that even the stern Calvinism of the Presbyterians and other dissenting sects, which they distrusted almost as much as they feared Catholicism, had a positive and constructive side to it. It was shown in the lives of the Quakers, who welcomed their children to 'this vale of misery' when they were born but nevertheless achieved great serenity and happiness.[13] It was also shown in the intellectual repercussions of Puritanism in European thought. La Rochefoucauld, whose elegant and merciless dissection of human folly helped to mould

29 (*Above*) Hogarth: *The Sleeping Congregation*, 1728. A comment on the apathy and lethargy of the eighteenth-century Anglican church.

28 (*Overleaf*) Hogarth: *Marriage à la Mode. The Death of the Countess*, 1745. Retribution, both divine and human: the Countess's sins are assumed to have resulted in her child being born crippled, while her suicide means that her jewellery will be forfeit unless her father can remove it before she stiffens.

eighteenth-century French philosophy, was deeply influenced by *The Mystery of Self-Deceiving*, an early seventeenth-century Puritan tract by the Englishman Daniel Dyke. Just as foreign visitors admired the honesty and integrity and charity of the Quakers and other dissenting communities, so foreign thinkers saw the value of the ruthless self-examination which English critics of Puritanism saw as merely morbid.

Towards the end of his life Hogarth decided to put into visual terms his hatred of religious enthusiasm and its melancholy effects. Oddly enough, he took as the basis of his design a painting which he had done more than thirty years before and which was a satire of a totally opposite sort – an attack on the worldly indifference and secularism of the eighteenth-century Anglican church. It was called *The Sleeping Congregation* (Plate 29) and it showed a parson preaching without interest or conviction a sermon which had already sent most of his listeners to sleep. This fairly typical English scene may have amused Hogarth when he painted it in 1728 but now he determined to show the alternative, which he found anything but amusing. The church was turned into a meeting house, suspiciously like the one in Tottenham Court Road where George Whitefield preached, and the parson's place in the pulpit was taken by a ranting enthusiast who held an image of a devil in one hand and a model of God the Father, suitably sustained by angels, in the other. This time the congregation did not sleep but gnawed like cannibals on doll-like figures of Christ. There were, as usual, many levels to the satire. The images were based on favourite themes in Italian art and were intended to damn the old masters still further by showing that they were idolatrous; while the dog howling under the lectern was labelled 'Whitefield', to show that Hogarth disapproved of the Methodist preacher in whose meeting house he had set this horrifying scene. But above all this drawing, which was entitled *Enthusiasm Delineated* (Plate 30), was intended as an attack on the Catholic church. The grimacing faces munching at the body of Christ, the parody of sacred art, the tonsured head appearing as the preacher's wig fell off – all helped to underline the object which was stated in the caption, 'to give a lineal representation of the strange effects of literal and low conceptions of Sacred Beings as also of the idolatrous tendency of pictures in churches and prints in religious books &c'.

This intention was never to be fulfilled for the print was not published in its original form. After an interval of nearly two years, during which he was ill and depressed, Hogarth took it in hand again and made some significant alterations. The edible images of Christ were removed, leaving the congregation a prey to morbid hysteria rather than blasphemous cannibalism. The preacher continued to rant in the pulpit, but now he held in his outstretched right hand a model of a witch on a broomstick instead of an image of God the Father. The devil remained, but the other references to Italian art were replaced by allusions to ghost stories and cases of popular gullibility. The woman lying on the floor in the foreground was robbed of her image of Christ and turned into Mrs Toft of Godalming, whom Hogarth had already satirized more than thirty years before for her claim to give birth to rabbits. The figure crouched over her, also now deprived of its sacred doll, became Richard Hathaway, the boy who was supposed to spew forth crooked pins in a miraculous manner. There were also references to the Cock Lane Ghost, a hoax which had been exposed only a month or two before. And the barometer in the corner, designed to register emotional rather than meteorological pressure, now included the significant word 'suicide'. Under its new title of *Credulity, Superstition and Fanaticism* the revised print (Plate 31) was published in the spring of 1762.[14]

The effect of these changes was to direct the main burden of the attack against the Methodists, whose particular brand of enthusiasm was represented as reviving the worst superstitions of popery and of ancient folklore. John Wesley was then about half-way through his remarkable progress from hated fanatic to accepted pillar of piety: he had preached his first open-air sermon in 1739 and he was to deliver a total of some 40,000 of these addresses before he died in 1791. Like those of George Whitefield, who collaborated with him in founding the Methodist movement before breaking away in the 1750s, Wesley's sermons often produced a startling effect. The colliers of Kingswood near Bristol, to whom he preached his first sermons in 1739, had been almost totally neglected by the official Anglican church, so that many of them had quite literally never heard the message of Christianity before. Even those in areas where churches were more plentiful and parsons more conscientious had never heard preaching like Wesley's and Whitefield's before. Instead of carefully composed dissertations on the reasonableness of Christianity, designed to buttress the social order rather than raise the level of spirituality, they now heard full-blooded descriptions of the rewards of paradise and the terrors of hell. David Garrick the actor was reputed to have said that he would give £100 to be able to say 'Oh' in the way Whitefield could say it;[15] and the amazing oratorical powers of both Whitefield and Wesley were used to build up word pictures of the love of God, of the infinite horror of eternal damnation and of the infinite mercy which would be shown to the truly contrite soul. Souls became contrite and bodies

30 Hogarth: *Enthusiasm Delineated*, c. 1760. Even Anglican apathy was preferable, Hogarth thought, to the excesses of the Catholics and the 'Idolatrous Tendency of Pictures in Churches', which he here satirizes.

31 Hogarth: *Credulity, Superstition and Fanaticism*, 1762. In this revised version of *Enthusiasm Delineated* the satire has been turned against the Methodists and their supposed association with the Cock Lange Ghost and other frauds.

became convulsed. Whitefield's first sermon was said to have sent fifteen people mad. Wesley became involved in violent controversy because he attributed the hysterical ecstasies and cataleptic trances of his followers to the workings of the Holy Ghost, whereas the horrified ecclesiastical authorities saw them as a mixture of insane fanaticism and deliberate exploitation of the simple-minded. It was this astonishing phenomenon of Methodism, public scandal and religious revival at one and the same time, that Hogarth now attacked.

By the time his print appeared Methodism was beginning to be respectable. At first both church and state, represented in the persons of parson and squire, had been vigorously opposed to it. Clergymen who neglected their flock in order to dance attendance on those who had patronage to bestow were infuriated to find their shortcomings shown up by itinerant preachers, while local landowners resented the challenge to the social order which the movement seemed to present. Justices of the peace often carried out deliberate victimization, drafting preachers into the army or the navy as vagabonds. But by the 1750s a new attitude was becoming apparent. Gentlemen were shocked by the turbulent riots which greeted the Methodists in many places and by the barbarity with which preachers were treated by the mob. The riots in Norwich in 1751 and 1752 were reported in the *Gentleman's Magazine* in a way which was far more sympathetic to the Methodists than would have been conceivable a decade earlier. In 1760 the magazine expressed nothing but disgust at the louts who had rolled a preacher in the ditch at Kingston in Surrey and nothing but admiration for the gentleman who had saved him by taking him into his house.[16] Methodist chapels in London were becoming popular and even fashionable. The Countess of Huntingdon's efforts to introduce the upper classes to Methodism were beginning to bear fruit, especially now that George III had begun his reign by issuing a proclamation against profanity and immorality and by making it clear that he expected his courtiers to be less frivolous and more godly than they had been in his grandfather's time. Most important of all, it was becoming clear that most rank-and-file Methodists were orderly and hard-working people, if anything more submissive rather than less to the social hierarchy now that they had a new and lively expectation of future bliss.

Hogarth, however, was not concerned with the social order but with the vale of tears, the perennial problem of the English malady and its manifestations. He had only two and a half years left to live and he was troubled by symptoms of the cardiac disease that was to kill him. It has been suggested that he was suffering from syphilis, in which case there was an unpleasant parallel between him and the rake he had consigned to Bedlam. The rake lay plunged in a melancholy caused by the venereal disease he had caught as well as by the loneliness and hopelessness which had resulted from his vain quest for social acceptance. Hogarth was subject to recurring fits of depression in which his physical condition and his bitter professional quarrels both played a part. There was a disgusted despair about much of what he drew and wrote in those last few years of his life; and it was intensified by the spectacle of the horrors and the absurdities which the Methodists seemed to be calling up. Although he had never achieved the grand style of painting which he had once envied and at which he now saw Reynolds succeeding, he had at least taught people to be rational and sceptical, to busy themselves with honest work and avoid morbid speculation about the world of spirits and shadows. And now here were the Methodists plunging the country back into superstition and melancholy. For Wesley did not only believe in the workings of the Holy Ghost, acting upon his people by means of his words and those of his fellow preachers; he also believed in the working of lesser ghosts and demons, as well as in the witches and warlocks who dealt in them. It was the Methodists who had publicized the story of the Cock Lane Ghost, saying that mysterious knockings heard in Richard Parsons' house there had been interpreted as messages from a dead woman accusing her murderer. Parsons, who was himself a Methodist, had given the details to the press and he had been backed up by two Methodist preachers. When the ghostly noises were found to be the work of his daughter, banging pieces of wood together under the bedclothes according to a prearranged code, the Methodists were seriously discredited and Hogarth's satire found a ready audience.[17]

As to witches, Wesley's own opinions were unequivocal: 'The giving up of witchcraft', he wrote angrily, 'is in effect, giving up the Bible.' In Cornwall in 1746 he listened solemnly and sympathetically to a woman who told him she had been bound to Satan 'in an uncommon manner' for seven years, ever since a malicious neighbour had paid a witch fourteen shillings to make the devil visit her one dark night in the middle of a thunderstorm. Wesley was glad to hear that the grace she had gained as a result of his sermon had forced the prince of darkness to leave her alone at last, instead of tearing her flesh with burning pincers as he had done methodically for seven years.[18] After many years of virtual disuse the laws against witchcraft had been repealed in 1736, but now there was a revival of accusations of witchcraft. At Tring in Hertfordshire in 1751 a publican called Butterfield announced that he had been bewitched by

Ruth Osborne, a destitute old woman who was at that time in the workhouse. He appointed a day on which he said he was going to have her ducked; and a crowd gathered which was so vast and so threatening that the parish authorities tried to hide the old woman and her husband for safety. The mob then threatened to kill the governor of the workhouse and set fire to the town, upon which Ruth and her husband were delivered up. They were stripped naked, dragged two miles to a stream and then repeatedly ducked, with their big toes and thumbs tied together in the approved manner. When they were half drowned and choked with mud, the woman was kicked and beaten with sticks until she was dead. Then her body was tied to her husband, who was still alive, and the two were put to bed together. The ringleader of the mob, a chimney sweep called Colley, then took a hat round among the crowd and was rewarded handsomely for the sport he had provided. Four months later he was hanged for murder, but the local people refused to attend his execution. Instead 'many thousands stood at a distance to see him go, grumbling and muttering that it was a hard case to hang a man for destroying an old wicked woman who had done so much mischief by her witchcraft'.[19]

Nobody could seriously suggest that the Methodists encouraged or even condoned atrocities of this sort, but cases of sorcery and demoniac possession continued to be heard of at their meetings and debated by Wesley himself. While the Methodists concerned themselves with bringing salvation and liberation to the victims of possession, people more ignorant or more malevolent cried for vengeance against its authors. When Susannah Haynokes of Wingrove in Buckinghamshire was accused of bewitching a spinning wheel in 1759 her husband insisted that she should be tried by being weighed against the church Bible, an altogether more satisfactory method from the point of view of the accused than ducking. 'She was stripped of all her clothes, to her shift and under-coat, and weighed against the Bible; when, to the no small mortification of the accuser, she outweighed it and was honourably acquitted of the charge'. Mrs Pritchers of West Langdon in Kent was less fortunate: she was dragged from her house in 1762, while London was already laughing at Hogarth's flights of fancy in *Credulity, Superstition and Fanaticism*, and badly scratched about the arms and face in the presence of the boy she was supposed to have bewitched. The crowd then threatened to duck her 'but some people of condition interposing, the poor woman's life was happily preserved'.[20]

From its earliest days Methodism had also been suspected of encouraging the sort of morbid religiosity which brought about some at least of the country's many suicides and attempted suicides. When a Methodist named James Taylor was saved from drowning in Southwark Park in 1747 his rescuers got scant thanks: he told them that he had tried to kill himself because 'he longed to be in heaven and the sooner the better'. In 1751 the *Gentleman's Magazine* reported that a woman Methodist from Ledbrook in Gloucestershire had cut her throat while fresh from her devotions, expiring within two hours in spite of efforts to sew her up. 'We have also been told,' the writer went on, 'of a man and his wife at Chatham, Methodists, who hanged themselves last month . . . In order to prove him a lunatic the friends produced to the coroner's jury the New Testament written on a roll of paper with his own blood – A more particular account of this affair would be acceptable.'[21] It would indeed, for this last detail cut both ways. If there was something morbid about a man who copied out the gospels in his own blood, there was something even more morbid about a society which had power to bury a suicide at a crossroads with a stake through his heart unless his friends could prove that he was of unsound mind when he killed himself. When a London bookseller called Barlow shot his two-year-old child and then himself in 1755, dying of his wounds in prison, he was foolish enough to leave behind him a note saying that he did it because of the pressure of his creditors. Deprived of the chance to plead insanity, his friends smuggled away the body and buried it in secret; but the lord mayor had the last word. He ordered the corpse to be dug up and reburied under Moorfields crossroads, with the traditional stake driven through it to prevent the man's ghost rising.[22] It seemed that the society which condemned the Methodists for believing in ghosts and promoting suicide was not entirely above believing in ghosts itself.

While Hogarth and the other satirists mocked at Methodist credulity and superstition, catering for the fickle London public who would undoubtedly be just as awed by the next supernatural sensation until they were told it was safe to laugh at it, moderate and reasonable men tried to steer a middle course between scepticism and superstition, between apoplexy and melancholy, between the dangers of self-indulgence and the even greater dangers of self-denial. According to the medical writers it was a relatively simple matter: all that you had to do was to keep your bowels open, take plenty of fresh air and exercise and make sure that your children were breast-fed. This would avoid the distressing extinction of opulent families which Cheyne bemoaned. According to Dr William Cadogan, writing in 1748, it would do more. If his advice were to be followed, he said, all disease, including madness and the King's Evil, would disappear within a generation or two. He banished the spectre of inherited disease, to his own satisfaction at least, by pointing out that most chronic diseases developed late in life 'when the business of love is pretty well over'.[23] If this was true it was a little surprising that a great part of the population died before it had even had a chance to make love.

On closer examination the simple and natural diets recommended by the medical manuals turned out to be a little puzzling. Cheyne advised abstention from all fermented liquors, which was pretty standard, but he also suggested an annual oscillation between carnivorous and vegetarian habits – meat in the winter, fruit and vegetables in the summer – which might have proved a little impracticable and unsettling. At the same time he declared that the ideal diet, one which was guaranteed to 'cure all chronic distempers', was a mixture of animal and vegetable products, milk and turnips, taken all the year round. Acute distempers, on the other hand, would yield best to 'teas made of saponaceous or aromatic seeds'. Then there was the question of where to live: everyone agreed that London's fog and smoke were terribly unhealthy, but the alternatives were not always clear. Kalm said that the coal-smoke gave everybody a cough when they first came to London, but that after a time they got used to it. Nevertheless he thought that in the long run the smoke caused lung disease and was better avoided; but at the same time an eminent English physician warned that 'the dark shades of thick woods, where vapours are contracted, occasion various diseases, and often death, to those who reside among them'.[24] Fifty years later, when Arthur Young's little daughter was taken ill with consumption, one of her physicians insisted that she must be taken away from the bracing air of East Anglia to a seaside resort where the climate was mild and humid. Other doctors disagreed and in the end she was transported to Boston, a journey which helped to kill her. Young reproached himself bitterly afterwards for paying attention to the medical advice he received: 'I did for the best and spared nothing, but had she been a pauper in a village she would, I verily think, have been alive and hearty. Such are the blessings of money: it has cost me £100 to destroy my child.'[25]

Strangely enough, most of the medical writers of the period would have agreed with him. Almost to a man they praised the virtues of the simple life and the health-giving properties of hard work. In 1732 the author of a facetious tract on the 'English malady' of spleen or melancholy pointed out that it had originally been limited to the ladies of the Court, until 'Dr Ratcliff, out of his well-known pique to the Court physicians, persuaded an ironmonger's wife of the City into it'. It had then travelled all over the country, but 'the industrious farmer, shepherd, ploughman and day-labourer are indeed safe from these evils, respect for their betters not suffering them to pretend to it'.[26] Cadogan, Cheyne and many others enthused over the superior health and vigour of the industrious poor. By the time Arthur Young's child died, in 1797, the work of Frederick Morton Eden was already making nonsense of the idealized view of 'a pauper child in a village';* but in the middle of the century it was still possible to believe that poverty and hard work bred good health and happiness. In the middle and upper classes, too, idleness was seen as the most debilitating thing of all. In 1734 there was an ironic account in the *Gentleman's Magazine* of a woman who had been miraculously cured of a chronic and apparently hopeless attack of the vapours by a startling new prescription: small beer only to drink, no social occasions and several hours' work a day.[27]

However much the leisured classes might admire and even envy the industry of the poor, it was not always easy for them to imitate it. 'Man of pleasure' was a title that conferred status, in spite of all that the moralists could do, but 'man of business' was hardly an occupation to which a gentleman should aspire. In the 1790s it was possible for Arthur Young to occupy himself in his grief by hoeing his dead daughter's garden, but few men of property in the middle of the century would have done so, at any rate while anyone might be looking. If they spent their leisure in organized enjoyments, hunting or racing or carousing or going to balls and assemblies, there was always the danger of dissipation and the diseases which sprang from excess and over-exertion; but if they spent it in solitary meditation there were even greater dangers. In the 1740s a country rector called Edward Young, clever and well connected but apparently too diffident to pursue the patronage and promotion which his friends thought he deserved, published the results of his own long and solitary reflections. The book was called *The Complaint, or Night Thoughts on Life, Death and Immortality* and it was enormously popular, even though it was one of the most melancholy poems of the period, full of reminders of death and reflections upon the empty and transient nature of human life. Several more works of the same kind followed within the next few years and very soon there was a fashion not only for reading about other men's meditations, but also for carrying out one's own – preferably in suitably melancholy settings such as churchyards or ivy-covered ruins. While Hogarth was battling against the superstitious melancholy which the Methodists were spreading among the labouring classes, men of letters

* See p. 99.

were popularizing a new kind of romantic melancholy among the leisured classes. Perhaps most sinister of all, they were making solitude itself seem attractive and even in some mysterious way ennobling. And solitude was a state which Hogarth rarely illustrated and even more rarely commended. The romantic cult of solitary meditation was even more inimical to his values than the Methodist cult of communal religious exaltation.

Dr Johnson, who feared solitude as much as any man, gave a hint as to the nature of its dangers. 'If you are idle,' he warned Boswell, 'be not solitary; if you are solitary, be not idle.' As to what thoughts might come if idleness and solitude were allowed to prolong their deadly partnership, he did not commit himself. Other writers, particularly medical writers, were less reluctant. 'I have already hinted', said Cheyne in 1742, 'at the chief source of infertility in the male sex.' By the end of the century hints had given way to open denunciation: masturbation, the child of solitude and idleness, was the unforgivable sin, the ultimate act of defilement, the greatest of all dangers to the health of the individual and of the race. Medical treatises abounded with cases of lost potency, hopeless sterility, diseased semen, incurable trembling and the draining away of spinal fluid – all caused by this unspeakable practice.[28] This was where all the talk of melancholy and suicide and the English disease had its source: it was self-abuse that paved the way to self-destruction.

In the first flush of post-Freudian enthusiasm some writers have been tempted to interpret all the aspects of eighteenth-century melancholy, from romanticism and the belief in ghosts to Methodism and the belief in eternity, as symptoms of some overwhelming national neurosis. Diagnosis of this sort is perhaps a little over-confident: it is difficult enough for the psychiatrist to define the neurosis of one patient whom he can interview, let alone that of several million who are already dead and have left only very limited records of their innermost thoughts. Some of those thoughts may have been more guilt-ridden than those of other nations because of the absence of the confessional, that useful spiritual equivalent of the psycho-analyst's couch; but beyond that it is hard to go with any real certainty. A readiness to believe in witches and ghosts is not in itself a sign of neurosis, though the form taken by these apparitions may sometimes be indicative of certain mental states. Even the eighteenth century's ability to face up to the reality and inevitability of death, which some have seen as evidence of neurotic morbidity, may have been healthier and more sensible than the desperate pretences about death which have been developed in some subsequent cultures. But the distrust of solitude and the reluctance to admit the value of self-examination or introspective thought do seem to have had an anxious and almost neurotic edge to them. It was unfortunate that the eighteenth-century Englishman's reaction against popery should also have involved him in a reaction against spirituality. It was even more unfortunate that this should have brought with it dark suspicions and guilty apprehensions about one of man's basic needs, the need for occasional solitude.

It was Young's *Night Thoughts* that provided, even in the midst of its images of melancholy and mortality, an indication of the way to make the contemplative life safe and respectable. Young hailed devotion as the 'daughter of astronomy': 'An undevout astronomer', he concluded, 'is mad.' Meditation on the movements of the heavens, contemplation of the vast, unerring clockwork of the universe, was the means whereby man could be reconciled to God and to himself, to life and to death. The important thing was to study the rational nature of the whole creation first, the mathematical precision with which God regulated the material world, before looking inwards at your own mind and soul. By this means you could be sure of preserving the sense of reason and symmetry which would show you how the nature of man reflected the nature of the universe. Man was the reasonable denizen of a reasonable world. How could the God who created all this be pleased by irrational religious enthusiasm, by stories of witches and devils and ghosts? How could He permit his rational and logical human creation to lose itself in morbid and superstitious introspection? If man would only be still and listen to the voice of God he would find that it was the voice of reason, the voice that spoke in Newton's rational explanation of the universe and Locke's equally rational explanation of the mind of man.

Unfortunately there were the wind and the earthquake and the fire to be explained, as well as the still small voice that followed them. An English country rector, looking out from his orderly and well-staffed house upon the symmetry that human labour had imposed upon the landscape, might find it possible to believe that the whole of God's creation, human as well as inanimate, was governed by logical and ascertainable laws. Those who were exposed to the full force of man's inhumanity or to the apparently capricious wrath of God found it more difficult. Natural disasters were not easy to account for: the Portuguese capital of Lisbon was devastated in 1755 by an earthquake which was accompanied by a great and strong wind and followed by a fire, as well as by enormous tidal waves, but not by any still, small voice. The fashionably optimistic assumption that the natural world was governed by rational laws was severely shaken by the Lisbon earthquake, which was used to deadly effect by Voltaire in his *Candide*, a fierce satire on those who still imagined that 'all was for the best in the best of all possible worlds'. Even in Britain there were landscapes that seemed to have been created by the demons of man's nightmares rather than by the reasonable God of his dreams. As late as 1768 Sir Harbottle Grimston was appalled by the dreary and inhospitable mountain scenery of North Wales, while the Highlands of Scotland made a similar impression on Dr Johnson five years later. 'How, sir, can you ask me what obliges me to speak unfavourably of a country where I have been hospitably entertained?' he said irritably to a gentleman in Auchinleck who asked for his opinions. 'Who *can* like the Highlands? I like the inhabitants very well.'[29]

But there was a change taking place in this as in every other aspect of man's relationship with nature. In 1774 a tourist in Snowdonia recorded impressions very different from those of Grimston: 'During our abode amid those superb mountains neither sun nor stars appeared to our sight for several days; and, wrapt up in an impenetrable mist, we were perpetually enveloped with a twilight obscurity. Our situation was like a scene of enchantment.' In the same year young Thomas Bewick, his apprenticeship as an engraver in Newcastle over, set off on a walking tour to the Scottish Highlands, where he found the 'beauty and severity' and the 'grandeur or terrific aspect' of the scenery awe-inspiring and extremely beautiful.[30] And while the new generation of travellers searched out the wild and uncharted corners of the land, a new generation of readers sought wild and uncharted corners of the human experience. They found them in what was later to be called 'romantic' literature: ancient (or supposedly ancient) ballads telling of heroic deeds in the remote and misty past, or blood-curdling tales of ghosts and vaulted tombs and hooded figures half-seen in the moonlight. On the surface the world remained practical and rational, believing with Newton and Locke that God had constructed a reasonable universe and put reasonable men into it. The organization of life and work, the direction of scientific enquiry, the conduct of business and politics were all based on these reasonable assumptions. But more and more people were seeking to escape from this tamed and symmetrical workaday world into another world in which things deeper than reason, dream images of enormous power and strange beauty, could be recognized and explored. Those who could afford it sought this world in space or in time or in the imaginations of others, by travel or study or reading. The rest had to make do with ghosts and witches and popular folklore, with hempseed laid down at midnight for their lovers or with the ancient magic of divine intervention and demoniac possession which had received new sanction from the Methodists.

The same confrontation between common sense and magic governed the bodily aspect of human misery, the physical ailments which were supposed to cause or to reflect the madness and melancholy between which man was balanced. Men of property and education could if they wished consult physicians when they fell ill. The Royal College of Physicians was a reputable body and it elected as Fellows only graduates of Oxford or Cambridge or Trinity College, Dublin: Dr William Browne asserted in 1753 that this was the only way of ensuring that physicians had the necessary 'approved learning and morals' and 'agreeable and social dispositions' for the proper performance of their duties.[31] Such men proceeded along apparently logical lines and the treatments they prescribed seemed to accord with a reasonable man's understanding of the reasonable world in which God had placed him. Their constant recourse to blood-letting was to seem strange to later generations, as was the treatment of madness by hot poultices applied to the shaven head 'to draw out the humours',* but in the light of current theories of the physical world these things could be logically justified. The schools of medicine at the Scottish universities and at Leyden in Holland were more progressive, even though their graduates were only allowed to be Licentiates, rather than fellows, of the Royal College. Surgeons, though an inferior class of beings, artisans who worked with their hands as opposed to the physicians who consulted their stores of learning, were often sensible and practical men who sought to repair and adjust the human body in the light of the knowledge they acquired by dissecting corpses. John Hunter, the most distinguished figure in eighteenth-century surgery, was often under attack for his supposed body-snatching and for the rather macabre museum of anatomical specimens which he established in Windmill Street; but he was also respected and honoured for his skill and knowledge. Since there were no effective antiseptics or anaesthetics surgery was often dangerous and always excruciating, but it was by no means unscientific.

The same could not be said for the kind of medical treatment received by the majority of the population. Sometimes employers called the physician and even the surgeon to their servants as well as to their family. In the 1740s the Duke of Bedford subscribed £200 a year to the first smallpox hospital founded in London, sending his servants there as

* This treatment was given to George III in 1788.

part of the bargain if they caught the disease.[32] Between 1720 and 1745 five great London hospitals were set up, in all of which the poor could get the latest treatment, though sometimes under appalling conditions and at the risk of being used for medical investigations of one sort or another. But the existence of good hospitals and considerate employers, in the provinces as well as in London, did not alter the fact that for the masses medicine usually involved more magic than science. In Cheshire in the 1740s an old woman called Bridget Bostock cured 'the blind, the deaf, the lame of all sorts, the rheumatic, King's Evil, hysteric fits, falling fits, shortness of breath, dropsy, palsy, leprosy, cancers, and, in short, almost everything, except the French disease, which she will not meddle with'. All she did was to pray over her patients and stroke them with her spittle (it had to contain no trace of food, so that she had to treat all her patients before she broke her fast), but it was said that they never failed to recover. Her refusal to treat syphilis, 'the French disease', was almost certainly based on religious scruples rather than on any lack of confidence in herself: she was given her miraculous powers by God and so she must not abuse them by curing those whom he had punished for their immorality.[33]

This intrusion of religion into medicine raised awkward questions. If people were to be allowed to believe in white witches who did good by the grace of God, why should they be forbidden to believe in black witches who did harm with the connivance of the devil? Wesley's own opinions on medicine do not seem to have been influenced very much by his belief in witches, even though some of his favourite remedies had a touch of ancient magic about them: the ague, he thought, was best treated with flowers and leaves picked in July and beaten together with salt before being applied to the head.[34] Many other traditional country remedies had their origins in pre-Christian pagan beliefs, and superstitions about the moon respected her ancient powers over man's body as well as over his mind. While simple people believed that madness was associated with the full moon, respectable gentlemen refused to have blood taken from them while the moon was on the wane. The rituals of popular medicine showed that the old beliefs, as well as the Christian religion which was supposed to have replaced them, could still call in question the idea that men lived by reason alone.

There were new religions, new forms of magic, as well as old. In London quackery was almost a religion in its own right – and one with many followers. In the countryside the travelling quack doctor did relatively little harm: he peddled bottles of coloured water at fairs or in taverns and many of those who bought them got better, either in the natural course of things or because of the power of their own belief. If they did not, then they were no worse off and they went to an apothecary, who gave them more reputable and possibly more effective drugs. In town and country alike the apothecary was the doctor of the poor. Officially his trade was to compound medicines, not to prescribe them, so that he only charged for the drugs he provided; but his advice was eagerly sought, even by those who could well afford to call in the physician. 'I ever thought a good honest apothecary a much safer person to apply to than half the physicians and surgeons in the kingdom,' wrote William Cole in 1766.[35] Unfortunately, however, not all apothecaries were good and honest. The few who exploited their knowledge, concocting miraculous preparations which claimed to cure every ill, tended to gravitate to London. Unlike Bridget Bostock, they had no scruples about treating 'the French disease': whereas she accepted no payment for her cures, they were in the miracle-working business for the money and could not afford to neglect this very numerous and lucrative class of patients. And the French disease was more intractable than the English: it would not yield to fresh air and milk and exhortatory remarks. The pills and potions of the London quacks had to have a real kick to them, so that they often included dangerous substances such as antimony or arsenic. This was the case with the celebrated pills compounded by Joshua Ward, a practitioner who was so successful that he was patronized by the king and queen and given special exemption from the Act of 1748 which forbade the preparation of medicines by unqualified persons.

Ward appeared, along with Mrs Mapp the bone-setter and John Taylor the eye-surgeon, in Hogarth's print called *The Company of Undertakers* (Plate 32), published in 1737. It was a savage satire on the medical profession as a whole: the anonymous doctors in the lower half of the picture, like the three recognizable quacks at the top, were represented as undertakers rather than physicians, agents of death rather than restorers of life. There were undoubtedly cases in which Ward's pills had led to blindness, paralysis and even death, but the case against John Taylor and Mrs Mapp was less clear.[36] Hogarth's successors at the end of the century were equally indiscriminate. When Dr Edward Jenner began to vaccinate with the comparatively harmless disease of cow-pox in the 1790s, a technique which was eventually to bring the much more terrible disease of smallpox under control, Gillray and others produced grotesque cartoons showing Jenner's patients sprouting cow-like appendages. Meanwhile, the quacks of London had developed and refined their own techniques. Exotic ingredients proved to be safer and more prestigious than dangerous

32 Hogarth: *The Company of Undertakers*, 1737. A group of doctors, headed by three notorious quacks, portrayed as undertakers.

33 Hogarth: *Tailpiece, or the Bathos*, 1764. His last engraving: Time himself is dying.

drugs: in 1739 Mrs Stephens, who compounded medicines with powdered snails and Alicante soap, got a special Act passed to ensure for her a reward of £5,000 from treasury funds. In 1770 John Ball recommended live woodlice or millipedes ground up with sugar and nutmeg in a mortar, as a cure for cancer.[37] But it was Dr James Graham, the inventor of the Celestial Bed, who saw that the real profits lay in rejuvenating the jaded rich rather than in selling potions to the genuinely ill. His courses of treatment in Bristol and Bath, involving electricity, milk baths and friction, were so successful that he was able to move to London and establish a 'Temple of Health' in the Adelphi. Like all good showmen, he introduced a touch of the occult into the spectacles he staged and the treatments he prescribed. The new generation of quacks were the priests of a health cult, initiating their patients into the arcane mysteries of a new religion.

In the 1780s, with the arrival in England of Cagliostro and the prophets of Mesmerism, the new movement reached its apogee. In Paris Mesmer himself was already being hailed as a secular Messiah whose discovery of the principle of 'animal magnetism' had given mankind a new insight into the nature of life itself. In Germany and in Italy the secret societies, the Freemasons and the Illuminati and many others, dabbled impartially in health cults, political theory and mystical experiences of one sort or another. Excited initiates, their bodies rejuvenated by electricity and magnetism and their minds filled with the prospect of a new heaven and a new earth, trembled on the brink of ever more amazing discoveries. This was the dawn in which, according to Wordsworth, it was bliss to be alive and very heaven to be young. When the people of Paris stormed the Bastille in July 1789 it seemed that the long night of ignorance and misery was at last over and that the sun was about to rise. After all the false starts, the morbid melancholy of the selfish and the frenzied enthusiasm of the superstitious, mankind could come out from the shadows and stretch its limbs in the healing light of the new day. There would be no more tears and no more ills, either social or individual, mental or physical.

When the French Revolution passed after a few years to extremes of violence which shocked even its most ardent apologists, the reaction which resulted was not just a matter of social and political conservatism. The pessimism of the late 1790s was as generalized and as undiscriminating as the optimism that had preceded it. There was no more talk of short cuts and easy panaceas, of a quick or certain escape from the vale of tears. The authorities began to ordain public fast days again, to implore God's forgiveness for past sins and to request his support in the war against the ungodly legions of the French revolutionaries. 'A fast,' wrote Coleridge bitterly in 1795, 'a word that implies prayers of hate to the God of love – and after these a turbot feast for the rich and their usual scanty morsel for the poor.'[38] The rich did not have to eat turbot if they did not want to, but they must take care not to give it to the poor. God had placed the rich man in his castle and the poor man at his gate, just as He had ordained that this transient life should be a vale of tears, a stern proving ground for the life to come. 'Seekers after improvement', as George III once called them contemptuously, would end by involving their fellow men as well as themselves in the righteous wrath of a God whose hierarchical and disciplinarian intentions were not to be mocked. What should it profit a man if he reformed the whole world and lost his own soul?

'Lyfe bee butt a littel thynge,' wrote Anne Hughes in February 1797, on her return from a neighbour's funeral, 'and I doe wonder whiles what doe lie beyond. Butt wee shall all see anon.'[39] A few months later the death of his beloved daughter led Arthur Young to think more deeply than ever before on 'what doe lie beyond'. Before she died she asked him to pray for her – "Do it now, papa," she said, 'on which I poured forth aloud ejaculations to the Almighty, that He would have compassion and heal the affliction of my child. She clasped her hands together in the attitude of praying and when I had done said, "Amen" – her last words.' The grief-stricken father prayed that he might have the grace to live the rest of his life as though she were watching him. 'Melancholy', he wrote, 'has produced in me a more earnest desire to be reconciled to God than any other event of my life and proves that of all the medicines of the soul, sorrow is perhaps the most powerful.'[40] More than thirty years before, Hogarth, an enemy to melancholy and a sceptic as to the immortality of the soul, had died unfortified by any such medicine. Like Shakespeare, he ended his work with a vision of the mortality of all things: in Shakespeare's last play Prospero foretells the dissolution of the great globe itself, while in Hogarth's last drawing Time himself is dying and the world is falling to pieces around him. It was in April 1764 that Hogarth advertised 'a print called FINIS, representing the Bathos, or Manner of sinking in sublime painting . . . It may serve as a Tail-piece to all the Author's Engraved works'. (See Plate 33.) He had already told his friends that the work would be his own epitaph[41] and it contained a broken palette which was as symbolic as Prospero's broken staff in *The Tempest*. Hogarth did not publish anything more and on 25 October, some hours after eating the freeborn Englishman's sacramental meal of beef-steak, he died. He had no daughter to meet, no expectations to be fulfilled. Time did not die with him, but the hope of exchanging time for eternity certainly grew mightily among Englishmen during the thirty years that followed his death. As it grew it leaned heavily on Hogarth's moralizing but it rejected his stoicism and his scepticism and much of his spontaneity. Later generations, less confident of immortality and less fastidious about the world of the flesh, may perhaps right the balance.

Notes

Full details are given of works cited for the first time: subsequent references are given in a shortened form. Place of publication is London unless otherwise stated. The following abbreviations are used:

AR	*Annual Register*
DNB	*Dictionary of National Biography* (new edition, 22 vols., 1970)
GM	*Gentleman's Magazine*
HMC	Historical Manuscripts Commission Reports. References to these are given in the form recommended in the Sectional Lists published by the Stationery Office
PH	Cobbett's *Parliamentary History of England*, 26 vols., 1807–20

Notes to Chapter 1

1. G. W. Prothero, *Select Statutes and other constitutional documents illustrative of the reigns of Elizabeth and James I*, 4th edition, 1963, p. 289.
2. D. Defoe, *Tour through the whole Island of Great Britain*, ed. G. D. H. Cole, 2 vols., 1962, ii, 15. Some historians, however, have seen the riots of the eighteenth century as part of a continuing dialogue between propertied and labouring men over traditional rights. See E. P. Thompson, 'The Moral Economy of the English Crowd in the Eighteenth Century', in *Past and Present*, no. 50, 1971, pp. 76–136.
3. M. D. George, *Hogarth to Cruikshank: Social Change in Graphic Satire*, 1967, p. 15.
4. *Ibid.*, pp. 16–17.
5. C. Williams (ed.), *Sophie in London 1786, being the Diary of Sophie von la Roche*, 1933, p. 95.
6. *Ibid.*, p. 86.
7. P. J. Grosley, *A Tour To London*, tr. T. Nugent, 1772, p. 85.
8. Hans Stanley to the Earl of Huntingdon, 15 June 1776, HMC 78, *Hastings III*, pp. 173–4.
9. George, *Hogarth to Cruikshank*, p. 14. For a fuller account of the Englishman's view of France – and the Frenchman's view of England – see Derek Jarrett, *The Begetters of Revolution: England's involvement with France 1759–1789*, 1973, pp. 18–41.
10. R. Paulson, *Hogarth: His Life, Art and Times*, 2 vols., New Haven and London, 1971, ii, 75–8.

11. *Ibid.*, ii, 76, 431–2. Paulson suggests that George Steevens, one of Hogarth's early biographers, was responsible for applying these words to the 1748 trip; but it is clear nevertheless that Hogarth habitually applied the phrase to France and to all things French.

12. The late 1750s saw prints referring to John Bull, including one which featured a bull-headed man among its characters; but it was not until 1762 that he appeared as the central figure. In *The Poor Man loaded with mischief, or John Bull and his sister Peg*, published 23 September 1762, he was a man with bull's horns and in *The Caledonian Slaughter House*, also published in September 1762, he was a bull. See *Catalogue of Prints and Drawings in the British Museum: Political and Personal Satires*, vol. III, pt. ii, 1877, nos. 3467, 3548, 3904, 3907.

13. *Poems of Swift*, ed. H. Williams, Oxford, 2 vols., 1958; i, 162. These verses, intended by Swift to discredit the Club, were probably more extreme than those it actually used.

14. *GM* 1735, p. 105. In fact the crowd's indignation seems to have been unfounded: the Club and its rituals were by this time comparatively harmless.

15. See Walter Arnold, *The Sublime Society of Beefsteaks*, 1871.

16. This trick is used in *Evening*, one of the paintings of *The Four Times of Day* which Hogarth did in 1738 to decorate boxes in the Vauxhall pleasure gardens.

17. Act I, scene i, lines 259–64.

18. Country gentlemen, especially those who sat for the counties, were a good deal less 'independent' than they pretended. Of the 180 who represented the English counties between 1747 and 1768 at least a third were place-hunters, successful or otherwise, and more than half were launched on their political careers by party leaders, boroughmongers or other great patrons. See my 'The Myth of "Patriotism" in Eighteenth Century English Politics', in *Britain and the Netherlands*, vol. v, ed. J. S. Bromley and E. H. Kossmann, The Hague, 1976, pp. 120–40.

19. See T. W. Perry, *Public opinion, propaganda and politics in eighteenth century England: a study of the Jew Bill of 1753*, Harvard, 1962; and R. J. Robson, *The Oxfordshire Election of 1754*, Oxford, 1949.

20. *Catalogue of . . . political and personal Satires*, vol. III, pt. ii, nos. 3208, 3209.

21. British Museum Additional Manuscripts 32952, fo. 200 (Duke of Newcastle's account of George III's conversation with Charles Yorke on 2 November 1763).

22. *Ibid.*, 32966, fo. 131 (Newcastle to the Archbishop of Canterbury, 31 March 1765).

23. Quoted in L. B. Namier and J. Brooke, *The History of Parliament: the House of Commons, 1754–90*, 3 vols., 1964, iii, 131.

24. *Correspondence of William Pitt and Charles, Duke of Rutland, 1781–1787*, Edinburgh and London, 1890, p. 7.

25. *Correspondence of Edmund Burke*, ed. T. W. Copeland *et al.*, Cambridge and Chicago, 9 vols., 1958–70, vi, 27, 28.

26. H. Fielding, *Amelia*, Book I, chapter ii.

27. A. Babington, *A House in Bow Street: Crime and the Magistracy, London, 1740–1881*, 1969, pp. 80–82.

28. J. Norris, *Shelburne and Reform*, 1963, p. 133.
29. *GM* 1788, p. 315.
30. HMC 64, *Verulam*, pp. 136 *et seq.*
31. J. Bowdler, *Reform or Ruin*, 2nd edition, 1797, pp. 1, 10.
32. V. Riquetti, marquis de Mirabeau, *L'Ami des Hommes*, 3 vols., The Hague, 1758, iii, 213–14.
33. *PH* xiv, 1318–22.
34. *Ibid.*, xxv, 598–601.

Notes to Chapter 2

1. *Boswell's Life of Johnson*, ed. G. B. Hill, revised L. F. Powell, 6 vols., Oxford, 1934, iii, 265.
2. *Ibid.*, iii, 155–6.
3. *Letters of Horace Walpole*, ed. Mrs P. Toynbee, 16 vols., Oxford, 1903–5, iv, 302, 327.
4. Samuel Johnson, *Selected Writings*, ed. R. T. Davies, 1965, p. 257.
5. T. S. Ashton, *Economic Fluctuations 1700–1800*, Oxford, 1959, p. 51.
6. R. R. Sedgwick, *The History of Parliament: the House of Commons, 1715–1754*, 2 vols., 1970, ii, 468–9; Namier and Brooke, *Commons 1754–90*, iii, 526.
7. George, *Hogarth to Cruikshank*, p. 104.
8. The account in these paragraphs is based on J. R. Western, *The English Militia in the Eighteenth Century*, 1965.
9. *AR* 1767, pt. ii, p. 171.
10. *Johnson's England*, ed. A. S. Turberville, 2 vols., revised edition, Oxford, 1952, i, 40.
11. *Ibid.*, i, 52.
12. These traditional devices are described in M. Lewis, *The Navy of Britain*, 1948, p. 356.
13. *Johnson's England*, i, 53.
14. T. Smollett, *Roderick Random*, Everyman edition, ed. H. W. Hodges, 1927, pp. 161–2.
15. HMC 47, 15th R., App. X, *Tillard*, p. 100.
16. *Boswell's Life of Johnson*, i, 348.
17. Lewis, *Navy of Britain*, pp. 312–13.
18. C. Mitchell (ed.), *Hogarth's Peregrination*, Oxford, 1952, pp. 11–12.
19. B. Williams, *The Whig Supremacy*, revised C. H. Stuart, Oxford, 1962, p. 215.
20. G. J. Marcus, *A Naval History of England: I, the formative centuries*, 1961, p. 389.
21. *Johnson's England*, i, 72.
22. *DNB* xx, 551–2.
23. *Collected Works of Oliver Goldsmith*, ed. A. Friedman, 5 vols., Oxford, 1966, ii, 458–65.
24. *Johnson's England*, i, 86.
25. *GM* 1748, p. 475.
26. For Woodforde's dealings with 'Moonshine' John Buck, the smuggling

blacksmith, see *The Diary of a Country Parson*, ed. J. Beresford, 5 vols., Oxford, 1924–31, i, 198, 282; ii, 39, 45, 77–8, 292; iii, 30, 86, 373, 377; iv, 99, 156, 160; v, 362n.

27. See N. Williams, *Contraband Cargoes*, 1959.
28. *Sophie in London*, pp. 235–6.
29. *DNB* ii, 1290–1.
30. *Calendar of Home Office Papers, 1760–75*, 4 vols., 1878–99, iii, no. 758.
31. *GM* 1755, p. 117.
32. The best account of the incident is that given by Burke, who raised the matter in Parliament. See *Speeches of Edmund Burke*, 4 vols., 1816, ii, 156–9.
33. See, for instance, the case of Mr J— D— of Banbury, reported in *GM* 1755, p. 328.
34. W. E. H. Lecky, *History of England in the Eighteenth Century*, new edition, 7 vols., 1892, ii, 137n.
35. *GM* 1789, p. 272.
36. Lecky, *History of England*, ii, 136n.
37. Babington, *House in Bow Street*, p. 17.
38. *GM* 1750, p. 235.
39. *Ibid.*, pp. 532–3.
40. Babington, *House in Bow Street*, p. 121.
41. *GM* 1765, pp. 302, 488; *Calendar of Home Office Papers*, i, nos. 1874, 1910, 1913, ii, nos. 896, 1361. See W. J. Shelton, *English Hunger and Industrial Disorders*, 1973.
42. *PH*, xxi, 592.
43. For a colourful account of the riots see C. Hibbert, *King Mob*, 1958.
44. *Last Journals of Horace Walpole*, ed. J. Doran, revised A. F. Stewart, 2 vols., 1910, ii, 312.
45. T. Gisborne, *An Enquiry into the Duties of Men in the Higher and Middle Classes of Society*, 1794, p. 279.

Notes to Chapter 3

1. Defoe, *Tour*, i, 266.
2. E. A. Wrigley, 'Family limitation in the pre-industrial age', *Economic History Review*, xix, 1966, pp. 82–109.
3. W. Cadogan, *Essay upon the Nursing and Management of Children*, 1748, p. 7.
4. H. Chapone, *Letters on the Improvement of the Mind, etc.*, 1827, p. 200.
5. Cadogan, *Essay upon Nursing*, pp. 21, 26.
6. W. Alexander, *The history of Women from the earliest antiquity to the present time*, 2 vols., 1779, i, 95–6.
7. Quoted in G. R. Taylor, *The Angel-Makers*, 1958, p. 328.
8. Cadogan, *Essay upon Nursing*, p. 14.
9. *Works of John Wesley*, 14 vols., 1872, i, 387.
10. Taylor, *Angel-Makers*, p. 325.
11. *GM* 1732, p. 556.
12. G. E. and K. R. Fussell, *The English Countrywoman*, 1953, p. 132.
13. Chapone, *Letters on Improvement*, p. 202.

14. I. and P. Opie (eds.), *Oxford Dictionary of Nursery Rhymes*, revised edition, 1952, p. 61.
15. G. S. Thomson, *The Russells in Bloomsbury, 1669–1771*, 1940, p. 198.
16. The only dissentient and dissatisfied voice on this point was that of Ashley Cowper, who decided after having his baby daughter painted by Hogarth that the artist must have 'an aversion to the whole Infantine Race, as he always contrived to make them hideous' (Paulson, *Hogarth*, i, 556).
17. *GM* 1731, p. 15.
18. French foundling hospitals continued to be praised well after the establishment of the English institution, with which they were favourably compared. 'The elegant neatness we found the children in here and the attention paid to them is not to be described,' wrote the future Lord St Vincent from France in 1772, 'and reflects disgrace on that similar Establishment in our own country, so shamefully mismanaged' (British Museum Additional Manuscripts 31192, fo. 11).
19. Paulson, *Hogarth*, ii, 39.
20. W. E. Tate, *The Parish Chest*, 3rd edition, Cambridge, 1969, p. 59.
21. *Ibid.*, p. 74; Taylor, *Angel-Makers*, p. 312.
22. *Ibid.*, pp. 305–7.
23. *The Life of Sir Samuel Romilly written by himself*, 3rd edition, 2 vols., 1842, i, 12.
24. *Narrative of the Life of Mrs Charlotte Charke*, 1755, pp. 29–30.
25. E. Gillett (ed.), *Elizabeth Ham by herself, 1783–1820*, 1945, p. 8.
26. D. Marshall, *English People in the Eighteenth Century*, 1956, p. 108.
27. G. F. Lamb, *The Happiest Days*, 1959, p. 182.
28. *Ibid.*, p. 48.
29. Marshall, *English People*, p. 110.
30. W. Turner, *The Warrington Academy*, Warrington, 1957, pp. 53–68.
31. S. Andrews, *Methodism and Society*, 1970, pp. 53–4.
32. Marshall, *English People*, pp. 136–7.
33. *Sophie in London*, p. 294.
34. *GM* 1735, pp. 17–18.
35. *GM* 1736, pp. 332–3.
36. Anon., *The Benefit of School Discipline*, 1741, pp. 3, 6, 14.
37. HMC 61, *Du Cane*, pp. 230–31.
38. Lamb, *Happiest Days*, pp. 73–80.
39. E. J. Climenson (ed.), *Elizabeth Montagu, her Correspondence from 1720 to 1761*, 2 vols., 1906, ii, 33–4.
40. *Ibid.*, ii, 48–9.
41. R. Halsband (ed.), *Complete Letters of Lady Mary Wortley Montagu*, 3 vols., 1965–7, iii, 22.
42. Charke, *Narrative of Life*, p. 26.
43. *AR* 1759, pp. 424–6.
44. Marshall, *English People*, pp. 237–8.
45. *GM* 1789, p. 489.
46. H. Cartwright, *Letters on Female Education*, 1777, pp. 45–6.
47. J. Moir, *Female Tuition*, Dublin, 1787, p. 185.
48. T. Gisborne, *An Enquiry into the Duties of the Female Sex*, 1797, p. 163.

49. *Ibid.*, p. 91.
50. *Sophie in London*, pp. 135–6, 246–50.
51. S. C. Carpenter, *Eighteenth Century Church and People*, 1959, p. 47.
52. Marshall, *English People*, p. 163.
53. *GM* 1734, p. 636.
54. See, for instance, J. Hampden (ed.), *An Eighteenth Century Journal, 1774–76*, 1940, p. 65.
55. HMC 52, *Astley*, pp. 414–15.

Notes to Chapter 4

1. P. Kalm, *Account of his Visit to England*, tr. J. Lucas, London and New York, 1892, pp. 191, 205–6, 82–3.
2. A. Young, *Travels in France during the years 1787, 1788 and 1789*, ed. C. Maxwell, Cambridge, 1929, pp. 46–8; Marshall, *English People*, pp. 172, 180.
3. Grosley, *Tour to London*, p. 63.
4. *Collected Works of Oliver Goldsmith*, ii, 298.
5. Namier and Brooke, *Commons, 1754–90*, iii, 199.
6. B. F. Duckham, 'Serfdom in eighteenth century Scotland', *History*, liv, 1969, pp. 178–97.
7. Kalm, *Account*, p. 438.
8. *Victoria History of the County of Derby*, ed. W. Page, 2 vols., 1905–7, ii, 364.
9. *Sophie in London*, p. 253.
10. Hampden, *Eighteenth Century Journal*, pp. 291–2, 295–6, 304, 313.
11. Marshall, *English People*, p. 207.
12. *Life of William Hutton by Himself*, 3rd edition, 1841, p. 4.
13. See, for instance, the account of the Leicester framework knitters in *The Victoria County History of Leicestershire: vol. iv, The City of Leicester*, ed. R. A. McKinley, 1958, pp. 168–78.
14. George, *Hogarth to Cruikshank*, p. 141.
15. Paulson, *Hogarth*, i, 239–40.
16. M. D. George, *Catalogue of Political and Personal Satires, British Museum, vol. v, 1771–83*, 1935, nos. 5808–13.
17. *Sophie in London*, pp. 205–6.
18. Moir, *Female Tuition*, p. 182.
19. Quoted in *Encyclopedia Britannica*, new edition, 1970, xviii, 395.
20. George, *Hogarth to Cruikshank*, p. 47; *PH* xxv, 889.
21. J. B. Leblanc, *Letters on the English and French Nations*, Dublin, 2 vols., 1747, i, 214.
22. Cited in Jarrett, *Begetters of Revolution*, p. 33.
23. C. B. A. Behrens, *The Ancien Régime*, 1967, p. 73.
24. For an account of the present state of historical scholarship on this point see G. E. Mingay, *English Landed Society in the Eighteenth Century*, 1963.
25. Marshall, *English People*, p. 223; W. H. Chaloner, *People and Industries*, 1963, p. 23.
26. Ashton, *Economic Fluctuations*, p. 41.
27. Hampden, *Eighteenth Century Journal*, pp. 200–201.

28. E. Robinson, 'Matthew Boulton and the art of parliamentary lobbying', in *Historical Journal*, viii, 1964, pp. 209–29.
29. Namier and Brooke, *Commons 1754–90*, iii, 533–6.
30. Carpenter, *Eighteenth Century Church and People*, p. 75n.
31. *GM* 1765, p. 296.
32. C. Hole, *English Home Life 1500 to 1800*, 1947, p. 138.
33. Hampden, *Eighteenth Century Journal*, p. 88.
34. C. de Saussure, *A Foreign View of England in the Reigns of George I and George II*, tr. and ed. M. van Muyden, 1902, pp. 179, 181.
35. Williams, *Whig Supremacy*, p. 364. (C. H. Stuart, editor of this revised edition, suggests that Williams was wrong in attributing this order to Pitt rather than to the Commander-in-Chief, Lord Ligonier.)
36. The phrase is from Horace Walpole's description of the sketch, which Hogarth gave to him many years later. See H. Walpole, *Anecdotes of Painting in England*, ed. James Dallaway, 4 vols., 1828, iv, 131. Neither Dallaway nor any subsequent commentator has explained why the figure in the drawing is labelled Huggins and not Bambridge. I hope to dig deeper into this puzzling episode in my forthcoming study of Hogarth's imagery.
37. *Memoir of Thomas Bewick written by Himself*, 1924, pp. 109–10.
38. Gisborne, *Enquiry into the Duties of Men*, pp. 279, 293, 624.
39. J. Tucker, *Reflections on the present low price of coarse wools*, 1782, pp. 9, 15.
40. Quoted in M. J. Quinlan, *Victorian Prelude*, New York, 1941, p. 42.
41. G. Himmelfarb, 'The haunted house of Jeremy Bentham', in *Ideas in History: Essays presented to Louis Gottschalk*, Duke University, 1965, pp. 204, 214.
42. R. Evans, 'Bentham's Panopticon: an incident in the Social History of Architecture', in *Architectural Association Quarterly*, iii, 1971, pp. 21–37.

Notes to Chapter 5

1. *GM* 1750, pp. 235–6.
2. A. Young, *Autobiography*, ed. M. Betham-Edwards, 1898, p. 361.
3. Alexander, *History of Women*, ii, 266.
4. Gisborne, *Enquiry into the Duties of Men*, p. 405.
5. *Collected Works of Oliver Goldsmith*, ii, 122–3.
6. *Boswell's Life of Johnson*, i, 463.
7. *Collected Works of Oliver Goldsmith*, ii, 84.
8. Alexander, *History of Women*, i, 123.
9. Gemelli's letter from London, 23 May 1686, printed in A. & J. Churchill, *Collection of voyages and travels*, 8 vols., 1752, iv, 644.
10. *DNB* iv, 298–301.
11. Quoted in Taylor, *Angel-Makers*, p. 296.
12. Gisborne, *Enquiry into the Duties of Female Sex*, p. 265.
13. Kalm, *Account*, pp. 327–8.
14. *Ibid.*, p. 328.
15. Fussell, *English Countrywoman*, pp. 151–2.

16. *AR* 1767, pt. i, pp. 190–97.
17. Hampden, *Eighteenth Century Journal*, pp. 169–70.
18. Babington, *House in Bow Street*, p. 16.
19. Kalm, *Account*, p. 327.
20. S. Beedell (ed.), *The Diary of a Farmer's Wife, 1796–97*, 1964, pp. 185–6.
21. *Ibid.*, pp. 45–6, 53, 120.
22. *Ibid.*, pp. 158–62, 143, 70–71, 123.
23. *Ibid.*, pp. 52, 56, 62.
24. R. Sedgwick (ed.), *Lord Hervey's Memoirs* (abridged one-volume edition), 1952, p. 247.
25. George, *Catalogue of Satires, 1771–83*, nos. 6105–6112, 6122–6124.
26. Climenson, *Montagu Correspondence*, i, 51.
27. Alexander, *History of Women*, i, 305.
28. L. E. Jones, *An Edwardian Youth*, 1956, p. 163.
29. M. Cockle, *Important Studies for the Female Sex*, 1809, pp. 149, 229.
30. W. Brodum, *A Guide for Old Age, or, a Cure for the Indiscretions of Youth*, 1795, pp. 66–7, 74.
31. S. Solomon, *A Guide to Health or Advice to both sexes*, 2nd edition, n.d., pp. 21, 97–9.
32. M. Wollstonecraft, *Vindication of the Rights of Woman*, 1792, p. vi.
33. W. Godwin, *Memoirs of the author of a vindication of the rights of woman*, 1798, pp. 7, 9–10, 109.
34. *GM* 1735, p. 93.
35. Paulson, *Hogarth*, i, 333–5.
36. J. S. Burn, *The History of the Fleet Marriages*, 1846, p. 7.
37. Tate, *Parish Chest*, pp. 82, 49.
38. *PH* xv, 39.
39. G. Crabbe, *Poems*, 3 vols., Cambridge, 1905–7, i, 184.
40. *PH* xv, 35.
41. *Collected Works of Oliver Goldsmith*, ii, 300.
42. *PH* xv, 19.
43. R. E. Leader, *Sheffield in the Eighteenth Century*, 1901, p. 42.
44. Hampden, *Eighteenth Century Journal*, p. 164.
45. Halsband, *Letters of Lady Mary Wortley Montagu*, ii, 32.
46. *GM* 1738, p. 591.
47. J. Casanova de Seingalt, *Memoirs*, 2 vols., 1922, ii, 228.
48. Climenson, *Montagu Correspondence*, i, 265.
49. *Universal Spectator*, 16 January 1731, no. 119, reproduced in *GM* 1731, pp. 14–15.
50. *Sophie in London*, p. 133.
51. F. A. Pottle (ed.), *Boswell's London Journal, 1762–63*, 1950, p. 240.
52. Casanova, *Memoirs*, ii, 163–4.
53. *Universal Spectator*, 25 November 1738, no. 529, reproduced in *GM* 1738, p. 591.
54. Saussure, *Foreign View of England*, pp. 277–9.
55. *DNB* v, 582–3.
56. J. Ashton, *Eighteenth Century Waifs*, 1887, pp. 185ff.
57. *DNB* xix, 325.

58. *Universal Spectator*, 25 November 1738, no. 529, reproduced in *GM* 1738, p. 591.
59. *Boswell's Life of Johnson*, i, 447.
60. *Ibid.*, iii, 46.
61. *DNB* xix, 407–9; Ashton, *Eighteenth Century Waifs*, pp. 321–2.
62. J. M. S. Tompkins, *The Popular Novel in England 1770–1800*, reprinted 1969, pp. 224, 234–6.
63. F. M. Smith, *Mary Astell*, New York, 1916; *DNB* i, 673–4.
64. The evidence for the 'dull and deep potations' of eighteenth-century Oxford and Cambridge is too extensive to be listed here. Homosexuality was less publicized, though in 1715 it was said to be 'very usual among the chief men in some of the colleges', with the result that 'it is dangerous sending a young man who is beautiful to Oxford'. Half a century later there was a sensational scandal at Wadham College, Oxford. See Taylor, *Angel-Makers*, p. 254; I. Bloch, *History of English Sexual Morals*, 1936, pp. 402–3.
65. *GM* 1786, pp. 321–2.

Notes to Chapter 6

1. *Swift's Poems*, ed. H. Williams, 3 vols., Oxford, 1958, i, 198.
2. It has recently been suggested that the series was even more fragmentary than had previously been thought. See A. S. Marks, 'William Hogarth's *The Happy Marriage*', in *The Art Quarterly*, xxxv, 1972, pp. 145–56.
3. Paulson, *Hogarth*, i, 13, 30.
4. *Poetical Works of Cowper*, ed. H. S. Milford, 4th edition reprinted, Oxford, 1950, p. 119.
5. Paulson, *Hogarth*, ii, 81.
6. Kalm, *Account*, p. 154.
7. *Diary of a Farmer's Wife*, p. 47.
8. Marshall, *English People*, p. 106.
9. Young, *Travels in France*, p. 24.
10. Marshall, *English People*, p. 165.
11. M. D. George, *London Life in the Eighteenth Century*, revised edition, 1965, p. 100.
12. George, *Hogarth to Cruikshank*, p. 98.
13. Thomson, *Russells in Bloomsbury*, p. 96.
14. *Ibid.*, pp. 186, 355.
15. G. Eland (ed.), *Purefoy Letters 1735–53*, 2 vols., 1931, i, 47–52. In 1973 a new volume with the same title, edited by L. G. Mitchell, aroused hopes of fresh material; but it turned out to consist for the most part of letters which had already been printed forty years earlier.
16. For an account of Pitt's plans for Burton Pynsent see Sir Tresham Lever, *The House of Pitt*, 1947, pp. 155–6.
17. *Purefoy Letters*, i, 53–60.
18. Kalm, *Account*, pp. 12–13.
19. Hole, *English Home Life*, p. 96.
20. Fussell, *English Countrywoman*, p. 133.

21. Gregory King's calculations are summarized in M. D. George, *England in Transition*, Pelican edition, 1953, pp. 150–51.
22. George, *Hogarth to Cruikshank*, p. 70.
23. A. Clarke, *Working Life of Women in the Seventeenth Century*, reprinted 1968, p. 68n.
24. *Diary of a Farmer's Wife*, pp. 21–2, 94–6.
25. C. Ryskamp and F. A. Pottle (eds.), *Boswell: The Ominous Years, 1774–1776*, 1963, p. 79.
26. *Diary of a Farmer's Wife*, pp. 16–17.
27. Marshall, *English People*, p. 128.
28. R. E. Schofield, *The Lunar Society of Birmingham*, Oxford, 1963.
29. *Sophie in London*, pp. 207–8.
30. Kalm, *Account*, p. 13; C. P. Moritz, *Journeys of a German in England in 1782*, ed. R. Nettel, 1965, p. 35.
31. Marshall, *English People*, p. 172.
32. *Diary of a Farmer's Wife*, p. 16; Paulson, *Hogarth*, ii, 82.
33. *Diary of a Farmer's Wife*, pp. 127–31.
34. Mitchell, *Hogarth's Peregrination*, pp. 8–9, 13.
35. *Ibid.*, p. 7.
36. Kalm, *Account*, pp. 143–4.
37. M. and C. H. B. Quennell, *History of Everyday Things in England, vol. iii, 1733–1851*, 5th edition, 1950, pp. 96–100.
38. *Diary of a Farmer's Wife*, p. 143.
39. Hole, *English Home Life*, p. 11.
40. Thomson, *Russells in Bloomsbury*, p. 350.
41. Fussell, *English Countrywoman*, pp. 118–19.

Notes to Chapter 7

1. Mitchell, *Hogarth's Peregrination*, pp. 7, 8, 10.
2. Saussure, *Foreign View of England*, pp. 294–5.
3. M. Letts, *As the Foreigner Saw Us*, 1935, pp. 72, 143–4.
4. Saussure, *Foreign View of England*, p. 180.
5. Hole, *English Home Life*, p. 136.
6. Saussure, *Foreign View of England*, pp. 281–2.
7. E. Dumont and S. Romilly, *Letters . . . translated from the German of Henry Frederic Groenvelt*, 1792, pp. 246–7, 301, 306.
8. W. B. Daniel, *Rural Sports*, 2 vols., 1801, i, 233.
9. *Spectator*, no. 477; Kalm, *Account*, pp. 142–3.
10. *Boswell's Life of Johnson*, iii, 162.
11. George, *Hogarth to Cruikshank*, pp. 66–8.
12. *Ibid.*, p. 52.
13. J. L. Fougeret de Monbron, *Preservatif contre l'Anglomanie*, 'à Minorque' 1757, pp. 57–8.
14. *Purefoy Letters*, ii, 407.
15. Saussure, *Foreign View of England*, p. 288.
16. Additional Manuscripts, British Museum, 32951, fo. 340.

17. See my article, 'The Regency Crisis of 1765', in *English Historical Review* lxxxv, 1970, pp. 282–315.
18. Saussure, *Foreign View of England*, p. 295.
19. H. Nicolson, *Good Behaviour*, 1955, p. 189.
20. Hampden, *Eighteenth Century Journal*, pp. 91, 176.
21. Marshall, *English People*, p. 47.
22. Paulson, *Hogarth*, i, 18.
23. *Ibid.*, i, 323.
24. *Ibid.*, i, 20–21.
25. *Johnsonian Miscellanies*, ed. G. B. Hill, Oxford, 1897, ii, 301.
26. P. Hartnoll, 'The Theatre and the Licensing Act of 1737', in *Silver Renaissance*, ed. A. Natan, 1961, pp. 165–86.
27. HMC 20, *Dartmouth III*, pp. 232–6.
28. Marshall, *English People*, p. 277.
29. *Collected Works of Oliver Goldsmith*, ii, 300.
30. *Boswell: The Ominous Years*, p. 339; Alexander, *History of Women*, ii, 96, 137–9.
31. *Diary of a Farmer's Wife*, p. 17.
32. *Ibid.*, p. 158.
33. George, *Hogarth to Cruikshank*, pp. 64, 14.
34. *Ibid.*, p. 64.
35. Chesterfield to his son, 9 March 1748; *Lord Chesterfield's Letters to his Son*, ed. O. H. Leigh, 2 vols., New York, 1948, i, 57.
36. Hampden, *Eighteenth Century Journal*, p. 59.
37. Leader, *Sheffield in the Eighteenth Century*, p. 28.
38. R. J. White, 'The Grand Tour', in *Silver Renaissance*, pp. 122–41.
39. For an account of this period of Fox's life, together with extracts from his correspondence, see *Memorials and Correspondence of Charles James Fox*, ed. Lord John Russell, 4 vols., 1853–7, i, 11–47.
40. Paulson, *Hogarth*, i, 139.
41. Marshall, *English People*, pp. 130–31, 258.
42. Taylor, *Angel-Makers*, p. 34.
43. *Universal Spectator*, 9 January 1731, no. 118, reproduced *GM* 1731, p. 14.
44. *The Poems of Alexander Pope* (one-volume edition of the Twickenham text), ed. J. Butt, 1963, p. 567.
45. Alexander, *History of Women*, i, 366.
46. *Diary of a Farmer's Wife*, pp. 19–20, 53–4.
47. *Letters of Horace Walpole*, vi, 190.
48. Taylor, *Angel-Makers*, pp. 77–9; Bloch, *History of English Sexual Morals*, pp. 126, 131, 307, 350, 425. *Satan's Harvest Home* came in due course to the notice of H. S. Ashbee, the nineteenth-century connoisseur of erotic literature. His account of it, with fairly extensive quotations, is reproduced in Peter Fryer, *Forbidden Books of the Victorians*, 1970, pp. 183–8.

Notes to Chapter 8

1. G. Cheyne, *The Natural Method of Cureing the Diseases of the Body and the Disorders of the Mind depending on the Body*, 1742, p. 276.
2. I. Macalpine and R. Hunter, 'A clinical re-assessment of the "insanity" of George III and some of its historical implications', in *Bulletin of the Institute of Historical Research*, xl, 1967, pp. 166–85.
3. British Museum Additional Manuscripts 20,842 ('*Etat actual du Royaume de la Grande Bretagne . . . rédigé par ordre du roi en 1756*'), fo. 20.
4. *GM* 1755, p. 43.
5. HMC 78, *Hastings III*, pp. 195–6.
6. *Fog's Journal*, 14 May 1737, reproduced *GM* 1737, pp. 289–90.
7. Book 14, Chapters xii, xiii.
8. Saussure, *Foreign View of England*, pp. 196–7.
9. *GM* 1755, p. 43.
10. *Sophie in London*, p. 170.
11. *Boswell's Life of Johnson*, iii, 178.
12. Saussure, *Foreign View of England*, pp. 157–8.
13. *Ibid.*, p. 325. Though a Protestant himself, de Saussure had little sympathy with either Presbyterians or Quakers, so that the occasional praise he gives them is all the more noteworthy.
14. For details of the allusions in this print, see Paulson, *Hogarth*, ii, 298–301, 354–7.
15. Carpenter, *Eighteenth Century Church and People*, p. 198.
16. *GM* 1752, pp. 90, 125, 239, 286; 1760, p. 151.
17. Paulson, *Hogarth*, ii, 355–7.
18. *Works of John Wesley*, iii, 324; *Journal of John Wesley*, Everyman's Library edition, 4 vols., 1906, i, 557.
19. *GM* 1751, pp. 186, 378, reproduced in part in C. Hole, *A Mirror of Witchcraft*, 1957, pp. 148–51.
20. Hole, *Mirror of Witchcraft*, pp. 172, 249–50.
21. *GM* 1747, p. 398; 1751, p. 183.
22. *GM* 1755, p. 423.
23. Cadogan, *Essay upon Nursing*, pp. 21–3.
24. Cheyne, *Natural Method*, p. 316; Kalm, *Account*, pp. 122, 138–9; *GM* 1750, p. 455.
25. Young, *Autobiography*, p. 277–8, 287.
26. *GM* 1732, pp. 1062–3.
27. *GM* 1734, p. 611.
28. Cheyne, *Natural Method*, p. 283; Brodum, *Guide for Old Age*, pp. 47–65; Solomon, *Guide to Health*, pp. 99ff.
29. J. Boswell, *Journal of a Tour to the Hebrides with Samuel Johnson*, ed. F. A. Pottle and C. H. Bennett, 1963, p. 371.
30. E. Moir, *The Discovery of Britain: the English Tourists 1540–1840*, 1964, p. 136: *Memoir of Thomas Bewick*, p. 75.
31. George, *Hogarth to Cruikshank*, p. 36.
32. Thomson, *Russells in Bloomsbury*, pp. 240–41.
33. Hole, *Mirror of Witchcraft*, pp. 224–5.

34. Hole, *English Home Life*, p. 158.
35. George, *Hogarth to Cruikshank*, p. 95.
36. Paulson, *Hogarth*, i, 391–4; Ashton, *Eighteenth Century Waifs*, p. 324.
37. *Ibid.*, pp. 293, 330–32.
38. George, *Hogarth to Cruikshank*, p. 86.
39. *Diary of a Farmer's Wife*, p. 138.
40. Young, *Autobiography*, pp. 279, 282–3.
41. Paulson, *Hogarth*, ii, 409.

Supplementary References

Chapter 1, n.2: see also M. J. Yelling, *Common Fields and Enclosure in England*, 1977 and M. Turner, *English Parliamentary Enclosure*, 1980.
Chapter 1, n.21 (also Chapter 3, n.18, Chapter 7, n.16 and Chapter 8, n.3): it should be noted that the Manuscript Department, part of the British Museum when this book was first published, is now part of the British Library.
Chapter 4, n.24: see also J. Cannon, *Aristocratic Century: the peerage of eighteenth-century England*, 1984.
Chapter 4, n.36: for the account referred to here see D. Jarrett, *The Ingenious Mr Hogarth*, 1976, pp. 77–82.
Chapter 4, n.42: see also C. F. Bahmueller, *The National Charity Company: Jeremy Bentham's Silent Revolution*, 1982.
Chapter 5, n.20: there are some puzzling features about this diary. It seems that the original cannot be traced: the published version is based on a typescript dating from 1937. It should also be said that no Herefordshire village can be found which fits the one described in the diary.
Chapter 6, n.16: see also D. Stroud, *Capability Brown*, revised edition, London, 1975.

Suggestions for Further Reading

Ashton, T. S., *An Economic History of England: the Eighteenth Century*, corrected reprint, Methuen, 1961.

Bayne-Powell, R., *Travellers in Eighteenth-Century England*, Murray, 1951.

— *Housekeeping in the Eighteenth Century*, Murray, 1956.

Beedell, S. (ed.), *The Diary of a Farmer's Wife, 1796–97*, Countrywise Books, *The Farmer's Weekly*, 1964

Boswell, J., *Life of Johnson*, ed. G. B. Hill, 6 vols., Oxford University Press, 1934.

The Yale Edition of the Private Papers of James Boswell, ed. F. A. Pottle and others, Heinemann, 1950–63. (*Boswell's London Journal, 1762–63*, 1950; *Boswell in Holland, 1763–64*, 1952; *Boswell on the Grand Tour, 1764*, 1953; *Boswell on the Grand Tour, 1765–66*, 1955; *Boswell in Search of a Wife, 1766–69*, 1957; *Boswell for the Defence, 1769–74*, 1960; *Boswell: the Ominous Years, 1774–76*, 1963; *Boswell's Journal of a Tour to the Hebrides, 1773*, 1963.)

Bovil, E. W., *English Country Life, 1780–1830*, Oxford University Press, 1962.

Brewer, J. and Styles, J. (eds.), *An Ungovernable People*, Hutchinson, 1980.

Briggs, A., *The Age of Improvement*, Longman, 1959.

Brooke, J., *George III*, Constable, 1972.

Byng, J., *The Torrington Diaries*, ed. C. Bruyn Andrews, 4 vols., Eyre and Spottiswoode, 1934–38.

Cannon, J., *Aristocratic Century*, Cambridge University Press, 1984.

Carpenter, S. C., *Eighteenth Century Church and People*, Murray, 1959.

Christie, I. R., *Wars and Revolutions: Britain, 1760–1815*, Arnold, 1982.

Corfield, P. J., *The Impact of English Towns, 1700–1800*, Oxford University Press, 1982.

Defoe, D., *A Tour through the Whole Island of Great Britain*, ed. P. Rogers, Penguin, 1971.

Eland, G. (ed.), *Purefoy Letters, 1735–53*, 2 vols., Sidgwick and Jackson, 1931. (See n.15 to Chapter 6.)

Flinn, M. W., *An Economic and Social History of Britain since 1700*, Macmillan, 1963.

Foss, M., *The Age of Patronage: the Arts in Society, 1660–1750*, Hamish Hamilton, 1972.

Fussell, G. E. and K. R., *The English Countrywoman, 1500–1900*, Andrew Melrose, 1953.

— *The English Countryman, 1500–1900*, Andrew Melrose, 1955.

George, M. D., *England in Johnson's Day*, Methuen, 1928.
— *England in Transition*, Pelican Books, 1953.
— *English Political Caricature*, 2 vols., Oxford University Press, 1959.
— *London Life in the Eighteenth Century*, revised edition, Methuen, 1965.
— *Hogarth to Cruickshank: Social Change in Graphic Satire*, Allen Lane, 1967.
Girouard, M., *Life in the English Country House*, Yale University Press, 1979.
Goodwin, A., *The Friends of Liberty*, Hutchinson, 1979.
Hampden, J. (ed.), *An Eighteenth Century Journal, 1774–1776*, Macmillan, 1940.
Hatton, R., *George I*, Thames and Hudson, 1978.
Hay, D. and others, *Albion's Fatal Tree*, Allen Lane, 1975.
Hecht, J. J., *The Domestic Servant Class in Eighteenth-Century England*, Routledge, 1956.
Hibbert, C., *The Grand Tour*, Weidenfeld and Nicolson, 1969.
Hickey, W., *The Memoirs of William Hickey*, ed. P. Quennell, Hutchinson, 1960.
Hole, C., *English Home Life, 1500–1800*, Batsford, 1947.
Jarrett, D., *Britain 1688–1815*, Longman, 1965.
— *The Begetters of Revolution: England's Involvement with France, 1759–89*, Longman, 1973.
— *Pitt the Younger*, Weidenfeld and Nicolson, 1974.
— *The Ingenious Mr Hogarth*, Michael Joseph, 1976.
Kemp, B., *King and Commons, 1660–1832*, Macmillan, 1959.
Knox, R., *Enthusiasm*, Oxford University Press, 1950.
Laslett, P., *The World We Have Lost*, Methuen, 1965.
Lewis, M., *The Navy of Britain*, Allen and Unwin, 1948.
Longrigg, R., *The English Squire and his Sport*, Michael Joseph, 1977.
Macdonald, J., *Memoirs of an Eighteenth Century Footman*, ed. J. Beresford, Routledge, 1927.
McKendrick, N. and others, *The Birth of a Consumer Society: the Commercialization of Eighteenth-century England*, Europa, 1982.
Malcolmson, R. W., *Popular Recreations in English Society, 1700–1850*, Cambridge University Press, 1973.
— *Life and Labour in England, 1700–1780*, Hutchinson, 1980.
Marshall, D., *English Poor in the Eighteenth Century*, Routledge, 1926.
— *English People in the Eighteenth Century*, Longman, 1956.
— *Eighteenth Century England*, Longman, 1962.
Mingay, G. E., *English Landed Society in the Eighteenth Century*, Routledge, 1963.
Moir, E., *The Discovery of Britain: the English Tourists, 1540–1840*, Routledge, 1964.
Moritz, C. P., *Journeys of a German in England in 1782*, ed. R. Nettel, Cape, 1965.
Namier, L. B., *The Structure of Politics at the Accession of George III*, revised edition, Macmillan, 1957.
— *England in the Age of the American Revolution*, revised edition, Macmillan, 1961.

Paulson, R., *Hogarth: His Life, Art and Times*, 2 vols., Yale University Press, 1971.
Porter, R., *English Society in the Eighteenth Century*, Pelican Books, 1982.
Pringle, P., *Hue and Cry*, Museum Press, 1955.
— *The Thief Takers*, Museum Press, 1958.
Quinlan, M. J., *Victorian Prelude*, Columbia University Press, New York, 1941.
Redwood, J., *Reason, Ridicule and Religion: the Age of Enlightment in England*, Thames and Hudson, 1976.
Rogers, P., *Grub Street*, Methuen, 1972.
— *The Augustan Vision*, Weidenfeld and Nicolson, 1974.
Rude, G., *Wilkes and Liberty*, Oxford University Press, 1962.
— *Hanoverian London*, Secker and Warburg, 1971.
Rule, J., *The Experience of Labour in Eighteenth-Century Industry*, Croom Helm, 1980.
Schwartz, R. B., *Daily Life in Johnson's London*, Wisconsin University Press, 1983.
Speck, W., *Stability and Strife: England, 1714–60*, Arnold, 1977.
Stone, L., *The Family, Sex and Marriage in England, 1500–1800*, Weidenfeld and Nicolson, 1977.
Summerson, J., *Architecture in Britain, 1530–1830*, Penguin (Pelican History of Art), 1953.
Tate, W. E., *The Parish Chest*, 3rd edition, Cambridge University Press, 1969.
Taylor, G. R., *The Angel-Makers*, Heinemann, 1958.
Thomson, G. S., *The Russells in Bloomsbury, 1669–1771*, Cape, 1940.
Thomson, E. P., *Whigs and Hunters*, Allen Lane, 1975.
Turner, E. S., *The Court of St. James's*, Michael Joseph, 1959.
Turner, T., *The Diary of a Georgian Shopkeeper*, ed. G. H. Jennings, Oxford University Press, 1979.
Waterhouse, E., *Painting in Britain, 1530–1790*, Penguin (Pelican History of Art), 1953.
Wearmouth, R. F., *Methodism and the Common People of the Eighteenth Century*, Epworth, 1945.
Wesley, J., *Journals*, Everyman's Library, 4 vols., Dent, 1906.
Western, J. R., *The English Militia in the Eighteenth Century*, Routledge, 1965.
Whinney, M., *Sculpture in Britain, 1530–1830*, Penguin (Pelican History of Art), 1964.
Williams, B., *The Whig Supremacy, 1714–60*, 2nd edition, revised C. H. Stuart, Oxford University Press, 1962.
Williams, C. (ed.), *Sophie in London 1786*, Cape, 1933.
Williams, E. N., *Life in Georgian England*, Batsford, 1962.
Williams, N., *Contraband Cargoes: Seven Centuries of Smuggling*, Longman, 1959.
Willey, B., *Eighteenth Century Background*, Chatto and Windus, 1950.
Wilson, F. M., *Strange Island: Britain through Foreign Eyes, 1395–1940*, Longman, 1955.
Woodforde, J., *The Diary of a Country Parson, 1758–1802*, ed. J. Beresford, 5 vols., Oxford University Press, 1924–31.
Wrigley, E. A. and Schofield, R., *The Population History of England, 1541–1871*, Arnold, 1981.

Index